The Holy Spirit

The Holy Spirit
Unbounded Gift of Joy

Mary Ann Fatula, O.P.

A Michael Glazier Book
THE LITURGICAL PRESS
Collegeville, Minnesota

A Michael Glazier Book published by The Liturgical Press.

Cover design by Kathryn Brewer.

	2	3	4	5	6	7	8

Library of Congress Cataloging-in-Publication Data

Fatula, Mary Ann.
   The Holy Spirit : unbounded gift of joy / Mary Ann Fatula.
      p.   cm.
   "A Michael Glazier book."
   Includes bibliographical references and index.
   ISBN 0-8146-5030-9 (alk. paper)
   1. Holy Spirit.   2. Catholic Church—Doctrines.   I. Title.
BT121.2.F33   1998
231'.3—dc21   97-49884
                                                                                CIP

For my past and present students at Ohio Dominican College,
on whose faces I have seen the Holy Spirit's joy

CONTENTS

Pentecost Sequence

Come, Holy Spirit, come!
And from your celestial home
    Shed a ray of light divine.

Come, Father of the poor!
Come, source of all our store!
    Come, within our bosoms shine!

You, of comforters the best;
You, the soul's most welcome guest;
    Sweet refreshment here below;

In our labor, rest most sweet;
Grateful coolness in the heat;
    Solace in the midst of woe.

O most blessed Light divine,
Shine within these hearts of yours,
    And our inmost being fill!

Where you are not, [we have] naught,
Nothing good in deed or thought,
    Nothing free from taint of ill.

Heal our wounds, our strength renew;
On our dryness pour your dew
    Wash the stains of guilt away.

Bend the stubborn heart and will;
Melt the frozen, warm the chill;
    Guide the steps that go astray.

On the faithful, who adore
And confess you, evermore
    In your sev'nfold gift descend.

Give them virtue's sure reward;
Give them your salvation, Lord;
    Give them joys that never end.
        Amen. Alleluia.

INTRODUCTION

"The disciples were filled with joy and with the Holy Spirit" (Acts 13:52). In his encyclical *Dominum et Vivificantem* ("Lord and Giver of Life"), Pope John Paul II solemnly placed the Church under the guidance of the Holy Spirit for the third millennium. The pope stressed that the Incarnation itself was accomplished through the Holy Spirit's power; so, too, the great Jubilee of the Incarnation has impelled the Church to turn its "mind and heart" to the Holy Spirit in facing with joy the challenges of the third millennium.[1] The pope thus made his own the call of Pope Paul VI to the entire Church, urging renewed devotion to and study of the Holy Spirit.[2] To the urgent question, "What is the greatest need of the Church today?" Pope Paul VI himself had responded, "The Holy Spirit." For it is the Holy Spirit who is the font of the Church's life and holiness, her unity and gifts, her comfort and strength, and, most of all, her joy.[3]

In a world marked not only by technological progress but also by growing sources of anxiety, many people today search for the secret of a happy heart. This book reflects on the Holy Spirit as the answer to our thirst for a joy that will not disappoint us (John 16:22). A previous work of mine, *The Triune God of Christian Faith*,[4] was devoted to the mystery of the Trinity as the fulfillment of our hunger for perfect gift-love. A central theme of that work is that we are meant to experience the transforming joy of intimate friendship with each divine person. This book continues these Trinitarian reflections. My own students

---

[1] Pope John Paul II, *Dominum et Vivificantem*, #49. Encyclical on The Holy Spirit in the Life of the Church and the World, May 30, 1986 (Washington, D.C.: United States Catholic Conference, 1986) 92.

[2] Ibid., #2; 5. The remarks of Pope Paul VI were published in *L'Osservatore Romano*, June 7, 1973.

[3] *L'Osservatore Romano*, November 30, 1972.

[4] Collegeville: The Liturgical Press, 1990.

constantly teach me that the Holy Spirit, least known and most elusive of the three divine persons, fascinates us in a way that we find difficult to resist. People often are amazed to discover that the Holy Spirit is not something but Someone, not a feeling but the divine person through whom we also grow close to the Father and Son. Most of all, many people are enchanted to discover that the sweetest fruit of closeness to the Holy Spirit is a happy heart.

In the Pentecost Sequence, the exquisite poem used at the Eucharist for Pentecost, we beg the Holy Spirit to flood us with unending joy, for the Spirit is the very person of the Father's and Son's happiness. It is this Spirit who eases our struggles, comforts our hearts, heals our wounds, and, in the words of Pope John Paul II, transforms our heart's desert into "fertile fields of grace and holiness."[5] Inspired by these sentiments of the Pentecost Sequence, the following chapters ponder the insights of Christian saints, mystics, and theologians of East and West, especially the Fathers of the Church, whose writings are so inspired by Scripture and so full of the Holy Spirit's anointing.

As we consider varied facets of the Spirit's alluring personality, the theme of the Holy Spirit as the giver of joy emerges as the underlying motif. In the first chapter we reflect on the Holy Spirit as the person of the Father's and Son's own joy, dwelling in our hearts to fill us with the happiness at the heart of God. The second chapter contemplates Jesus' death, resurrection, and ascension as the source for the Holy Spirit's joyful outpouring at Pentecost. In this chapter we also trace in Scripture and early Church writings the development of belief in the Holy Spirit's divinity and unique personhood. The third chapter focuses on the Holy Spirit as the giver of life lavished on us at our baptism and confirmation. We also consider movements such as the Charismatic Renewal through which the Holy Spirit helps us to reclaim the Trinity's own joy as our baptismal heritage.

The fourth chapter reflects on the Holy Spirit as the Father's and Son's love in person, dwelling at the center of every true love and friendship, uniting us also to the Father, to Jesus, and to one another. The fifth chapter considers the Holy Spirit at the heart of the Church and sacraments, giving each member special gifts to build up the Church as a community of love. In the sixth chapter we examine contemporary theological approaches to the Holy Spirit, especially in light of our focus on intimate friendship with the Holy Spirit. The seventh chapter ponders the Holy Spirit as our healer and comforter, while the eighth chapter contemplates the Holy Spirit as our inmost teacher and guide. The ninth chapter considers the Holy Spirit at the heart of prayer that

---

[5] *Dominum et Vivificantem,* #67; 138.

draws us into intimacy with each divine person. In the tenth chapter we reflect in more detail on deepening closeness to the Holy Spirit. Finally, in chapter eleven we contemplate the Holy Spirit at the heart of our death and of our risen life in heaven's joy.

Many persons in my own life have been sacraments of the Holy Spirit's joy for me. To them I owe my gratitude for inspiring this book and helping to bring it to fruition. In a special way, I give all of my love and thanks to my parents, Michael and Rita Hyzy Fatula, for the gift of their profound faith and selfless love. My Dominican congregation of St. Mary of the Springs, and particularly my community of Dominican sisters at St. James the Less Convent, have been an undeserved grace for me. Finally, my students at Ohio Dominican College have constantly shown me how enchanting the Holy Spirit is to the human heart. Many other persons deserve my debt of thanks, especially John Fatula, Ennio Mastroianni, Rita Fatula Mastroianni, and Sr. Mary Michael Spangler, O.P., who, in the joy of friendship, have helped me with many valuable suggestions.

I consecrate this book to the Holy Spirit, Giver and Gift of true joy. May this Spirit of tenderness anoint these pages, so that readers may be helped to enjoy the Spirit's sweetness in their own lives. Through closeness to the Holy Spirit, may we grow in that friendship with the Trinity and one another which allows us to taste heaven's joy even now.

ABBREVIATIONS

AA   *Apostolicam actuositatem*, Vatican II Decree on the Apostolate of the Laity.

CG   Thomas Aquinas, *Summa contra Gentiles. On the Truth of the Catholic Faith.* Trans. Pegis, Anderson, Bourke, O'Neil. 5 vols. New York: Doubleday, 1955–57. Reprint, Notre Dame University Press, 1975.

DS   H. Denzinger and A. Schönmetzer, *Enchiridion Symbolorum. Definitionum et Declarationum de rebus fidei et morum.* 36th ed. Freiburg im Breisgau: Herder, 1976.

DV   *Dei Verbum*, Vatican II Dogmatic Constitution on Divine Revelation.

GS   *Gaudium et spes*, Vatican II Pastoral Constitution on the Church in the World.

LG   *Lumen gentium*, Vatican II Decree on the Church.

NPNF   *Nicene and Post-Nicene Fathers.* First and Second Series. New York: Charles Scribner's Sons, 1886–1912. Reprint, Grand Rapids, Michigan: Wm. B. Eerdmans, 1976–83.

LH   *Liturgia Horarum. Book of Prayer: A Short Breviary.* 4th rev. ed. Monks of Saint John's Abbey. Collegeville: Saint John's Abbey Press, 1975.[1]

PG   *Patrologia cursus completus. Series Graeca.* Jacques Paul Migne, ed. Paris: J. P. Migne, 1857–87.

---

[1] When possible, I cite this reference along with primary sources in order to illustrate how frequently the Office of Readings (from the Church's Liturgy of the Hours) is drawn from early Christian writings on the Spirit. This particular version is useful because it contains the Office of Readings in one compact volume.

PO   *Presbyterorum ordinis,* Vatican II Decree on the Life and
         Ministry of Priests.

SC   *Sacrosanctum concilium,* Vatican II Constitution on the Sacred
         Liturgy.

ST   Thomas Aquinas, *Summa theologiae.* 60 vols. Blackfriars edi-
         tion. New York: McGraw Hill, 1964.

UR   *Unitatis redintegratio,* Vatican II Decree on Ecumenism.

VC   *Vatican Council II: The Conciliar and Post Conciliar Documents.*
         Rev. ed. Austin Flannery, O.P., ed. Northport, New York:
         Costello Publishing Company, 1996.

1

Spirit of Joy

The Living Joy of the Risen Lord

The sweetest fruit of knowing the Holy Spirit is a happy heart. Luke tells us that Jesus himself "rejoiced in the Holy Spirit" (Luke 10:21) and that his disciples were "filled with joy and with the Holy Spirit" (Acts 13:52). The early Christian writer, Eusebius, recounts how those who believed in Christ were "happy beyond telling, and God's joy radiated from every face."[1] This same joy has filled Christians throughout the ages. Martyrs have gone to their deaths radiant with joy,[2] and countless saints, known and unknown, have lived lives filled with gladness. We ourselves may be blessed to know people who shine with this happiness of the Spirit. A dear friend of mine who always seems to have a peaceful heart and a smiling face once told me, "I don't think that God worries about things. And if God does not worry, why should I?" People like this, filled with the Holy Spirit's good cheer, are irresistible to us. Like sunshine flooding a dark room, they spread the Trinity's light in our lives.

We may envy persons such as these, wishing that we could taste their joy in our own hearts. And Jesus himself assures us that we can: "Ask, and you will receive, so that my joy may be in you, and that your joy may be complete" (John 16:24; 15:11). This is an astounding promise to us. As much as we might want to, we ourselves could never hand over as a gift to a dear one's soul the very same joy that fills us. Yet this is precisely what Jesus promises us: the joy that floods his own

[1] Eusebius, *The History of the Church*, 10.2; LH 147/1.
[2] *Narrative on the Passion of the Carthaginian Martyrs*, 18; LH 1524.

heart. It is a gift that no one else can give us, a treasure no one can steal from us: "Your hearts will rejoice, and no one will take your joy from you" (John 16:22). This happiness is no fleeting emotion that fills us at one moment and slips away the next. No, the joy of Jesus is eternal, unbounded; his uncreated joy is Someone, God the Holy Spirit.

We ourselves know this Spirit, just as we intuitively know the air we breathe and without which we cannot live, for the Spirit lives with us and is deep within us (John 14:17). Though we may not always realize it, we experience the Holy Spirit's closeness when we are near our loved ones and our life feels good and sweet to us. We feel the Spirit's joy, too, as we savor the perfumes of springtime, when nature all around us bursts into bloom. Even hard times bring us the Holy Spirit's fragrance, for all that the Spirit touches is anointed with joy (1 Thess 1:5-6).[3] Augustine tells us that this Spirit who is the very "depths" of the Trinity's heart (1 Cor 2:10) is the Father's and Son's own communion,[4] their wondrous embrace of love and rapturous joy, the sweetness of their love in person.[5] As the divine "we" in whom the Father and Son forever embrace one another, the Holy Spirit eternally "blossoms" as the exquisite "flower" of their persons, the intoxicating "perfume" of their love.[6] Nothing created—not even the greatest ecstasy nor the most exquisite tenderness—can describe this happiness which the Holy Spirit *is* at the heart of the Trinity.[7]

To speak of the Holy Spirit, the Scriptures often use lovely but impersonal images such as breath (John 20:22), wind (Acts 2:2), water (John 7:38-39), tongues of fire (Acts 2:3), anointing (1 John 2:27, Acts 10:38), finger of God (Luke 11:20), dove (Luke 3:22), seal (Eph 4:30), gift (Acts 11:17), peace (John 20:21-22), and love (Rom 5:5). Yet early Christians recognized in faith that these impersonal images suggest the unfathomable beauty of the Holy Spirit precisely as Someone. The Holy Spirit is the third divine person whose tenderness we experience like a gentle breeze caressing our face, like the sun bathing us in warmth,

---

[3] Seraphim of Sarov, *The Revelations;* in Vladimir Lossky, *The Mystical Theology of the Eastern Church* (New York: St. Vladimir's Seminary Press, 1976) 229.

[4] Augustine, *On the Trinity,* 5.11; trans. Stephen McKenna (New York: Fathers of the Church, 1954) 190.

[5] Augustine calls the Holy Spirit the Father's and Son's *complexus* (embrace), *perfuitione,* and *usus,* (enjoyment); *On the Trinity,* 6.10.11; McKenna, 213–14.

[6] Karl Adam, *Christ Our Brother* (London: Sheed and Ward, 1937) 148. Adam notes that he draws these images from Matthias Scheeben.

[7] Maurice Landrieux, *Le divin Méconnu* (Paris: Beauchesne, 1921); in Yolande Arsène-Henry, *Les plus beaux textes sur le Saint-Esprit,* rev. ed. (Paris: Lethielleux, 1968) 279.

like love itself deep within us. And just as we cannot live without breath or water, without freedom or love, we cannot live without the sweet joy of the Spirit.

In his book, *A New Pentecost*,[8] Cardinal Suenens paints a beautiful portrait of what it means for us to know the Holy Spirit's sweetness deep within our hearts. In our thirst for love we are like a lone traveler who gets lost in a storm. Just as we are ready to despair, however, we spy a beautiful little home, filled with warmth. We creep up to the windows and peer inside; love and kindliness shine on the faces of the family within. They are snuggled around a blazing fire, their faces bathed in its sweet glow. We ourselves can stay outside, dying of the cold, or we can go inside and let the warmth of that family's love and of that sweet hearth fill our soul. We need only knock at the door— "How much more will the heavenly Father give the Holy Spirit to those who ask" (Luke 11:13)—and let ourselves be welcomed with open arms. We will not be greeted as strangers at that hearth. We are accepted as a family member. We are a son, a daughter of God, and this is our home; we were made for its love. Filled with this realization, we knock at the door and find ourselves greeted with joy. Once we are inside, everything becomes different for us. The gentle flames of the fire leap up to warm us. In its soft glow we see the love on the family's faces as they gather to embrace and welcome us. Their affection envelops us, and our face, too, lights up in the glow. We are not alone anymore. We are home.

When we ourselves begin to know the Holy Spirit, we discover that we, too, have come "home." Because of God's own Spirit in our hearts, we live in God and God lives in us (1 John 4:12-13, 3:24): the Trinity who is "all welcome, light, and warmth" is our home, and the Holy Spirit is its inmost joy.[9] And just as the Holy Spirit pours out on us the gift of created love or charity, the same Spirit fills our hearts with the gift of joy as the inseparable effect of this love. Thomas Aquinas tells us that our beloved's presence fills us with the joy that is delight, contentment, and a deep inner satisfaction; in the presence of our beloved, our heart's desires are fulfilled. All the more is this true of the joy the Holy Spirit gives us. Since we are always in the presence of our beloved God through the Spirit's love within us (Rom 5:5), this same love gives us a joy that no created force can wrest from us.[10]

---

[8] Léon Joseph Cardinal Suenens, *A New Pentecost?*, trans. Francis Martin (New York: Crossroad Seabury, 1975).

[9] Ibid., 68–69.

[10] Aquinas, ST II–II, 28, 1–4.

The Holy Spirit Within Us

We possess this Spirit of love and joy not in a place external to us, but at the most intimate level of our being, for the Spirit dwells within us (John 14:17). Cardinal Manning writes that if we truly realized that the Holy Spirit dwells within us, permeating us more intimately than our soul fills our body, listening to our every breath and heart's sigh, we would cry out in joy, "My own soul is the house of God, and my own heart is to me the gate of heaven."[11] In the very depths of our heart the Spirit who is the Father's and Son's own "heart" has come to dwell.[12] Again and again, Paul assures us of this very truth: "God has sent the Spirit of his Son into our hearts" (Gal 4:6); "God's love has been poured into our hearts by the Holy Spirit that has been given to us" (Rom 5:5); God has given us the Spirit "in our hearts" as a guarantee (2 Cor 1:22).

Our "heart" is the secret core of our being, the very center of who we are, the place within us where we are most at "home."[13] Moreover, the triune God has created this human heart of ours for an exquisite solace, the gift of finding ourselves completely at home in another's heart. Because we were made for communion by the God who is a Trinity of love, the core of our own being cannot help crying out for the joy of giving ourselves completely to another.[14] A loving mother holds her baby to her heart; a tender father carries his child tight in his arms. Children and friends, spouses and lovers, walk arm in arm. The countless ways that we find to be physically close to those we love express our deeper thirst to be emotionally close to another, to be fully known and loved, in every part of who we are.

And we were made to be cherished not as second best, but with a love totally centered on us, as if we were the only person in the world. Our nearest experience of this kind of love is the rapt attention—bordering on "adoration"—which loving parents lavish on their newborn child. We all desire to be loved and "adored" in this way at every moment. But as we grow older, we discover that our dear ones cannot be with us always, caring for our every need. Even if we are physically close to those we love, we can feel lonely, and our dreams of closeness can be shattered by the pain of unmet needs and broken relationships.

[11] Henry Edward Manning, *The Internal Mission of the Holy Ghost*, 5th ed. (New York: P. J. Kenedy, 1904) 34–35.

[12] F. X. Durrwell, *Holy Spirit of God: An Essay in Biblical Theology*, trans. Sr. Benedict Davies, O.S.U. (London: Geoffrey Chapman, 1983) 26.

[13] Ibid.

[14] Luis M. Bermejo, S.J., *The Spirit of Life: The Holy Spirit in the Life of the Christian* (Chicago: Loyola University Press, 1989) 46.

The Holy Spirit of love, however, dwells in us as our inseparable and intimate friend, our beloved "Paraclete" and counselor, our advocate and helper, our comfort and consoler. This Spirit at the depths of the Trinity (1 Cor 2:10) comes to live in us not in a shallow or superficial way, but permanently and in our inmost depths: "I will put my spirit within you" (Ezek 36:27, 37:14). Through thick and thin, the Spirit abides with us always (1 Cor 3:16, 1 Cor 6:19, Rom 8:9, 11; John 14:16-17; 1 John 4:13). Dwelling in us more deeply than we ourselves do, the Holy Spirit draws us to our own heart, to find within us the contentment we seek outside ourselves. As we experience the Holy Spirit's closeness, we begin to take joy in our own company, for we know that we are not alone. Enveloped by the person who is the Father's and Son's own love, we discover that even our bodies are the temple of this sweet Spirit (1 Cor 6:19). The early Church historian, Eusebius, tells us the touching story of Leonides, the father of Origen, who would reverently kiss the breast of his sleeping child in the conviction that he was the temple of the Holy Spirit.[15] Through our own baptism, we, too, bear deep within us this person of joy at the heart of the Trinity. The Father and Son thus pour out on us not only the peace and joy given by the Holy Spirit (Rom 14:17; 1 Thess 1:6), but also the very person of the Spirit, who is their "heart" and "joy," their "wealth" and "kingdom." Indeed, the kingdom of God is within us (Luke 17:21; Vulgate), because the Holy Spirit dwells deep within us (John 14:17).

Our Peace

"My peace I give to you" (John 14:27). Jesus promises us the Holy Spirit not only as the person of uncreated joy who floods his own heart, but also as the person of uncreated peace who fills his own soul: "Peace be with you . . . receive the Holy Spirit" (John 20:19, 22). We know that love, joy, and peace are created gifts of the Trinity to us. But many Church Fathers interpreted these beautiful words of John to mean that the uncreated peace which Jesus lavishes on us is the very person of the Spirit. Following Augustine, Thomas Aquinas reflects on peace as the tranquility of order, the calm within and among us that flows from love.[16] And just as children nourished with their parents' affection become peaceful in their arms, we, too, grow contented when we let the Spirit of love embrace our whole being. As we begin to enjoy

---

[15] Eusebius, *The History of the Church*, 6.2.11; trans. G. A. Williamson (Baltimore, Md.: Penguin Books, 1965) 241.
[16] ST II–II, 29, 1–3.

the Spirit's peace and presence within us, we grow less anxious and more trusting in the Father's care for us: "May the God of hope fill you with all joy and peace in believing, so that you may abound in hope by the power of the Holy Spirit" (Rom 15:13).

Initially we may not recognize the peace we feel as the Holy Spirit's own gift to us.[17] Yet as we grow to savor the Spirit's sweetness, all that lacks the Holy Spirit begins to lose its attraction for us. In contrast to worldly pleasures which always leave us restless and empty, the Holy Spirit's contentment completely satisfies us.[18] The sweetness of this peace has inspired Christians to describe the Holy Spirit as the fulfillment of Scripture's loveliest images and most alluring promises. The Spirit is the kingdom of God and our spouse, the precious pearl and grain of mustard seed, the living water and fire deep within us.[19] As our true protector, the Holy Spirit dwells in us to save and heal, to teach and advise, to strengthen, console, and illumine us. With a presence that is always "gentle and sweet-scented," the Holy Spirit offers us a yoke that is exceedingly light,[20] for the Spirit is all gentleness and peace, compassion and mercy, solace and joy.[21] The Holy Spirit becomes our "clothing," our rest and joy, our delight and life, our heart's sweetness and brother,[22] our father, mother, bridegroom, and friend.[23]

As we give ourselves completely to this Spirit of love, we begin to live from an overflowing source of joy and peace within us. The Holy Spirit's contentment in our heart then sheds its radiance in all of our relationships. With the Spirit's "merciful unction" filling us, we gain

---

[17] St. Mary Magdalene de Pazzi, *On Revelation* and *On Spiritual Trials*; LH 1580.

[18] John of the Cross, *Ascent of Mount Carmel*, 1.6.3; 1.7.3; 1.7.4; 2.17.5; in *The Collected Works of St. John of the Cross*, trans. Kieran Kavanaugh, O.C.D., and Otilio Rodriguez, O.C.D.; intro. Kieran Kavanaugh (Washington, D.C.: ICS Publications, 1973) 85, 88–89, 157.

[19] Symeon the New Theologian, *Sermon Ninety*; in Vladimir Lossky, *The Vision of God*, trans. Asheleigh Moorhouse (Bedfordshire: American Orthodox Book Service, 1963) 120.

[20] Cyril of Jerusalem, *Catechetical Lectures*, 16.16; NPNF 2.7, 119.

[21] Symeon the New Theologian, *Hymn Twenty-Two*; in George Maloney, S.J., trans. and intro., *Hymns of Divine Love* (Denville, N.J.: Dimension Books, 1975) 111.

[22] Macarius, *Sermon Seven*, 5–6; PG 34, 527; in Lossky, *The Vision of God*, 92–93.

[23] Yves Congar, O.P., *I Believe in the Holy Spirit*, trans. David Smith (New York: Seabury Press, 1983) 3:157. Congar notes that some Syrian writers, using the feminine word for "spirit" in Syriac, have called the Holy Spirit "mother." See E.-P. Siman, *L'experience de l'Esprit par l'Eglise d'après la tradition syrienne d'Antioche* (Paris, 1971), 155. See also R. Murray, "The Holy Spirit as Mother," in *Symbols of Church and Kingdom: A study in Early Syriac Tradition* (Cambridge, 1975) 312–20.

the "oil of innate kindness,"[24] becoming more compassionate toward ourselves and others. And because we are happy with who we are in God, we also grow more open, trusting, and self-giving. Our closeness to the Spirit in this way frees us from a self-centered life and draws us to communion with those around us. In the Holy Spirit's loving unity, our life and relationships become anointed with the Spirit's own "bond of peace" (Eph 4:3), and the description of the Jerusalem community becomes increasingly true of us: The company of those who believed "were of one heart and soul" (Acts 4:32).

In her lovely prayer to the Holy Spirit, St. Mary Magdalene de Pazzi begs the Spirit of love to come ever more deeply to us as the treasure containing all peace and consolation:

> Come, Holy Spirit!
> Come, Bond with the Father and
> Beloved of the Word . . .
> reward of the blessed,
> the soul's refreshment,
> light in darkness,
> the wealth of the poor,
> the treasure of lovers.
> You fill the hungry and
> console the pilgrim;
> in you all treasures are stored up.
> Come, and take from us whatever keeps us from being one
> with you.[25]

Our Gift

"Wealth of the poor": this tender name by which Mary Magdalene de Pazzi addressed the Holy Spirit echoes the sentiments of Luke: nothing we do can merit the gift of the Spirit, yet the Spirit is ours for the asking (Luke 11:13). The more needy we are, the more the Holy Spirit longs to fill us with the joy of God's heart: "Ask and you will receive, so that your joy may be complete" (John 16:24). The Holy Spirit is lavished on us, not because we are worthy, but because the Father is so good to the weak and poor. This truth surely underlies one of the most frequent scriptural images for the Holy Spirit as the "gift" (Acts 11:17): "You will receive the gift of the Holy Spirit" (Acts 2:38); "The gift of the Holy Spirit had been poured out even on the Gentiles" (Acts

---

[24] Bernard of Clairvaux, *On the Song of Songs*, 44.6; in *The Works of Bernard of Clairvaux*, trans. Kilian Walsh, O.C.S.O. (Kalamazoo, Mich.: Cistercian Publications, 1976) 3:229.

[25] St. Mary Magdalene de Pazzi, *On Revelation* and *On Spiritual Trials*; LH 1580.

10:45); "If you knew the gift of God, and who it is that is saying to you, 'Give me a drink,' you would have asked him, and he would have given you living water" (John 4:10).

Both eastern and western Church Fathers had special affection for this scriptural image of "gift" as a name for the Holy Spirit. Basil the Great reflects on the Spirit as the gift of life who frees us (Rom 8:2), the gift of power who transforms us: "You shall receive power when the Holy Spirit has come upon you" (Acts 1:8).[26] Cyril of Alexandria comments that since the Father's and Son's perfect gift is a sharing in the Holy Spirit, this same Spirit is their "good donation" to us.[27] Poured out on us who have communion with Jesus, the Holy Spirit is the living "drink" whom Jesus received as a gift from the Father and whom he has lavished on all of us.[28]

Insights such as these echo the truth of a key passage from Luke. Matthew had written that if we who are parents know how to give good gifts to our children, how much more will our Father in heaven "give good things to those who ask" (Matt 7:11). Luke, however, changes this passage to read: "How much more will the heavenly Father give the Holy Spirit to those who ask" (Luke 11:13). For Luke, the Holy Spirit is, in person, everything we could want for ourselves and our loved ones—life and peace, wholeness and love, contentment and joy. Hilary of Poitiers urges us to rejoice in this Spirit as the gift dwelling within us, the "light of our minds, the sun of our souls," "the solace of our waiting," and the guarantee of heaven's joy. Because the Holy Spirit is the living gift whose power we are meant to use, and whose presence we were made to enjoy, the more we desire the Holy Spirit's blessings, the more abundantly we receive them.[29]

Since the very nature of love is to be a gift, western writers such as Hilary, Augustine, and Thomas Aquinas call the Holy Spirit "Gift" precisely because the Holy Spirit is the person of love. We know from experience that what we give in any gift to a dear one is ultimately our love. In his own reflections on the Spirit as the risen Lord's gift lavished on us, Augustine stressed that no gift is greater than love. Our self-giving love is the ultimate gift through which and because of which we give all other gifts. But the Holy Spirit is the very person of love through whom God's own love is poured into our hearts (Rom 5:5). The Spirit, then, is called "Gift" for no other reason except love.

---

[26] Basil the Great, *On the Holy Spirit*, 24.57; NPNF 2.8, 36.

[27] Cyril of Alexandria, *On the Trinity*, 3.

[28] Irenaeus, *Against the Heresies*, 3.17.2.

[29] Hilary, *On the Trinity*, 2.35; in J. Patout Burns and Gerald M. Fagin, eds., *The Holy Spirit* (Wilmington: Michael Glazier, Inc., 1984) 112.

As the one who is the Father's and Son's intimate communion, the Holy Spirit is also their gift, "givable" from all eternity, and given to us in time (Acts 8:20).[30] Most especially, the Spirit is the gift through whom the Father and Son love us and dwell in us, the living gift through whom we also love and dwell in them. And since "God gives us nothing less than God," the Holy Spirit, Augustine tells us, is both gift and giver of himself and of every other gift.[31]

As he contemplated these themes from Augustine, Thomas Aquinas pondered another truth dear to our experience: we give as a gift to our loved ones only what is first ours to give, and we give it so that it may truly belong to them. We are offended if our dear ones return our gift, for we give it precisely so that it really may be theirs. These insights moved Thomas to reflect on the mystery of the divine persons giving themselves to us as their own most precious gift so that we might "possess" them completely, delighting in them through grace-filled knowledge and love.[32] In a special way, the Spirit who proceeds eternally from the Father and Son as their love in person is also their most precious gift to us, their inmost treasure whom they give to belong to us, to be truly ours as our Spirit and our gift.[33]

The Trinity's Glory Shining in Us

The Spirit is not only the Father's and Son's living gift but also the radiant glory whom they lavish on us: "The glory that you have given me I have given them, so that they may be one, as we are one" (John 17:22-23). Eastern Church Fathers recognized the Holy Spirit as the Father's living beauty, the shining splendor whom the Father eternally gives to his beloved Son. Moreover, through the most intimate love, Jesus now shares this precious gift, their living glory, with us.[34] Irenaeus tells us that the glory of God is the human person fully alive with God's own radiant life.[35] As the Father's and Son's "glory," the Holy Spirit is not only their inmost heart, but also their self-giving ecstasy in person, shared in friendship love with us so that our lives, too, might radiate the Trinity's glory.

---

[30] Augustine, *On the Trinity*, 15.19.37; 15.18.32; Burns and Fagan, *Holy Spirit*, 195, 193–94, 187. See also Aquinas, ST, I, 38, 1, ad 4.

[31] Augustine, *On the Trinity*, 15.19.35; 15.19.36; Burns and Fagan, *Holy Spirit*, 194.

[32] Aquinas, ST, I, 38, 1.

[33] Ibid., I, 37, 1; I, 38, 1–2. See also Augustine, *On the Trinity*, 5.14.15; Burns and Fagan, *Holy Spirit*, 189–90.

[34] Gregory of Nyssa, *Sermon Fifteen on the Song of Songs*; LH 390–91.

[35] Irenaeus, *Against the Heresies*, 4; LH 1616.

The Spirit of joy thus becomes within us the glorious giver of life, for we were created to enjoy our life not merely as self-motion in a physical way, but as the power of activity flowing from our own deepest self. The more free and self-directed we become, the more alive we feel. We learn by experience, however, that we are never so alive as when we love. Love makes us free, because the motivation and power for our activity come from deep within our own soul. We know too well how a spirit of fear can dampen our creativity, holding us back from becoming the person we were meant to be. But loving friendship with the Holy Spirit frees the creative energy of joy within us. As we grow close to the Holy Spirit, we become confident and unafraid. The Spirit inspires us to speak and write, to paint and compose from the depths of our soul, which is the Spirit's own home. We begin to feel the inner satisfaction of creating something beautiful with our life, through our work and words, through poetry and art, dance and song, through creative undertakings of any kind that form a melody of love to the Lord: "Be filled with the Spirit . . . making melody to the Lord in your hearts" (Eph 5:18-19). Augustine even urges us to make our whole life a song of joy to God.[36] Ambrose, too, invites us to ponder Mary's joy in surrendering herself to the Holy Spirit, and to ask for her heart to rejoice in the Lord (Luke 1:47).[37]

Leo the Great encourages us to pray for the Holy Spirit's joy as the full flowering of our baptismal grace. No one is cut off from this happiness, for saints and sinners alike have received God's sweet gift of mercy.[38] In her poem on Pentecost, Gertrude von Le Fort describes the joy of the Spirit as a blossoming in our heart more gorgeous than nature in springtime. As we experience the delights of Pentecost, our faces begin to shine with gladness, and joy becomes our very name. The same Spirit who fills the countryside with wondrous plenitude thus enables us, also, to burst into bloom. Like fields overflowing with grain and ablaze with blossoms, we, too, flower through the enchanting Spirit of God.[39]

This sweet flowering of the Spirit in our hearts is described in an especially lovely way by the nineteenth-century Cardinal Henry Manning. Even when we forget the Holy Spirit, Manning writes, the Holy Spirit never forgets us, filling us with comfort when we least expect it: "O how abundant is your goodness" (Ps 31:19). When we are sad or

---

[36] Augustine, *Sermon Thirty-Four*; LH 342.

[37] Ambrose, *Commentary on Luke*, 2; LH 67.

[38] Leo the Great, *Homily on the Lord's Birth*; LH 74.

[39] Gertrude von Le Fort, "Pentecôte," *Hymnes à l'Eglise* (Paris: Casterman); in Arsène-Henry, *Les plus beaux textes*, 330.

grieving, depressed or lonely, an unexplainable peace may flood our heart, "like the soft breath of evening," like the "sweet fragrance" of fields blessed by God. We may think that the comfort we feel comes from a natural cause—our dear ones' affection, or perhaps a call or note from a friend. But hidden in this consolation is the Spirit of joy who alone brings such peace to our heart. If only we would recognize that the "giver of all sweetness" dwells within us, we would waken as from sleep and cry out with Jacob (Gen 28:16-17): "God is in this place and I knew it not: all my life long I have been unconscious. Now I know that my own soul is the house of God, and my own heart . . . the gate of heaven." For this very reason, Manning urges us not to let a day pass without adoring and giving ourselves, with all of our freedom, mind, heart, and will, to the Spirit of love.[40] Indeed, this is the purpose of every spiritual treasure in the Church: to enable us to be possessed by the Spirit of God.[41]

Symeon the New Theologian stresses this same truth especially dear to eastern Christians when he urges us to give ourselves completely to the Holy Spirit as our life's deepest meaning.[42] In one of his prayers, Symeon praises the Lord who has become human in order to give us his Spirit who makes us "divine."[43] Symeon's words echo the sentiments of Athanasius: God the Word has become a "flesh-bearer" so that we might receive from him the Holy Spirit and become "Spirit-bearers," totally possessed by the Spirit.[44] We are called, then, not to a mere "devotion" to the Holy Spirit, but to a life of "living and breathing" the Holy Spirit.[45] As we ourselves live "aglow" (Rom 12:11; RSV) with the Spirit, giver of the Trinity's own joy, our very lives will shine with Christ's light in the world.[46]

---

[40] Henry Edward Manning, *The Internal Mission of the Holy Ghost*, 356; 34, 35.

[41] Lossky, *Mystical Theology*, 196–97.

[42] Symeon the New Theologian, *Sermon Seven*; in Congar, *I Believe*, 2:70.

[43] *Hymn Fifteen*; Maloney, *Hymns of Divine Love*, 54.

[44] Athanasius, *On the Incarnation and against the Arians*, 8; PG 36, 996c. Athanasius stresses that Jesus became a "bearer of our flesh" (*sarkophoros*) so that we might become "bearers of the Spirit" (*pneumatophoroi*); Vladimir Lossky, *Mystical Theology*, 179.

[45] *The Holy Spirit, Lord and Giver of Life*, prepared by the Theological-Historical Commission for the Great Jubilee of the Year 2000, trans. Agostino Bono (New York: Crossroad, 1997) 141–42.

[46] Gregory Nazianzen, *Homily Thirty-Nine: On the Baptism of Christ*; LH 112.

2

SPIRIT OF GOD POURED
OUT BY THE RISEN LORD

Jesus has come to pour out on us his Spirit of joy as the most wondrous fruit of his resurrection. Our reflections on the Holy Spirit thus lead us to contemplate the source of our joy in the Lord's paschal mystery—his death, resurrection, ascension, and their culmination in the Spirit's glorious outpouring at Pentecost. We then reflect on how the early Church came to know and confess the Holy Spirit's identity as the third divine person, giver of God's joyous life to us.

God's Spirit in the Hebrew Scriptures

The Holy Spirit's own anointing inspired early Christians to recognize that their Easter joy was the fruit not of something but of Someone bestowed on them by the risen Lord. They were helped to reach this faith-filled conviction by their Jewish heritage. *Ruah* is the Hebrew word for "spirit," "wind," or "breath." For the Israelite people living in a parched land, the image of winds bringing rain to the earth provided a striking symbol for God's creative power. In Genesis 1:2-3, God's "breath" or "wind" accompanies God's Word *(dabar)*, hovering over the abyss, and calling all of creation to life. The people found another image of God's *ruah* in our own life-breath that comes from God and returns to God at our death (Gen 2:7; Exod 15:8, 10; Ps 33:6; Ps 104:29-30; Job 34:14-15). Deprived of this life-giving Spirit, human efforts are like cut grass which withers and dies (Isa 40:6-8; Ps 104:29).[1]

---

[1] Ambrose, *On the Holy Spirit*, 2.5.33; in *The Holy Spirit*, eds. J. Patout Burns and Gerald M. Fagin (Wilmington: Michael Glazier, Inc., 1984) 143.

Those without this breath lack God's energy and power: the Egyptians' horses "are flesh, and not spirit" (Isa 31:3). Wherever new life springs up and endures, however, the Spirit of God is at work, giving life and renewing the face of the earth (Ps 104:30). This "Spirit" is "holy" (Ps 51:11), belonging to God alone.

Just as we ourselves describe someone who brims with creative vigor as "full of spirit,"[2] the Hebrew authors also envisioned God's creative power as God's "breath" or "Spirit" which came upon chosen leaders. Persons such as Moses (Num 11:25), Joshua (Num 27:18), and Saul (1 Sam 10:6) were depicted as full of God's Spirit enabling them to perform powerful deeds on behalf of the people (Judg 6:34; 1 Sam 11:6; Judg 13:25; 15:14-15). Furthermore, just as our own breath allows us to give voice to our thoughts, God's *ruah* or Spirit was pictured as entering the prophets, empowering them to speak God's own word to the people (Mic 3:8; Ezek 2:2). The ecstatic states of the early prophetic bands thus were attributed to this "breath" of God which no force can manipulate or control: "The spirit of the Lord will possess you . . . and you will be turned into a different person" (1 Sam 10:6; see also 1 Sam 19:20-24). Before the time of David, God's *ruah* was thought to come only for a limited time upon chosen people. With David, however, the Spirit's outpouring was no longer viewed as a sudden, temporary event, for the Spirit remained with David, God's chosen king (1 Sam 16:13).

The prophet Ezekiel was inspired to envision God's life-giving Spirit in still another way. As he contemplated the tragic destruction of Jerusalem and the exile of many people in Babylon, Ezekiel prophesied a joyous return by using the image of a nation raised from the dead. Through the power of God's Spirit who alone gives life, those who had become like a skeleton's bones would rise and live again. They would return from their exile to a whole new life in their homeland: "I will put my spirit within you, and you shall live" (Ezek 37:14). Far from being a transitory power given only to certain individuals to work a mighty deed or to speak God's word, the Spirit was now envisioned as God's life-giving power placed deep within the entire people to transform their hearts: "A new heart I will give you, and a new spirit I will put within you" (Ezek 36:26, 27).

After Zechariah and Malachai, prophecy ceased in the land, and the people grieved the loss of prophets inspired by the Spirit (Ps 74:9; 1 Macc 14:41). With time, however, there arose a fervent expectation that God's Spirit would visit them again. Joel even prophesied that the

---

[2] Walter Kasper, *The God of Jesus Christ*, trans. Matthew J. O'Connell (New York: Crossroad, 1986) 199.

Spirit would be lavished not only on a few but also on everyone (Joel 2:28-29). At the time of Jesus, many looked forward to this new outpouring of God's Spirit which they believed would usher in the eschatological era.

Jesus Anointed with the Spirit

As they reflected on Joel's words, early Christians discovered in their own lives the fulfillment of his prophecy: "In the last days I will pour out my Spirit upon all flesh" (Acts 2:17). In faith they were inspired to identify the source of their new life as the same Spirit of God who filled Israel's leaders and prophets and in whose power Jesus had been raised from the dead. Their own experience of the risen Lord's life within them also impelled them to reflect backward from Jesus' resurrection to the start of his public ministry, and even to the beginning of his human life. They began to recognize in Jesus the figure Isaiah had foretold, the one "anointed" *(messiah)* with the Spirit of God (Isa 42:1; 11:2). The evangelists depict the baptism of Jesus as the beginning of this eschatological age prophesied by Joel—the end time in which the Spirit would be poured out on all the people (Acts 2:33). In their accounts of the baptism of Jesus, the Gospel writers echo marvelous apocalyptic themes found in the Hebrew Scriptures: rending of the heavens, the sound of God's voice, and the coming upon Jesus of the Spirit promised for the end time (Mark 1:9-11; Matt 3:16-17; Luke 3:21-22; John 1:33). Jesus, messianic bearer of the Spirit, has inaugurated the eschaton, the final days of salvation.[3] John stresses that the Spirit of God does not simply visit Jesus but rests upon him permanently (John 1:32). And Paul so closely associates the Holy Spirit with Jesus that he assures us, "Any one who does not have the Spirit of Christ does not belong to him" (Rom 8:9).

Luke, especially, emphasizes the inseparable relation between Jesus and the Holy Spirit. Adopting a key theme from Isaiah, Luke identifies Jesus as so completely anointed with the Spirit that he fulfills and infinitely surpasses all that the prophets could have imagined: "The Spirit of the Lord is upon me, because he has anointed me" (Luke 4:18; Isa 11:2; 61:1). Conceived by the overshadowing of the Holy Spirit upon Mary, Jesus was filled with the Holy Spirit from the moment of his conception (Luke 1:35). Led into the desert by the Spirit (Luke 4:1-2), he cast out demons by the power of this same Spirit (Matt 12:28), and thrilled with joy in the Holy Spirit (Luke 10:21). Now, as risen Lord, he is entirely "anointed with the Holy Spirit and with power" (Acts 10:38).

---

[3] Ibid., 203.

The Holy Spirit and the Death of Jesus

Luke portrays Jesus as living his whole life in the Spirit's anointing (Luke 3:22; 4:1, 14). The evangelist John, however, gives us still another perception of the relation between Jesus and the Holy Spirit. John views the death of Jesus, to which his whole life was leading, as the defining event during which the Holy Spirit is abundantly outpoured. When John writes that Jesus "gave up his spirit" as he died (John 19:30), he uses the Greek word for "spirit," *pneuma,* in several profound and related senses. At his death, Jesus "breathes his last" and so gives to the Father his life-breath. But he also breathes forth on us— "gives over" to us—his Holy Spirit. It is this death, inspired by love, filled with love, and breathing forth love, that John views as the supreme moment of the Holy Spirit's outpouring. The abyss of God's heart is invisible to our eyes. But it is unveiled to us in the love poured out at Jesus' death, the uncreated love that Christians came to recognize as the very person of the Holy Spirit.

We ourselves carry within us depths of goodness that often go unseen. At poignant moments in which the secrets of our heart are manifested, however, the love within us becomes visible. For John, the crucifixion is the supreme moment in which the unseen depths of Jesus' heart are not only revealed but also poured out upon us. His death, full of love and forgiveness, lavishes upon the world the same Spirit of love who filled his heart. The cross, therefore, unveils to us first of all the infinite love between Jesus and his Abba. Jesus surrenders himself into the pit of emptiness which is his death, and trusts that his Father's tender arms will embrace and receive him. But the death of Jesus also unveils the unimaginable depths of his love for us. Catherine of Siena assures us that the flesh of Jesus was nailed to the cross, not by the spikes, but by his own love. No instrument of torture could keep God the Son nailed to the wood if his own love had not kept him there.[4]

The figure of Jesus on the cross—his arms outstretched, his feet nailed—presents a striking contrast to our own reaction to hurt. We are like boxers, with our hands poised to strike out at those who attack us, our feet ready to withdraw from those who hurt us. But the arms of Jesus are extended on the cross in a posture that says, "I will love you always." With his feet nailed to the cross Jesus promises that he will never leave us, regardless of the enormity of our sin. Before he dies, he

---

[4] *Letter 253* to Trincio De' Trinci da Fuligno and Corrado, his brother (Tommaseo edition); Mary Ann Fatula, *Catherine of Siena's Way,* rev. ed. (Collegeville: The Liturgical Press, 1990) 126.

speaks his love in these words full of compassion: "Father, forgive them" (Luke 23:34). Thomas Aquinas tells us that it was the Holy Spirit who filled Jesus' human heart with such tenderness that he freely chose to die this tortured death for us.[5] According to John, then, Jesus' crucifixion culminated his life, for the same Spirit of love who pervaded his life also permeated his death, transforming his human existence into risen life in the Spirit. By his very crucifixion, Jesus has given us communion with the Spirit of love.[6]

On the cross, as he suffered an excruciating death by asphyxiation, Jesus was not able to speak fully the words which would convince his disciples that he freely chose his death for us. During his last meal with his disciples, however, he communicated the meaning of his death in words and actions which anticipated his death and made it present in mystery before it happened. "Having loved his own in the world, he loved them to the end" (John 13:1)—to the very depths that love can go. At a meal which the evangelists associate with the Passover, Jesus took bread, and in the very gesture of breaking it, spoke the meaning of his death: "This is my body which I break for you." In giving them the cup of wine, Jesus proclaimed the mystery of his love for them and for us: "This is my blood which I freely shed for you" (see Luke 22:19-20).

Who can understand love like this? There are depths of sacrifice to which our own love impels us to go for someone dear to us. We read of a mother trapped with her child in the ruins of an earthquake. In her love, she slashes her wrist so that her little one, dying of thirst, can drink her blood. We are touched to the heart by such a story, and yet we can understand love like this—a parent's love for his or her own child. What we cannot understand is love in God infinitely more intense, even "insane," to use Catherine of Siena's remarkable image.[7] To feed our heart's hunger for love, God the Word gives himself to us as our food. In the meals we ourselves prepare for our dear ones, our food symbolizes our love. But in the Last Supper which Jesus shares with his disciples, the meal which he continues to share with us through the Eucharist, we, his beloved friends, feed not simply on a symbol of Jesus' love but on Jesus himself. Here in this Last Supper with his friends, and in the Eucharist which makes the Last Supper present until the end of time, we see unveiled the depths of love in the

---

[5] Aquinas, ST III, 7, 6.

[6] F. X. Durrwell, *Holy Spirit of God: An Essay in Biblical Theology*, trans. Sr. Benedict Davies, O.S.U. (London: Geoffrey Chapman, 1983) 137.

[7] *Prayer Seventeen*; in *The Prayers of Catherine of Siena*, trans. Suzanne Noffke, O.P. (New York: Paulist Press, 1983) 148.

heart of Jesus: "As the Father has loved me, so I have loved you" (John 15:9).

The Holy Spirit and the Resurrection of Jesus

In his death on the cross and his Last Supper anticipating this death, Jesus' entire being was filled with love: love for his Abba and love for us (John 15:13). This created love that filled his human heart had its source not only in his own uncreated person but also in the very person of love who is the Holy Spirit. Before his resurrection, the limitations of Jesus' human existence enabled him only to "contain" the Holy Spirit. Jesus is God the Word whose divine nature is unbounded love, but his human existence, like ours, needed to be opened beyond the limits imposed on him by time and space, and by a specific culture and nation. The Spirit who is the person of infinite life and love had to transform Jesus' humanity so that he could be present to all people, at all times and in all ages. This is precisely the wonder which the Holy Spirit accomplished in the resurrection of Jesus. Through the love which filled his death, the Holy Spirit broke the chains of his death and filled his humanity with new, unconquerable life. This is why Paul stresses that it was by the power and glory of the Holy Spirit that Jesus was raised from the dead (Rom 8:11). His limited human existence was transformed in this way into a Spirit-permeated existence. In the risen humanity of Christ, the Holy Spirit's love reached its greatest intensity, and the Holy Spirit's power achieved its greatest wonder.[8]

Prepared by their own Jewish heritage, early Christians recognized the resurrection of Jesus as the work of God's own Spirit. As we have seen, the exile of the people in Babylon had prompted Ezekiel to prophesy their return through the image of a corpse raised from the dead by God's Spirit. Ezekiel had first pictured the ravaged people of Israel as a pile of decayed bones no longer forming even a corpse. When the Spirit of God breathed over these bones, however, they not only came together but also formed a body that gloriously lived again (Ezek 37:1-14). We ourselves cannot live without air flowing through our lungs. And when someone we love is dying, though we yearn to take our dear one into our arms and breathe life into him or her, our breath is powerless. The Spirit of life, however, can make the dead live again.

In Jesus' resurrection, early Christians recognized the fulfillment of Ezekiel's words: "You shall know that I am the Lord, when I open your graves and bring you up from your graves, O my people. I will put my

---

[8] Durrwell, *Holy Spirit*, 22.

spirit within you, and you shall live" (Ezek 37:13-14). The Spirit breathed unconquerable life into Jesus' human existence, so transforming it that it became the source of our own future glory, the risen life that will be ours forever. Jesus' resurrection, therefore, is not a resuscitation to the same limited life, but rather a magnficent transformation of his entire humanity. Like our own bodies now, the pre-risen body of Jesus was limited by time and space, by suffering and death. The risen Lord, however, no longer lives with the same limited body he had before. The most magnificent sunrise or sunset, setting the sky ablaze with brilliant colors, can only suggest the indescribable beauty of the risen Lord, transfigured by the Spirit's glory. The Church's cry that the Lord is risen expresses our joy in the Lord who is freed of the limitations of time and space even in his human body, and who bestows his marvelous life on us. The risen Jesus is now *Kyrios*, "Lord," and *Christos*, the One so entirely "anointed" with the Holy Spirit that he pours out this same Spirit on those joined in faith to him.

An ancient Easter homily attributed to St. John Chrysostom pictures the baptismal life poured out on us by the risen Lord as the sumptious Easter feast. All are welcome, those who have come at the last hour as well as those who have come at the third or ninth hour (Matt 20:1-6). The "table is full-laden" and the Lord's mercy is lavished on all: "Let none lament their poverty or transgressions, for pardon has dawned from the tomb!" Christ is risen, and the demons are conquered, angels rejoice, and all are made free. Christ is risen, and "there are none dead in the tomb!"[9] God's eschatological promise thus is fulfilled in this dazzling light of Christ's glory. Through the risen Lord, the full outpouring of the Spirit promised by Joel is accomplished: "I will pour out my Spirit on all flesh" (Joel 2:28).

Pentecost

Jesus' glorious resurrection in this way cannot be separated from Pentecost, the outpouring of the Spirit by the risen Lord. The Holy Spirit has so transformed Jesus' humanity that he has become not only the living one, but also, in his risen humanity, "life-giving spirit" (1 Cor 15:45), that is, giver of the Spirit to us. Eastern Christian writers have reflected with special insight on this outpouring of the Spirit as the culmination of the Lord's paschal mystery: the purpose of our redemption is Pentecost. Jesus lived, died, and was raised to unending

---

[9] *Paschal Homily,* attributed to St. John Chrysostom (PG 49, 721–24); in Vladimir Lossky, *The Mystical Theology of the Eastern Church* (London: James Clarke and Co., 1957) 248–49.

life in order to lavish on us the same Spirit who permeated and transformed his own human existence. When we encounter the risen Lord in faith, then, we experience Pentecost—the flooding of our hearts with the same Spirit of love the Father has poured out on the Son from all eternity.

Luke and John give us two different perspectives on this great mystery of Pentecost. Because John views the paschal mystery of Jesus as one event with various facets, he depicts the resurrection, ascension, and Pentecost as happening on "one great day." John tells us of the Pentecost that is the risen Lord's outpouring of the Spirit upon the apostles on the very day of the resurrection (John 20:19). Reflecting John's perspective, eastern Christians continue to call Easter "the Great Day," and Easter week, "Bright Week." Luke, however, reflects on the mystery of Pentecost from a different vantage point. The word *Pentecoste,* meaning "fiftieth," is a Greek word applied to the Hebrew Shabuoth or "Feast of Weeks," a harvest festival beginning with the feast of Unleavened Bread and continuing for seven weeks. For Luke, the Feast of Weeks symbolized the abundant life in the Spirit which the early community experienced as a result of the Spirit's outpouring by the risen Lord. The number "seven" symbolizes fullness; one more than seven times seven connotes inconceivable plenitude. Pentecost occurs seven times seven days after Easter, and even one more day beyond that, not only as the fullness of time but also as the always new "day without evening."[10]

Using this symbolism of fifty days, Luke combines into one great "Pentecost" two distinct events: the apostles' reception of the Spirit, and the outpouring of the Spirit on the people who believed the apostles' preaching as the crowds assembled in Jerusalem for the Jewish feast of Pentecost (Acts 2:1-42). Rich with symbolism, Luke's account compares the division of peoples resulting from the sin of Babel (Gen 11:1-9) with the unity accomplished by the Spirit at Pentecost. At Babel, the spirit of pride caused a confusion of languages so that peoples could no longer communicate with each other. At Pentecost, however, the Holy Spirit bestowed by the risen Lord completely reversed this alienation. Peoples of many nations, speaking different languages, were so united by the Spirit of love that they all understood the marvelous word of God preached to them. The confusion of languages at Babel was thus reversed by the gift of tongues at Pentecost.[11] The Spirit poured out on all flesh has fulfilled the prophecy of Joel

---

[10] Alexander Schmemann, *The Vespers of Pentecost* (Orthodox Church in America, Department of Religious Education, n.d.) 1.

[11] Cyril of Jerusalem, *Catechetical Lectures,* 17.16-17; NPNF 2.7, 128.

2:28-29: all peoples are made one through *koinonia*, the loving communion of the Holy Spirit (Acts 2:42-47).

Adopting the perspective of Luke, the Church throughout the centuries has joyfully celebrated the Lord's resurrection during one long "feast," beginning on Easter Sunday, and culminating fifty days later on the "Great Sunday" of Pentecost. Pentecost is thus the fulfillment of the entire paschal mystery, the birth of the Church in the Spirit. Cyril of Jerusalem remarks that it was on this great day of Pentecost that "the Comforter came down from heaven, the Guardian and Sanctifier of the Church, the Pilot of the tempest-tossed."[12] Jesus' resurrection, culminating in the Spirit's outpouring on us, means that nothing in God is held back from us. Jesus now speaks to us the precious words he addresses to his Father: "All that is mine is yours" (see John 17:10). And "all" that belongs to Jesus, all of the riches poured out on him by his Father, are contained in the person of the Spirit. Jesus, risen Lord, gives us "all" of his treasure, the Spirit who is the Father's and Son's very "heart." Pentecost, then, is the great feast of the triune God's intimacy with us. The Spirit who is the Father's and Son's own heart is now lavished on us, to be our heart as well. Our life is now "Christ-ian" life, completely anointed with the Spirit of love bestowed on us by the risen Lord.

The Gospel of John tells us that before the Lord's death and resurrection "the Spirit had not yet been given, because Jesus was not yet glorified" (John 7:39). Early Christian writers such as Cyril of Jerusalem interpreted this passage to mean that before Pentecost, only certain people shared in the Spirit, and only partially; now, however, all are completely immersed, "baptized," in the Holy Spirit. Those who had mocked the apostles at Pentecost accused them of being inebriated with "new wine." Yes, Cyril of Jerusalem assures us, they were full of the "new Wine" who is the Holy Spirit. This Spirit is like the thriving vine that bears ever new fruit; having filled the prophets, the Holy Spirit now accomplishes an even more wonderful work in us.[13]

The Holy Spirit in the Christian Scriptures

Nearly two decades after the great outpouring of the Spirit on the pilgrims gathered at Jerusalem, Paul began writing his epistles to the communities he had evangelized. Approximately fifty years after Pentecost, Luke wrote his two-volume work, his Gospel and the Acts of the Apostles. Perhaps ten years after this, John's Gospel was com-

---

[12] Ibid., 17.13; NPNF 2.7, 127.
[13] Ibid., 17.18; NPNF 2.7, 128.

posed. Yet each of these authors wrote about his community's experience of the Holy Spirit with the same joy and vigor that characterized that first Pentecost. We summarize here some of the key insights these authors were inspired to articulate about the Spirit they experienced so powerfully at work in their hearts and communities.

Paul, the earliest New Testament writer, emphasizes that the Holy Spirit is the very heart of our Christian life and belief (Rom 8:1-11; Gal 5:16-26). The Spirit is Christ's own Spirit (Rom 8:9; Phil 1:19; Gal 4:6) in whose power he was raised from the dead (Rom 8:11) and who now dwells in us through baptism, in order to lead us to Jesus (1 Cor 12:3). From his own experience, Paul was convinced that without this Spirit our human life is mere "flesh" whose pitiful "works" are strife, anger, jealousy, dissension, envy, drunkenness, carousing, enmity, immorality (Gal 5:19-21). But the Holy Spirit poured out by the risen Lord enables us to live in a totally different way (Rom 7:6), with a joy and peace (Rom 14:17), a power and freedom (Gal 5:13-16) that infinitely surpass what our own efforts could accomplish.

The Spirit unites us so intimately with Jesus that we now have a radically new power to pray (Rom 8:26), and to address the first divine person with the same intimate name which Jesus himself used when praying, *"Abba"* (Gal 4:6). No longer strangers and slaves filled with the spirit of fear, we are sons and daughters of the Father, filled with the Holy Spirit of God (Rom 8:15-16). This Spirit does not form us into isolated individuals but into a community of people in loving relationship, living in the "communion" *(koinonia)* of the Holy Spirit with the triune God and one another (2 Cor 13:14). We enter into this communion by drinking of the one Spirit, that is, by being baptized into the one body of Christ, the Church (1 Cor 12:13). In the body of Christ, each member is important, for the Spirit gives to each one his or her own gifts, ministry, and part to play in fostering the growth of the entire body (1 Cor 12:4-11). Infusing all these gifts is the Spirit's own charity (Rom 5:5; 1 Cor 13:1-13) which enables us to give ourselves to one another in unselfish love and service (Gal 5:13). Our very baptism, then, transforms us into persons who are "spiritual," that is, "Spirit-permeated" (1 Cor 2:13-15): "You are not in the flesh, you are in the Spirit, since the Spirit of God dwells in you" (Rom 8:9). Even now, this Spirit is the "guarantee" within us of heaven, where our mortal bodies will be "swallowed up by life" (2 Cor 5:4, 5) and we will share completely in the Spirit-permeated life of the risen Christ (1 Cor 15:42-44).

The above insights of Paul are complemented by those of John and Luke. As we have seen, Luke stresses that Jesus has poured out on us the Holy Spirit as the entire treasure of the Father's heart (Luke 11:13), the eschatological gift in answer to all of God's promises (Acts 2:33). Just as Jesus himself "rejoiced in the Holy Spirit" (Luke 10:21), all of us who believe in Jesus are meant to be filled with the same Spirit of joy (Acts 13:52). Luke's Acts of the Apostles, sometimes called the "Gospel of the Holy Spirit," recounts the power and joy of this Spirit filling the Church, spreading its boundaries to the ends of the earth. Peter proclaimed to the people assembled at Jerusalem that they, too, would receive the same "promise" and "gift" of the Spirit who had been poured out on the apostles (Acts 2:33, 38). Later, Peter and Steven preached the Gospel in the power of the Spirit (Acts 4:8; 7:55), who also instructed Philip where to go and to whom to preach (Acts 8:39). Saul's own conversion was accompanied by the outpouring of this same Spirit (Acts 9:17).

Luke summarizes the first part of Acts by describing how the Holy Spirit worked powerfully not only in these apostles but also in all the early Christians: "The church throughout Judea, Galilee and Samaria had peace and was built up. Living in the fear of the Lord and in the comfort of the Holy Spirit, it increased in numbers" (Acts 9:31). In the second part of Acts, Luke shows the Church spreading out from Jerusalem, with the Holy Spirit inspiring both Paul's mission to the Gentiles and Peter's acceptance of Gentiles into the Church (Acts 10:19-20). When, for example, Peter preached to Gentiles who thereafter spoke in tongues and extolled God (Acts 10:44-46), "the circumcised believers who had come with Peter were astounded that the gift of the Holy Spirit had been poured out even on the Gentiles." Luke also recounts how Paul's discourse was the occasion for the Spirit's outpouring on still other Gentiles, so that they, too, spoke in tongues and prophesied (Acts 19:6). The same Holy Spirit led Paul to Jerusalem (Acts 20:22-23), and from there ultimately to Rome, the very heart of the empire, where he would proclaim the Lord Jesus Christ to everyone he encountered (Acts 28:31).

Not only Luke's writings but also John's Gospel and epistles stress the centrality of the Holy Spirit in the life of the Church. We will see various themes of John developed in the following chapters, but here we simply point out some key emphases of John. Jesus has received the Spirit "without measure" (John 3:34) in order to lavish this same Spirit upon the apostles (John 20:22), and on us through our baptism (John 7:39; 1:33; 3:5). This "Spirit of truth" is the Paraclete, our "Counselor" and "Advocate" with us forever (John 14:16), the "Anointing" within us, teaching and guiding us into all truth (John 14:16-17; 1 John 2:26-27). Even more, we can experience God's intimate presence within us only because we have received God's own Spirit (1 John 3:24; 4:13).

The Spirit Is Someone, Not Something

In a number of these passages from Paul, Luke, and John, the Holy Spirit is depicted, not as something, but as Someone who is divine. In other places of the New Testament, however, the impersonal pronoun "it" is used in referring to the Holy Spirit. This practice is explained both by the early Christians' gradual realization of the Spirit's personal identity, and also by the fact that while the word "spirit" is a feminine noun in Hebrew and Syriac, it is a neuter noun in Greek, the language of the New Testament. Nevertheless, several verses in John refer to the Holy Spirit with the masculine personal demonstrative (John 14:17, 26; 16:7-8, 13-14).[14] We have also seen Luke's emphasis on the Holy Spirit directing the apostles in the spread of the Church to the Gentiles. Passages such as these, in which the Spirit speaks, are common in Acts: "While they were worshipping the Lord and fasting, the Holy Spirit said, 'Set apart for me Barnabas and Saul for the work to which I have called them.'" After hands had been laid on them, they were "sent out by the Holy Spirit" (Acts 13:2-4). It was also the Holy Spirit who directed Peter to consult those who would expand his vision of Church to include the Gentiles (Acts 10:19).

When New Testament writers refer to the Holy Spirit in this personal rather than impersonal way, they do so from a Jewish background that prepared them to identify the Holy Spirit not as something but as Someone. As we have seen, the "Spirit of God" in the Hebrew Scriptures refers to God's creative life-giving power. But from Proverbs 8:22-31 to the Book of Sirach, the Spirit is increasingly "personalized," so to speak. For example, the Spirit is sometimes identified with wisdom (Wis 1:6; 7:7, 22, 25), often portrayed as a person (Sir 1:1-10; 4:11-19; 15:1-8; 24:1-22).[15] In contrast with wisdom, however, the Spirit of God is characterized by energy and the power to transform. In apocryphal and rabbinical writings, too, the Spirit of God is described as speaking, crying, admonishing, grieving, weeping, rejoicing, and comforting. The Spirit of God in this way came to be viewed as a personal and even angelic being within Palestinian Judaism.[16]

Continuing this tradition of attributing personal characteristics to God's Spirit, the authors of New Testament texts such as Hebrews 3:7 and 1 Peter 1:12 refer to the Holy Spirit as speaking in the Hebrew Scriptures. Paul, in particular, tells us that the Spirit is present and act-

---

[14] Kasper, *God*, 210–11.

[15] Ibid., 210.

[16] Yves Congar, O.P., *I Believe in the Holy Spirit*, trans. David Smith (New York: Seabury Press, 1983) 1:9-11.

ing freely in all of creation, especially in us who are persons. The Spirit groans and prays in us, pleading for us (Rom 8:26), bearing witness to our spirit (Rom 8:16), and giving us gifts as he chooses (1 Cor 12:11). Finally, the Gospel of John assures us that the Holy Spirit is our helper (John 15:26) and teacher (John 14:26; 16:13-14), breathing when and where he wills (John 3:8). For early Christian writers such as Cyril of Jerusalem, scriptural passages such as these show clearly that the Holy Spirit is not something but Someone, God the Spirit.[17]

Eastern Patristic Writings: The Spirit Divinizes Us

During the first three centuries after Pentecost, the words of Ezekiel 36:26-27 took on a profound, new meaning for the early Christians: "A new heart I will give you, and a new spirit I will put within you . . . I will put my spirit within you." Inspired by the Holy Spirit and based on their own experience of this Spirit as the giver of life within them, these Christians were drawn to confess in a public way the Holy Spirit's personal identity.

For a half-century after the Council of Nicaea's profession of faith in the divinity of Jesus (325 A.D.), the Church had struggled with Arian "Pneumatomachians" or "Spirit-fighters," who did not acknowledge the Holy Spirit's divinity and personal identity. In response to the Arians who had denied the divinity of Jesus, eastern Church fathers had argued, "If Christ is not God, we are not saved." Now, in defending the Spirit's divinity, they spoke again from the depths of their own faith experience: "If the Spirit is not God, we are not divinized." In their baptism they had been filled with the joy and power of the Trinity's own life—the reality which eastern Christians call "divinization." They knew that they had been baptized into the Father, Son, and Holy Spirit, and that they prayed "in" the Spirit (John 4:24), worshipping the Spirit with the Father and the Son. Through their baptismal formula and prayer, therefore, they were already acknowledging the Holy Spirit's equality with the Father and Son. By the time of the fourth century, their experience of the Spirit as the "giver of life" (2 Cor 3:6; John 6:63) in baptism, conferring on them a whole new way to live, would not allow them to keep silent or ambiguous about the One who imparts so great a gift. Cyril of Alexandria stresses that in baptism the Holy Spirit gives us a new birth to the very life of God. Uniting us intimately to Christ as his brothers and sisters, the Holy Spirit transforms us into beloved sons and daughters, heirs of our Father.[18] We

---

[17] Cyril of Jerusalem, *Catechetical Lectures*, 17.28; NPNF 1.7, 131.
[18] Cyril of Alexandria, *Commentary on John*, 10; Burns and Fagan, *Holy Spirit*, 164.

thus receive from the Spirit the power to live in an entirely new way, exceeding all that our own efforts could accomplish. It is a life so full of the Trinity's own love, joy, and truth that it is called "divinization," "being made like God."

Saints such as Athanasius, Basil the Great, and Gregory Nazianzen became convinced that the Holy Spirit can "divinize" us, giving us a share in the Trinity's own life, only because the Holy Spirit is God and must be adored as God.[19] The living seal and anointing we receive at our baptism is not a creature but the person of the Holy Spirit who has the very same divine nature as the Father and the Son. It is through this Spirit that we become "partakers" of Christ and of the Father (see 2 Pet 1:4). Athanasius tells us that our baptismal "commingling" with the Holy Spirit unites us so intimately to the Father and Son that if we confess that the Son is divine, we must also confess that the Spirit is divine. Otherwise, we deny not only the Spirit's divinity but also the Son's, for the Spirit is the Son's own divine icon or image: those "whom he foreknew, he also predestined to be conformed to the image of his Son" (Rom 8:29). As the Son's living icon, the Holy Spirit who is proper to the Son is not alien to God.[20] Since the Spirit has the same relation to the Son as the Son to the Father, the Spirit cannot be a creature, for the Spirit is the giver of holiness and new life: "When you send forth your spirit, they are created" (Ps 104:30).[21] Another early writer, Cyril of Jerusalem, invites us to go with him beyond all that we can see of the Spirit's power and loveliness here on earth and to ascend into the heavens. Let us picture in our mind all of the spirits and angelic beings, the myriads of angels, archangels, and the entire heavenly host. As marvelous as these are, however, the Holy Spirit is still more wonderful, for the Holy Spirit is God, the third divine person overshadowing them all as their sanctifier, teacher, and comforter.[22]

The fourth century Cappadocians, Basil the Great, Gregory of Nyssa, and Gregory Nazianzen, dedicated themselves to defending the Holy Spirit's divinity and personal identity. They did so especially by reflecting on their own baptism, and, in the light of this profound gift, by searching the scriptural passages referring to the Holy Spirit. Basil the Great writes that Scripture itself proclaims the Spirit's divinity and personhood by calling the Spirit the "anointing" who is inseparable

---

[19] Athanasius, *Letter to Serapion*, 1.24, 25; Burns and Fagan, *Holy Spirit*, 104, 105; Gregory Nazianzen, *Fifth Theological Oration*, 4 and 28; NPNF 2.7, 319, 327; Basil, *Against Eunomius*, 3.5.

[20] Athanasius, *Letter to Serapion*, 1.24, 25; Burns and Fagan, *Holy Spirit*, 104, 105.

[21] Ibid., 1.22, 23; Burns and Fagan, *Holy Spirit*, 102.

[22] Cyril of Jerusalem, *Catechetical Lectures*, 16.23; NPNF 2.7, 121.

from the Lord. Since the Father himself has anointed Jesus with the Holy Spirit (Acts 10:38), this Spirit is not a creature like us. We are enslaved to sin, but the Spirit sets us free (Rom 8:2); we need life, but the Spirit gives us life (John 6:63); we need to be taught, but the Spirit teaches us (John 14:26); we need to be made holy, but the Spirit makes us holy (1 Pet 1:2). Giving us a profound understanding of the things of God, the Holy Spirit distributes wonderful charisms to us, making us citizens of heaven, giving us companionship with the angels, everlasting joy, and, the most profound gift of all, "being made God." This experience of "divinization" impelled Basil to plumb the depths of meaning contained also in 2 Corinthians 3:6 and John 6:63: "The Spirit gives life." At our baptism we receive an intimate communion with the Holy Spirit who shines in us, bestowing on us God's own life, and making us "spiritual" *(pneumatikoi)*, that is, persons entirely permeated with the Holy Spirit.[23]

Gregory of Nyssa argues that those who deny the Spirit's divinity set themselves against their own life which they have received in baptism. Nothing is more precious than this gift of sharing in the Trinity's life; how, then, can we not adore as God the One who gives God's life to us. Those who refuse to acknowledge the Spirit's divinity "insult the Life-giver" while cleaving to the Spirit's gift of life. Such people want to be holy without acknowledging the giver of this holiness (1 Pet 1:2). Gregory further stresses that, since we are baptized into all three persons, Father, Son, and Holy Spirit, each of them, and not simply one of them, is truly God. Those who deny the Spirit's divinity, therefore, attack not only the Holy Spirit but also the entire Trinity. Since the Father, Son, and Holy Spirit all create us, they all have the one same divine nature. And since grace flows down in an unbroken stream from the Father through the Son and in the Spirit, unbelief in the Holy Spirit extends to the entire Trinity, making faith in the Father and Son impossible also.[24] Unbelievers call the Spirit a creature. On the contrary, Gregory argues, the fact that Jesus is called "Christ," shows how inseparably the Son is united to the Holy Spirit, the living anointing and kingship with whom the Father has anointed Jesus. Scripture itself proclaims the Holy Spirit to be divine by describing the Spirit as infinitely good, all-powerful, wise, glorious, and eternal. Indeed, Gregory concludes, the Spirit is goodness and wisdom, power and holiness, everlastingness, and every other magnificent name that can be imagined.[25]

[23] Basil the Great, *On the Holy Spirit*, 9.23; NPNF 2.8, 16, 15.

[24] Gregory of Nyssa, *On the Holy Spirit*; NPNF 2.5, 323, 322, 324; *On the Trinity*; NPNF 2.5, 329.

[25] Idem., *On the Trinity*; NPNF 2.5, 330; *On the Holy Spirit*; NPNF 2.5, 321, 316–17.

The third Cappadocian, Gregory Nazianzen, gives us a beautiful summary of the Holy Spirit's glory as Scripture itself proclaims it. This Spirit is the Father's own Spirit as well as the Spirit of Jesus, the Spirit of adoption, truth, and freedom, creating and permeating the universe, making us holy through the sacraments, teaching and divinizing us, and drawing us to unending life in heaven.[26] Cyril of Alexandria asks how it is possible to call "created" the very Spirit by whom the "image and seal" of the Trinity's own life and nature (2 Pet 1:4) are "engraved" in the depths of our being. And the Spirit does not imprint God's nature in us as an artist paints a picture. On the contrary, the very person of the Spirit is impressed in our hearts as though in wax, "in the manner of a seal" (Eph 4:30). We are the humble recipients, therefore, of the Holy Spirit's own unconditional self-giving to us; "assimilated" with the very person of the Spirit, we are filled with God's glory and remade in God's own image.[27] Commenting on this beautiful theme, Symeon the New Theologian tells us that the Holy Spirit makes us "shine" with a love and joy that are God's own, for the glory within us is the very person of the Spirit. This is precisely the reason that God the Word has become flesh, to bestow on us his own Spirit so that we might become "God" through grace: "What dignity, what glory!"[28]

The Council of Constantinople and the Filioque

Influenced by Athanasius and the Cappadocians, and convoked under the leadership of Gregory Nazianzen, the Council of Constantinople in 381 A.D. proclaimed the Church's belief in the Holy Spirit as "Lord and Giver of Life." Because the debate between Arians and Nicene believers had divided his empire, the emperor Theodosius himself had called the council to settle the issue of the Spirit's divinity. A half-century earlier, the Council of Nicaea in 325 had professed belief in the Son's divinity by re-defining Greek philosophical language in response to Arius' use of philosophical terms. Against Arius, the Council of Nicaea had affirmed that the Son is divine, "God [the Son] from God [the Father]," begotten, not created, and of the same nature or substance *(homoousios)* as the Father. The Nicene Creed also had professed belief simply "in the Holy Spirit." For years after Nicaea, the meaning of the philosophical term used to defend the Son's divinity, *homoousios*, occasioned constant debate.

---

[26] Gregory Nazianzen, *Fifth Theological Oration*, 29; NPNF 2.7, 327.

[27] Cyril of Alexandria, *Thesaurus*, 34; in Congar, *I Believe*, 2:97, n. 41.

[28] Symeon the New Theologian, *Hymn Twenty-Five*; in *Hymns of Divine Love*, trans. and intro., George Maloney, S.J. (Denville, N.J.: Dimension Books, 1975) 136.

Over five decades of controversy prompted the bishops gathered at the Council of Constantinople to avoid the technical language that had provoked so many arguments after Nicaea. In contrast with the philosophical language used at Nicaea, the Council of Constantinople affirmed belief in the Spirit's divinity by adding to the Nicene Creed words drawn from Scripture, as well as from the community's baptismal and liturgical experience: The Holy Spirit is "Lord and Giver of life" (2 Cor 3:6; John 6:63) who proceeds from the Father (John 15:26). Drawing from Matthew 28:19—"baptizing them in the name of the Father, Son and Holy Spirit"—the Council also proclaimed that the Holy Spirit "together with the Father and Son is worshipped and glorified."

Finally, after four centuries of theological struggle about the personal identity of the Holy Spirit, the Council of Constantinople solemnly proclaimed the Church's belief in the Holy Spirit, not as an impersonal force or personification of God's power, but as truly God, the third divine person of the Trinity. And while the Council did not use the technical word "person" (*hypostasis*) of the Spirit because it is not a scriptural term, Christian writers began to apply this word to the Holy Spirit, for person is what is most perfect in all of reality. Indeed, all that is best in what is meant by "person"—reality that is Someone, not something—is found in the divine persons in an unimaginable way. Not only are the Father and the Son persons, therefore, but the Holy Spirit also is a person—not as we are, created and limited, for example, by gender—but in a way that infinitely transcends all that we can think or imagine.[29]

The Council of Constantinople proclaimed the Church's belief in the divinity and personal identity of the Spirit. But an issue that continued to occasion theological debate was the question of how the Holy Spirit is distinct from the Son. In John 15:26 we read that the Spirit "proceeds from the Father," yet we also read that the Son comes from the Father (John 8:42). Why, then, are the Spirit and Son not the same person? As we shall see, in the West, Augustine of Hippo stressed that the Holy Spirit is the very bond of love between the Father and Son, eternally proceeding from the Father "and from the Son" (*filioque*). In this way Augustine tried to guard the Holy Spirit's distinction from the Son. At the same time, he wanted to defend the Son's divinity against the Arians by professing the Son's equality with the Father.

In contrast with western writers such as Hilary and Augustine, however, eastern Christians distinguished the Spirit from the Son by using

---

[29] Aquinas, ST, I, 29, 3.

scriptural language only. The Son is the divine person who is "begotten of the Father," (John 1:18), but the Spirit is the one who "proceeds from" *(ekpourouetai)* the Father (John 15:26).[30] Although eastern Christians speak of the Spirit as the one who "proceeds from" the Father, the Cappadocians tell us that the manner of this proceeding cannot be understood by our minds nor described in our feeble words. Rather, we believe that the Father, Son, and Spirit are distinct because of their unique relationship to one another.[31] Gregory of Nyssa describes the Holy Spirit as holy, radiant with beauty, working everywhere in the world, teaching us the truth, searching "even the depths of God" (1 Cor 2:10), "proceeding from the Father" (John 15:26), and "receiving" from the Son (John 16:15).[32] In speaking apparently of the "temporal mission" rather than the eternal origin of the Spirit from the Father, Athanasius writes also that the Spirit "shines forth, and is sent, and is given" from the Son.[33]

As we have seen, the Nicene-Constantinopolitan Creed professed the Church's belief in the Spirit "who proceeds from the Father." By using only biblical language, the Council in this way avoided the controversy that surrounded the philosophical term *homoousios* used of the Son in the Nicene Creed. The Councils of Ephesus in 431, Chalcedon in 451, and III Council of Constantinople in 680–81 further declared that anyone who dared to add anything to the Nicene Creed was "anathema." In Spain, however, the Third Synod of Toledo in 589 used Augustine's theological formulation, "the Holy Spirit proceeds from the Father *and from the Son*" *(filioque)* to confess the Son's divinity and the Spirit's personal identity as distinct from the Son. Later, the Visigoth King Recaredo, a former Arian, mandated the addition of the *filioque* to the Creed. In this way he intended to fight against Arianism by professing the Son's divinity and equality with the Father. In 633 A.D., the Fourth Synod of Toledo sanctioned this addition to the creed recited in Spain.

Nearly two centuries later, Charlemagne was crowned in Rome as emperor of the Holy Roman Empire. But he also wanted to exert his power over the eastern empire, whose capital was Constantinople. Part of his strategy may have included using the *filioque* as a political weapon. Even though Pope Leo III would not include the *filioque* in the creed recited at Rome, Charlemagne ensured that the *filioque* was added to the creed in other parts of his empire. Furthermore, in 807 he

---

[30] See Walter Kasper, *God*, 217.
[31] Gregory Nazianzen, *Fifth Theological Oration*, 9; NPNF 2.7, 320.
[32] Gregory of Nyssa, *On the Holy Spirit*; NPNF 2.5, 319.
[33] Athanasius, *Letter to Serapion*, 1.20; Burns and Fagan, 101.

called a council which charged the eastern empire with heresy because it "omitted" the *filioque* from the creed. In the same century the patriarch of Constantinople, Photius, responded by insisting that the Spirit proceeds from the Father alone, and charging the West with heresy in using the *filioque*. Two centuries later, in 1014, the Germanic emperor Henry II was crowned at Rome by Pope Benedict VIII. At his coronation Mass, he used the Germanic liturgical rite, including the Germanic form of the creed containing the *filioque*. From that time onward, the *filioque* remained in the Creed recited at Rome.

The political power struggle between the two empires culminated in the schism between eastern and western Christians in 1054. In that year, Cardinal Humbert, the legate of Pope Leo IX, excommunicated the patriarch of Constantinople, Michael Caelularius. One of the several charges of heresy included that the Church centered in Constantinople had "suppressed" the *filioque* from the Creed. Caelularius in turn excommunicated the pope and declared that the bishop of Rome had no authority over the eastern Churches. The situation worsened in 1203 and 1204 when knights on the fourth crusade attacked and conquered Constantinople. Years later, the Councils of II Lyons in 1274 and Florence in 1439 tried to reconcile East and West. The attempts, however, produced no lasting union. One reason is that both of these western councils showed little understanding of eastern approaches to the Spirit and tried to demonstrate that eastern Church Fathers had professed belief in the *filioque*. In addition, the Council of Florence held out the promise of aid to the East as it faced attacks from the Turks. When Constantinople was betrayed by the West and fell to the Turks in 1453, the schism between East and West was sealed.[34]

Other eastern Churches linked to Constantinople were included in the schism. In 988 Russia had been converted to eastern Christianity after Prince Vladimir, a pagan of Viking descent, asked Constantinople to send missionaries to his empire. Married to Anna, sister of the Byzantine emperor Basil II, Vladimir is said to have fallen in love with the beauty of the liturgy celebrated in Constantinople. When Constantinople separated from Rome, the schism had repercussions in Russia also. Today, key Orthodox ("Right Belief") Churches are established in Russia, Greece, Cyprus, Bulgaria, Albania, North America, and other parts of the world. Some Orthodox Christians—for example, the Nestorians and Monophysites—had withdrawn from communion with Rome in the fifth century because of differing beliefs about the divinity and humanity of Jesus. But over the course of the centuries,

[34] See José Comblin, *The Holy Spirit and Liberation*, trans. Paul Burns (Maryknoll: Orbis Books, 1989) 166–75.

other eastern churches returned to communion with Rome. Among these were the Maronites, Ukrainians, Carpatho-Rusyns, Lebanese and Syrian Melkites, Romanians, and Bulgarians. Although the Orthodox generally remain critical of these unions, the ecumenical dialogues inspired by Vatican Council II are helping to bring about increased understanding and cooperation between Catholic and Orthodox Christians.

The Ever-Present Joy of Pentecost

Tragically, the division between western and Orthodox Christians which continues today centers in part not only on disputes over authority but also on differing understandings of the eternal origin of the Spirit, the source of our unity. The Holy Spirit who worked miracles of love in the early Church, however, is the same Spirit at work among us today, drawing us to experience the continuing miracle of Pentecost among us. In a beautiful poem, Paul Claudel voices the incredible wonder of this ever new and always present feast of the Holy Spirit's Pentecostal joy in our hearts. When we commune with Jesus in the Eucharist we, too, are plunged into the grace of Pentecost, and we, too, are consumed by the fire of the Spirit who conquers death. This Spirit of life comes to us with tenderness, filling our soul and senses like the fragrance of an intoxicating perfume, alluring us always to greater and sweeter good. For us who are permeated by the Spirit, every day is Pentecost. How, then, can our souls not sing for joy, and the wings of our heart refuse to take flight![35]

All of us are meant to experience daily this Pentecostal joy of the Spirit poured out by the risen Lord, for the grace of the paschal feast is the "beginning of a new existence."[36] This is why St. Athanasius urges us to ask for a greater outpouring of the Spirit every day of our lives. As we shall see in the following chapter, the Spirit of God is the living water whose power within us makes every day a new beginning.[37]

[35] Paul Claudel, "Hymne de la Pentecôte," *Ecoute, ma Fille* (Paris: Gallimard, 1934); in Yolande Arsène-Henry, ed., *Les plus beaux textes sur le Saint-Esprit*, rev. ed. (Paris: Lethielleux, 1968) 307–11.

[36] *Easter Homily of the Early Church*; LH 318.

[37] Athanasius, *Fifth Paschal Letter*; LH 282.

3

SPIRIT OF LIFE

The early Christians discovered by experience the inseparable relationship between Pentecost and baptism, the sacrament through which the Spirit of life bestowed by the Lord at Pentecost continues to be poured out on us today.

Spirit of Life Poured Out at Pentecost

In the midst of the lavish beauty of spring we celebrate Pentecost as "the last and great day," the beginning and culmination of our redemption. During the brilliance of springtime, the myriad voices of nature break out in the joy of living to announce this feast of the Spirit, great distributor of life![1] During the Vespers of Pentecost, eastern Christians sing to the Holy Spirit, "O Comforter, Treasury of Blessings and Giver of Life, Fountain of goodness, Come and abide in us!"[2] In churches decorated with lovely blossoms and young green branches, these Christians hold flowers in their hands to symbolize the ecstatic explosion of life that is Pentecost's eternal springtime.

Spring itself is the irrepressible feast of life. Who can resist its bounty, its beauty? Against all odds, delicate buds blossom forth, pushing their tender way through hard ground, from in between rocks, and in desert land. Everywhere, winter's cold night is conquered by glorious life. All three divine persons create this life, but earth's beauty is accomplished in a special way by the Spirit of life who adorns all of creation with

---

[1] Karl Adam, *Christ Our Brother* (London: Sheed and Ward, 1937) 145.
[2] Alexander Schmemann, *The Vespers of Pentecost* (Orthodox Church in America, Department of Religious Education, n. d.) 11, 20.

loveliness.[3] Not simply a few flowers, nor even a few kinds of flowers spring to life, but myriads of them, every one of them different. Glorious colors and intoxicating fragrances perfume the air with profusion and plenitude—gorgeous daffodils and hyacinths, lilies of the valley and violets, splendid magnolias and delicate apple blossoms. The mark of springtime is the casting off of restraint.

At the very beginning of time, the creation of the universe was a first springtime and a first "Pentecost," an outpouring of the Spirit of life into the void.[4] Genesis pictures the world being brought to birth by God's powerful *ruah*: "The spirit of God swept over the face of the waters" (Gen 1:2). This breath of God's life hovered over the waters like a mother bird bending over the nest of her little ones, calling them to live and to grow. The biblical authors further depict creation itself as wonderfully alive: the earth cries out with joy, the waters clap their hands, and the hills sing (Ps 98:8, 9)![5] Paul would later say that all of creation is "groaning" to share in the full Pentecostal life of God's children (Rom 8:19-22). Surely the source of creation's profusion is no cold, impersonal force, measuring out life in stingy drops. Rather, the Spirit is the infinitely generous giver of life: "When you send forth your spirit, they are created" (Ps 104:30). Wherever new life "seethes and bubbles" the Holy Spirit is present, filling the world with marvelous beauty (Wis 1:7; 7:22–8:1).[6] Cardinal Newman tells us that the Holy Spirit is the life-breath not only of the physical world but also of the spiritual world. Our every noble effort and deed, our every good thought, word, and desire comes from this Spirit who inspires the angels' praise, and raises the dead to life.[7]

Baptismal Experience of the Spirit

Early Christians came to know this Spirit of life through the wondrous grace of their baptism. As we have seen, Luke tells us in the Acts of the Apostles the marvelous story of Pentecost, the outpouring of the Spirit on the apostles and on those to whom they proclaimed the risen Lord (Acts 2:1-36). Inspired by the Holy Spirit, people began to re-

---

[3] *The Demonstration of the Apostolic Preaching,* 5; in J. Patout Burns and Gerald M. Fagin, eds., *The Holy Spirit* (Wilmington: Michael Glazier, Inc., 1984) 42.

[4] F. X. Durrwell, *Holy Spirit of God: An Essay in Biblical Theology,* trans. Sr. Benedict Davies, O.S.U. (London: Geoffrey Chapman, 1983) 19.

[5] Adam, *Christ Our Brother,* 145.

[6] Walter Kasper, *The God of Jesus Christ,* trans. Matthew J. O'Connell (New York: Crossroad, 1986) 202.

[7] John Henry Cardinal Newman, *Meditations and Devotions* (London: Longmans, Green and Co., 1953) 309–10.

spond to the apostles' witness with a faith that cried out, "We, too, repent of our sin and want this new life which we see in you, this gift of the Spirit lavished on you." The Church swelled with more and more believers who were transformed by the baptismal gift of the Spirit. Their lives were turned upside down as they entered into communion with the Trinity and one another through the Spirit of love. In the sweet power of this Spirit, these early Christians claimed their identity as God's own family, brothers and sisters in the risen Lord (Acts 2:37-47).

Gregory of Nyssa contemplates the miracle of baptism as the victory of the Holy Spirit destroying death and filling us with God's own radiant life. Conceived by faith, we are born anew in baptism as the Father's beloved children. Our sweet mother, the Church, receives us into her tender arms, feeds us with her teaching and discipline, and nourishes us with the heavenly food of the Eucharist. Fed by the Lord's body and blood, we grow strong by a holy way of life. Intimacy with wisdom becomes our marriage, God's kingdom our home, hope our child, and the delights of paradise our inheritance. We are destined not for death but for glorious life, since Jesus, first-born from the dead, has promised us, "I am ascending to my Father and your Father, to my God and your God" (John 20:17). The wondrous mystery of God's closeness to us is that Jesus remains with us and yet goes to his Father, taking all of us with him.[8]

To understand more deeply the meaning of their own sacramental baptism, early Christians pondered the biblical accounts of Jesus' symbolic baptism by John. As Jesus was plunged into the waters of the Jordan, the Holy Spirit assured his human heart of his identity as the Father's only beloved Son. Church Fathers such as Cyril of Alexandria stressed that it was not for himself that Jesus underwent this baptism. On the contrary, the Spirit is his from all eternity as God the Son, and it is from him that we receive the Spirit's grace. But because he bears us in himself, Jesus, the Word made flesh, received the Spirit for all of us, so that we, too, could become the Father's beloved sons and daughters in him.[9]

As they recognized this intimate connection between Jesus' baptism and ours, early believers began to celebrate his baptism as the Spirit's transformation of the entire universe: "Today earth and sea have shared the Savior's grace, and the whole world is flooded with joy." At

[8] Gregory of Nyssa, *Sermon One: On the Resurrection of Christ;* LH 366.

[9] Cyril of Alexandria, *Commentary on John,* 5.2; in Burns and Fagan, *Holy Spirit,* 162–63. See also Raniero Cantalamessa, *The Holy Spirit in the Life of Jesus: The Mystery of Christ's Baptism,* trans. Alan Neame (Collegeville: The Liturgical Press, 1994).

the ancient flood a dove brought an olive branch, but at Christ's baptism the Holy Spirit appears in the form of a dove to make known the immense mercy of God. Noah's flood destroyed our race, but the new flood of baptismal waters now brings the dead to life.[10]

A remarkable fifth-century inscription, perhaps composed by Leo the Great, adorns the baptistry of the Church of St. John Lateran, the mother Church at Rome. Its words describe the wonders which the Holy Spirit accomplishes in every place where the sacrament of baptism is celebrated:

> Here is born in Spirit-soaked fertility a brood destined for another City, begotten by God's blowing and borne upon this torrent by the Church their virgin mother. Reborn in these depths they reach for heaven's realm. . . . This spring is life that floods the world, the wounds of Christ its awesome source. Sinner sink beneath this sacred surf that swallows age and spits up youth. Sinner here scour sin away down to innocence, for they know no enmity who are by one font, one Spirit, one faith made one. Sinner shudder not at sin's kind and number, for those born here are holy![11]

The Baptismal Rites

As the above inscription suggests, early Christians were plunged into Jesus' death and resurrection by celebrating a baptismal rite that flooded not only their souls but also their senses with the loveliness of the Spirit, giver of life.[12] By the fourth century, baptism was celebrated in many communities during the Easter vigil with rites that permeated the catechumens with the delights of the Spirit symbolized by nature's lavish beauty: water to bathe their bodies and oil to soothe their skin, the sweet aroma of chrism filling the air, the taste of freshly baked bread and sweet wine, and milk mixed with honey. Often they had prepared for their baptism for several years as catechumens. During the all night paschal vigil which culminated their years of preparation, they were prayed over with exorcisms, anointed with oil, fed with salt to signify the Spirit's wisdom, and signed with the cross. After being baptized in water and clothed in new garments, they were presented to the bishop who laid hands on them, anointed them with oil, and presented them to the whole community gathered for the Eucharist.

This procession of the newly baptized into the midst of the community evoked a "huge surge of sentiment among the whole gathering as

---

[10] St. Proclus of Constantinople, *On the Epiphany;* LH 104–5.

[11] Aiden Kavanagh, *The Shape of Baptism: The Rite of Christian Initiation* (New York: Pueblo Publishing Company, 1978) 49.

[12] *The Apostolic Tradition, Gelasian Sacramentary,* and *Roman Ordo.*

the neophytes—still damp, oily, fragrant, and dressed in new garments"—were led into the assembly. Haunting melodies and jubilant ovations greeted them as they received the community's kiss of peace and felt their embrace of welcome into the Trinity's own family. Fed with milk mixed with honey to symbolize the sweetness of the Lord, the newly baptized Christians feasted, as the climax of all, on the body and blood of the Lord in the Eucharist; the newborn children of God savored the banquet who is God. Early Christian communities thus realized that the very richness of baptism into Christ "demands enough water to die in, oil so fragrant and in such quantity that it becomes the Easter aroma, kisses and *abrazos*, bread and wine enough to feed and rejoice hearts. And rooms of glory filled with life."[13]

Symeon the New Theologian praises the Holy Spirit for the joy he himself found through being inundated with the Trinity's love at his baptism. His prayer recounts his joy at being so completely baptized by the very person of the Spirit that the water itself seemed resplendent with light.[14] As he reflects on these sacred mysteries, another early believer invites us to taste for ourselves these baptismal joys bestowed by the Spirit. When we plunge into the baptismal waters with faith, we renounce Satan, and pledge ourselves to Christ. Throwing off our slavery, we become children of God and heirs with Christ; we rise from the waters "radiant as the sun."[15]

Hilary of Poitiers comments that though we can never capture in words the Spirit's infinite beauty as the source of this new life,[16] we can experience an exquisite baptismal joy as the Spirit's own gift to us. Baptism floods us with the Spirit who becomes, in person, a "river" of joy within us, a fountain of life inebriating us with happiness, causing streams of grace to flow from us.[17] Eastern writers also attest to this same outpouring of baptismal joy bestowed by the Spirit of God.[18] An eighth-century Syrian Christian, for example, writes of the Spirit who floods our hearts with jubilation,[19] and Cyril of Jerusalem urges us to unite our baptismal joy with the gladness of the whole universe. All

---

[13] Kavanagh, *The Shape of Baptism*, 65, 178, 179, 180.

[14] Symeon the New Theologian, *Catecheses*, 36; in *Symeon the New Theologian: The Discourses*, trans. C. J. De Catanzaro (New York: Paulist Press, 1980) 372.

[15] *On the Epiphany*, attributed to St. Hippolytus; LH 102–3.

[16] Hilary, *On the Trinity*, 12.56; Burns and Fagan, *Holy Spirit*, 113.

[17] Hilary, *Commentary on the Psalms*, 64.14–15; LH 642, 641.

[18] Cyril of Jerusalem, *Catechetical Lectures*, 21.2; NPNF 2.7, 149; LH 322.

[19] Joseph Hazzaya; in Kilian McDonnell, O.S.B., and George T. Montague, S.M., *Christian Initiation and Baptism in the Holy Spirit: Evidence from the First Eight Centuries* (Collegeville: The Liturgical Press, 1991) 302.

are called to the feast, for the Lord is bounteous, and desires to be wedded to each one of us through the baptismal consecration.[20]

The Spirit's New Life Given in Baptism

John Chrysostom reminds us that we ourselves have received this lavish outpouring of the Spirit.[21] In the presence of myriads of angels, we have been sealed at our baptism with the very person of the Spirit.[22] Baptized into the living streams of the Father, Son, and Holy Spirit, we have entered into the Lord's joy and are called to savor the "peace of mind and heart" which the Spirit gives.[23] Commingled with the Spirit through baptism, we are nourished to life at the breast of our mother, the Church, and we feast on the banquet of the Eucharist.[24] As one community united through faith and adoration of the Trinity, we ourselves are called to sing the psalm of Easter joy: "This is the day that the Lord has made; let us rejoice and be glad in it" (Ps 118:24).[25]

Early Christian writers such as Tertullian, Cyril of Jerusalem, and Gregory of Nyssa invite us to ponder still further depths of our baptism as an ever present grace. At every Easter Vigil we implore the same Spirit who hovered over the waters at the world's creation to descend upon the baptismal font and to make it a "living spring." As Gregory of Nyssa comments, the baptismal water of itself has no power to give us life until it is filled by the very person of holiness, the Holy Spirit who alone "gives life" (2 Cor 3:6; John 6:63).[26] Tertullian recalls how, after the ancient torrential floods had ravaged the earth, a dove heralded the reign of God's peace (Gen 8:10-12). So, too, when the minister of baptism welcomes the Spirit into our hearts, the Holy Spirit joyfully comes from the Father, filling the baptismal waters as though revisiting his primal dwelling-place, and bringing God's own peace to the "earth" of our flesh.[27] This Spirit of life comes to us not as a miser, but as the one who completely satiates us with life. When we enter into the baptismal pool, then, we are encompassed on all sides by the water. As the water flows around our body, however, our inmost self is flooded with the Holy Spirit, the living water.[28] We need to open

[20] Cyril of Jerusalem, *Catechetical Lectures*, 3.1–3; NPNF 2.7, 14; LH 1530–31.
[21] John Chrysostom, *Commentary on Matthew*, 11; NPNF 1.10, 71.
[22] Cyril of Jerusalem, *Catechetical Lectures*, 3.1–3; NPNF 2.7, 14; LH 1530–31.
[23] Ambrose, *On the Mysteries*, 8–11; LH 494.
[24] Irenaeus, *Against the Heresies*, 3.24.1; Burns and Fagan, *Holy Spirit*, 36.
[25] *Easter Homily of the Early Church*; LH 319.
[26] Gregory of Nyssa, *On the Holy Spirit*; NPNF 1.5, 322.
[27] Tertullian, *On Baptism*, 8; Burns and Fagan, *Holy Spirit*, 52.
[28] Cyril of Jerusalem, *Catechetical Lectures*, 17.14; 16.11; NPNF 2.7, 127–28, 118.

the eyes of our heart, then, to see beyond the human minister of baptism. With all of heaven present, the very person of the Holy Spirit baptizes our inmost being "into himself," completely recreating us.[29]

Without this Spirit of life, we would count ourselves among the living dead. But baptism so transforms us into "one spirit" with Jesus (1 Cor 6:17), that we can "walk in newness of life" (Rom 6:4),[30] and live completely in him: "We know that he abides in us by the Spirit that he has given us" (1 John 3:24). The baptismal font thus becomes both a grave for our old self and a second womb, bringing us to birth as children of God. At every baptism, the Holy Spirit hovers over the sacramental water, while angels sing with joy at the lost who are found in it.[31] We ourselves, reborn from the Church's font, are clothed in the newness of little children. Our entire person is inundated with God's radiant life by the One who is the very Spirit of life.

Our reflections on the power of our own baptism lead us to contemplate further dimensions of this sacrament as an ever present grace. In three immersions and invocations of the Spirit, our great baptismal mystery is accomplished: our old self dies and we are filled with new life through the Holy Spirit's presence permeating the water.[32] As we are plunged into the water, the Holy Spirit's own joy inundates our hearts, and we are reborn in the living springs of the Trinity.[33] With the Father breathing into us the life-giving Spirit, we become "divine," intimately sharing in the Trinity's life and bearing within us the Spirit as pledge of our full inheritance, our own resurrection with the risen Lord.[34] Washed in baptism's "saving bath," we emerge from the waters completely cleansed, inside and out, by the person of the Spirit.[35] And since all that the Spirit touches is made holy, we ourselves become clothed in the Spirit's own loveliness.[36] This Spirit is the fire with whom Jesus promised to baptize us (Matt 3:11; Luke 12:49),[37] the transforming flame who changes us from creatures and slaves into sons and

---

[29] Didymus of Alexandria, *On the Trinity*, 2.12; LH 379.

[30] Irenaeus, *Against the Heresies*, 5.9.3; Burns and Fagan, *Holy Spirit*, 41.

[31] Ephrem, *Hymns on Virginity*, 7.7; 7.8; in Sebastian Brock, *The Harp of the Spirit* (London: Fellowship of St. Alban and St. Sergius, 1983) 50.

[32] Basil, *On the Holy Spirit*, 15.35; LH 303.

[33] Jerome, *Sermon on Psalm 41: To the Newly Baptized*; LH 471–72.

[34] *On the Epiphany*, attributed to St. Hippolytus; LH 103.

[35] *Gelasian Sacramentary*; Congar, *I Believe*, 1:105.

[36] Tertullian, *Prescription Against the Heretics*, 36; McDonnell and Montague, *Christian Initiation*, 100.

[37] Symeon, *Homily Forty-Five*, 9; in Vladimir Lossky, *The Mystical Theology of the Eastern Church* (New York: St. Vladimir's Seminary Press, 1976) 171.

daughters of our Father, and sisters and brothers of Jesus. Sharing his inheritance and joy, we cling so closely to him like branches on the vine that Jesus himself cares for us as our tender nourisher, mother,[38] and beloved spouse.[39] The Holy Spirit in this way breaks the chains of our sin and death, filling us with grace, and restoring to us the beauty for which we have been created from all eternity.[40]

Water of Life

As we have seen, when the early Christians tried to speak of the personal identity of this Spirit whom they received at their baptism, they discovered by experience the poverty of our human comprehension and language. They resorted, therefore, to the use of images such as breath and air, water and fire, ointment and seal to suggest the profound depths to which the Holy Spirit penetrates our being. As a blazing fire ignites dry wood, as water saturates a sponge, the Holy Spirit completely permeates our being.[41] In a special way, the image of baptismal water inspired early Christians to envision the Holy Spirit as the living fountain of life within us. From the time of the exile, Hebrew writers already had used this symbol of water for the Spirit of God. In countries burnt by the sun, people tormented by thirst treasure water as the most precious and lavish of God's gifts. Life is engendered in water—water in the womb and water flowing through all of creation as its life-blood. Because of water, everything lives.[42]

The Spirit of God, however, is more life-giving and lavish than even the miracle of water flowing in a desert. For the Spirit is not a parsimonious giver, bestowing life in meager quantities, as one would measure out drops of water in a drought-besieged land. On the contrary, the Spirit is bestowed in a lavish, unrestrained flooding of our entire being: "I will pour my water on the thirsty land . . . I will pour my spirit upon your descendants" (Isa 44:3; see also Isa 32:15; Zech 12:10). In speaking of the Holy Spirit as this extravagant "living water" flooding them in baptism, early Christians also drew inspiration from the celebration of the Jewish Feast of Weeks. At the time of Jesus, this festival was the most spectacular of the Jewish holy days, celebrating

---

[38] Cyril of Alexandria, *Commentary on John*, 10.2; LH 368.

[39] St. Pacian, *Sermon on Baptism*, 5–6; LH 556.

[40] Didymus of Alexandria, *On the Trinity*, 2.12; LH 379.

[41] Luis M. Bermejo, S.J., *The Spirit of Life: The Holy Spirit in the Life of the Christian* (Chicago: Loyola University Press, 1989) 109.

[42] Maurice Landrieux; *Le divin Méconnu* (Paris: Beauchesne, 1921); in Yolande Arsène-Henry, ed., *Les plus beaux textes sur le Saint-Esprit*, rev. ed. (Paris: Lethielleux, 1968) 279.

God's wondrous deed of drawing water from the rock for the chosen people to drink on their desert journey. This feast also anticipated the days when God would cause a spring of water to well up in profuse abundance for all the chosen people. When the Spirit is lavished on the entire nation (Ezek 36:25-27), the outpouring will be like waters gushing through the desert land (Isa 43:20).

Drawing upon these images from the Hebrew Scriptures, the Gospel of John recounts a story about a woman to whom Jesus promised this very gift of the Spirit as the living water to quench her soul's thirst. Jesus asked her for a drink of water. And yet, as Augustine comments, Jesus in fact thirsted for her faith so that he could lavish on her the gift of the Spirit. He made his way to the woman's heart, teaching her gently and kindly: "If you knew the gift of God, and who it is that is saying to you, 'Give me a drink,' you would have asked him, and he would have given you living water . . . a spring of water gushing up to eternal life" (John 4:10, 14).[43] Extravagant fountains of living water will flow from Jesus: "He said this about the Spirit, which believers in him were to receive" (John 7:39).

The Holy Spirit was compared in this way, not to fearful sea waters, but rather to abundant springs and refreshing rain.[44] The Spirit of life is infinitely more profuse than the best spring rain soaking the earth and making it blossom with life (Isa 44:3; Ezek 47:1-12; Rev 22:1, 17). This Spirit is the living water through whom the world has been wonderfully created and even more wondrously re-created.[45] Irenaeus tells us that the Lord himself received the Spirit as a gift from his Father so that he could pour out the Holy Spirit as "living rain" on all of us (John 4:7-26). Deprived of this Spirit, we are like barren earth or dead branches, but with the Holy Spirit our life blossoms into an abundant harvest. Irenaeus compares us also to dry wheat that can be shaped into dough only by being mixed with water. We are the many grains of wheat who need the "heavenly water" of the Spirit to become the sweet tasting "bread" of God.[46]

Baptismal Anointing

Early Christians spoke of the Holy Spirit not only as the living water but also as the living anointing with whom they were "sealed" (Eph 4:30) and anointed: "The spirit of the Lord God is upon me, because the Lord has anointed me" (Isa 61:1). Cyril of Jerusalem reflects on

---

[43] Augustine, *Commentary on John*, tract. 15; LH 259–60.
[44] Durrwell, *Holy Spirit*, 20.
[45] Ambrose, *On the Holy Spirit*, 2.5.34; Burns and Fagan, *Holy Spirit*, 143.
[46] Irenaeus, *Against the Heresies*, 3.17.2; Burns and Fagan, *Holy Spirit*, 34–35.

Jesus' own baptism as the Father's anointing him with the Holy Spirit, the "oil of spiritual joy" and the source of all delight:[47] "God, your God, has anointed you with the oil of gladness beyond your companions" (Ps 45:7). Oil is a wonderful symbol of the Spirit because it penetrates everywhere and makes everything it touches function well. Believers began to realize that the Holy Spirit is the living "oil of gladness," completely permeating us with a new and holy life.[48] They recognized that the very word "Christian" means that we are "anointed" with the Holy Spirit, as Jesus himself was anointed: "The Father anoints, the Son is anointed, and the Spirit is the anointing."[49] As the living anointing, the Holy Spirit is bestowed on us by Jesus to transform our inmost self. For this reason, by the third century, many Christian communities were including in their initiation rites both pre-baptismal and post-baptismal anointings with perfumed oil or "chrism." Baptism, often administered by deacons or deaconesses, was not witnessed by the rest of the community because catechumens descended unclothed into the water. But the initiation rite concluded as the bishop laid hands on the newly baptized and anointed them with chrism in the midst of the entire community gathered to celebrate the Eucharist.

Cyril of Jerusalem tells us that we become "christs" through this anointing with the Spirit,[50] the "oil of gladness" who delights us with God's own blessings.[51] Other Christians were inspired by Paul to view the Holy Spirit not only as the living oil but also as the living perfume who transforms us into the sweet "fragrance of Christ." Just as precious ointment exudes a wonderful fragrance, the Holy Spirit, Christ's living anointing, permeates us with the ravishing scent of Christ's presence: "We are the aroma of Christ" (2 Cor 2:15).[52] Clement of Alexandria urges us to be fragrant not with costly oils but rather with the infinitely sweeter scent of the Spirit.[53] Like fine perfume that clings to us, permeating our skin and clothing, the Holy Spirit pervades our entire being with the fragrance of his person. Cyril of Alexandria uses still other images for the Holy Spirit when he compares the Spirit to the sweetness of honey or the fragrance of a spring blossom. Jesus is the flower and the Holy Spirit his fragrance; Jesus is the "honey," and

---

[47] Cyril of Jerusalem, *Catechetical Lectures,* 21.2; NPNF 2.7, 149; LH 322.

[48] Congar, *I Believe,* 1:11-12.

[49] Irenaeus, *Against the Heresies,* 3.18.3.

[50] Cyril of Jerusalem, *Catechetical Lectures,* 21.1-3; NPNF 2.7, 149–50.

[51] Ibid., 21.2; NPNF 2.7, 149.

[52] Athanasius, *Letter to Serapion,* 1.23; Burns and Fagan, *Holy Spirit,* 103.

[53] Clement of Alexandria, *Pedagogia,* 2.8; in Paul Galtier, S.J., *Le Saint Esprit en nous d'après les Pères Grecs* (Rome: Gregorian University, 1946) 70.

the Holy Spirit his sweetness. We taste sweetness when we eat honey, since the very essence of honey is to be sweet. So, too, we taste the Spirit's sweetness when we acknowledge Jesus as our Lord, for the Holy Spirit "receives" from Jesus (John 16:15) not as a creature receives from God, but as God receives from God. Like the sweetness of honey, or the warmth of fire, or the refreshing coolness of water, the Holy Spirit is distinct from the Father and Son and yet is one God with them and inseparable from them.[54]

This Spirit is the sweet "anointing" (Acts 10:38), the "oil of gladness" (Ps 45:7) the Father has bestowed on Jesus, and on all of us united to him.[55] We ourselves receive the living oil of the Spirit especially through our sacramental celebrations. Unlike ordinary oil, therefore, sacramental oils are filled with the Holy Spirit. This is why, at a special "Chrism" Mass during Holy Week, the bishop invokes the Spirit's power upon the oils which will be used for baptism, confirmation, holy orders, and anointing of the sick. This practice of invoking the Spirit upon the sacramental oils dates back to the early Church. Cyril of Jerusalem writes that the Eucharistic bread, after the invocation of the Holy Spirit, is no longer mere bread but the body of Christ. So, too, the ointment after the invocation of the Spirit is no longer simple ointment but is rather Christ's gracious gift, giving us his divinity and intimate communion with him. As our bodies are anointed outwardly with oil, our inmost beings are anointed by the Spirit of holiness,[56] so that hearts stained with sin are made white with forgiveness.[57] In our communion with Jesus, the Father's beloved Son, therefore, we, too, become the Father's dear "anointed ones," bathed by the Holy Spirit in heaven's glory.[58]

Early Christian writers interpreted our baptismal anointing also as a "sealing" with the very person of the Holy Spirit. "You . . . were marked with the seal of the promised Holy Spirit" (Eph 1:13); "You were marked with a seal for the day of redemption" (Eph 4:30). As we are anointed, Cyril of Jerusalem tells us, we are not to think of the one we see. Rather, with the eyes of our heart we are to behold the Holy Spirit invisibly present, sealing our soul, casting out all demons and destructive forces,[59] and enabling us to grow strong against all evil.

[54] Cyril of Alexandria, *Commentary on John*, 11.2; *Thesaurus*, 34; in Galtier, *Le Saint Esprit*, 260, 261.

[55] Cyril of Jerusalem, *Catechetical Lectures*, 21.2; NPNF 2.7, 149.

[56] Ibid., 21.3; NPNF 2.7, 150.

[57] Ephrem, *Hymns on Virginity*, 7, 8; Brock, *Harp*, 50.

[58] Hilary, *On Matthew*, 2:6; SC 254:110.

[59] Cyril of Jerusalem, *Catechetical Lectures*, 17.35, 36; NPNF 2.7, 132, 133.

Like a signet ring impressed upon wax, the Holy Spirit so completely claims us in our baptism that we belong completely to God.[60]

The Sacrament of Confirmation

In contrast to the practice of the early Christians, this "sealing with the Spirit" is often celebrated today in the western Church not as a rite integral to baptism but as a separate sacrament. As we have seen, by the third century, sacramental initiation into the Christian life comprised what we now know as the three sacraments of baptism, confirmation, and Eucharist. The first part of the initiation rite, baptism with water, was "completed" when the bishop laid hands on the newly baptized and anointed them with oil. These actions symbolized the acceptance of the baptized not only into the local community but also into the universal Church represented in the person of the bishop. As the Church in the West grew in numbers, however, and the practice of baptizing infants became common, this second part of the initiation rite, the anointing with chrism, was often separated from the baptism to which it was integral, and administered at a later time when the bishop could be available. In contrast, eastern Christians have maintained the inseparability of baptism, chrismation, and the Eucharist, even for the baptism of infants. Since the bishop is viewed as present through the oil he has consecrated, in the absence of the bishop, eastern priests conduct the entire initiation rite.

In Rome during the fourth and fifth centuries, however, the baptismal anointing usually was reserved to the bishop. As the growth of his local church made it increasingly impossible for him to visit all local communities, many baptized people did not receive this anointing at all, or they would receive it long after their baptism. In other parts of the West, especially France, priests were permitted to baptize children and anoint them with chrism consecrated by the bishop. The bishop would later visit local communities when possible and "confirm" these baptisms by a laying on of hands. The name "confirmation" for the rite that had originally "completed" baptism was first used in France at the Councils of Riez in 439 and Orange in 441. Bishop Faustus of Riez was one of the earliest writers who tried to explain theologically the meaning of this episcopal "confirmation," now celebrating a rite divorced from the baptism to which it once had been integral. In a sermon for Pentecost, Bishop Faustus urged parents to bring their children for the episcopal "confirmation." He explained that the bishop's laying on of hands gave baptized children the Spirit's

[60] Ephrem, *Hymns on Virginity*, 7, 6; Brock, *Harp*, 50.

grace to be more fully Christian and the strength to battle with sin as an adult member of the Church.

By the ninth and tenth centuries, this Roman practice of episcopal "confirmation" had spread throughout the West. In the ninth century, Charlemagne established a policy of adherence to a uniform liturgy throughout his empire. He adopted Roman liturgical practices, including that of reserving to the bishop the right of "confirming" baptisms through the laying on of hands and anointing with oil. Often, rural people waited for years to receive this confirmation, or did not present themselves at all for this rite. "Confirmation" in this way was pushed even further away from the time of baptism.[61]

In the twelfth century, Peter Lombard, compiler of *The Four Books of Sentences,* the standard theological text based on previous authorities, explained the existing practice of confirmation by using the theology of persons such as Bishop Faustus of Riez and Rabanus Maurus, abbot of Fulda in Germany. In the thirteenth century, Thomas Aquinas pondered the meaning of confirmation as a sacrament giving us the Spirit's grace for spiritual maturity in the Church, for combat against evil, and for courage in publicly professing the faith. In 1274, the date of Thomas' death, the Second Council of Lyons officially named confirmation as one of the seven sacraments of the Church.

Three centuries later, reformers argued that confirmation is not a sacrament because there is no scriptural evidence for its institution by Christ. The Council of Trent in 1547 counter-argued that confirmation is no pious ceremony but a true sacrament. In the centuries that followed Trent, this rite of "anointing with the Spirit" which originally had been integral to baptism as its "completion" continued to be viewed as a separate sacrament of "strengthening" or "confirmation" in the western rites of the Catholic Church. In contrast, the East maintained the tradition of administering together three sacraments as parts of the one initiation rite. Although the practice is changing in some places, most eastern priests continue to baptize, confirm, and give Holy Communion to infants by placing a small portion of the sacred host on their tongues.

For a long time in the West, the traditional order of baptism, anointing, and Eucharist was kept, though often separated by long time lapses. Usually children were baptized as infants, "confirmed" between the ages of seven and twelve, and given their first Communion in young adolescence. In 1910, however, this order changed. Prompted in part by the conviction that receiving Holy Communion is integral to

---

[61] Joseph Martos, *Doors to the Sacred: A Historical Introduction to Sacraments in the Catholic Church* (Garden City: Doubleday Image Books, 1982) 205–14.

attendance at Mass, Pope Pius X permitted reception of the Eucharist at an earlier age. In the West, the original order of the sacraments of initiation—baptism, chrismation, Eucharist—thus became completely disrupted. The result was the sequence: baptism, Eucharist, and confirmation, with each sacrament separated from the preceding one by at least several years. Eventually, the sequence became baptism, reconciliation, Eucharist, and confirmation.

One step toward restoring the original sacramental order occurred with the promulgation of the Vatican II Rite of Christian Initiation of Adults. This process reestablished the integral connection of confirmation with baptism and restored the words of the eastern formula: "Be sealed with the Gift of the Holy Spirit." However, Vatican II documents also offer as an explanation of this rite the medieval theology of "confirmation" as a strengthening of baptized persons, binding them more closely to the Church and enabling them to profess the faith courageously as witnesses of Christ.[62] There is today in the West, therefore, both a theological ambiguity about the meaning of confirmation and a diversity of practice in conferring it. Those who adopt a "liturgical" approach stress the integral unity of the three sacraments of baptism, confirmation, and Eucharist as inseparable parts of the one initiation rite. Explaining confirmation as the "completion" of the baptismal process, they advise keeping the order of the sacraments as it was in the early Church—baptism, anointing, and Eucharist—even when infants are baptized. Others adopt a "pastoral" approach, based on the medieval understanding of this sacrament as a "strengthening" of baptized persons for adult witness in the Church. Proponents of this approach advise the reception of confirmation at a later age, in adolescence or young adulthood, as a way for those baptized as infants to assent freely to the responsibilities of their baptism as adult members of the Church.[63]

The Charismatic Renewal and the Sacraments of Initiation

In reflecting on early Christians' experience of the Spirit's power and joy, many of us may realize that we do not even remember our own baptism or confirmation. It is a cause of deep gratitude for us, however, to know that the Holy Spirit is inspiring wonderful means of releasing within us the graces of our baptism and confirmation. The

---

[62] LG 11.

[63] Martos, *Doors to the Sacred*, 205–29. See also Gerard Austin, *Anointing with the Spirit: The Rite of Confirmation. Vol. II of Studies in the Reformed Rites of the Catholic Church* (New York: Pueblo, 1985).

liturgical reform initiated by Vatican II, as well as movements of renewal such as Cursillo, RENEW, Marriage Encounter, and Scripture and prayer groups, along with studies such as the work of Kilian McDonnell, O.S.B., and George Montague,[64] are helping us to reclaim the Holy Spirit's power and joy as our baptismal and confirmation heritage.

One significant means of this reclaiming is the Charismatic Renewal. *Charis* is the Greek word for "gift," a personal name applied to the Holy Spirit. All other gifts flow from this Spirit who is gift in person. The word "charismatic," therefore, does not refer first of all to gifts of the Spirit such as praying in tongues and prophecy, about which Paul speaks in 1 Corinthians 14. In its deepest sense, the term "charismatic" refers to those who give themselves to the Holy Spirit poured out in their hearts through the sacraments of baptism and confirmation, and therefore who are open to experience the power, joy, and gifts of the Spirit in their lives. In this sense, every Christian is meant to be a "charismatic" Christian and to experience the "baptism in the Holy Spirit," that is, the "renewal" or "release" of the graces of baptism and confirmation in their lives.

The forerunner of the Charismatic Renewal in the Catholic Church was the Pentecostal movement which flowered through the ministry of the Methodist pastor Charles P. Parham. Before Parham, various nineteenth-century "holiness" groups in America had taught their members to pray for the "Baptism in the Spirit" which the early Church had experienced at Pentecost. Convinced by his own study of Scripture that the gift of tongues is the one clear sign of receiving the Holy Spirit, Parham and his students invoked the Spirit for this grace over a period of time. On New Year's Day, 1901, in Topeka, Kansas, they prayed over a woman student who received the gift of tongues. Parham himself, along with other students, prayed in tongues soon afterward. Several years later the same blessings were granted to people who had gathered at the Mission at 312 Azusa Street in Los Angeles after preparing for this outpouring of the Spirit by ten days of prayer. Christians such as these, eventually driven out of their denominations, established in their place "Pentecostal churches" founded on the belief that the graces of Pentecost are meant for believers today. A second phase in this growth of the Pentecostal movement occurred in the 1950s, when mainstream Churches—Anglican, then Lutheran and

---

[64] Kilian McDonnell, O.S.B., and George T. Montague, S.M., *Christian Initiation and Baptism in the Holy Spirit: Evidence from the First Eight Centuries* (Collegeville: The Liturgical Press, 1991).

Presbyterian—experienced the outpouring of the Spirit in a movement called the "new Pentecostalism."[65]

The charismatic renewal began in the Catholic Church in February, 1967 at a retreat of students and faculty of Duquesne University. They had prepared for the weekend by praying daily the Pentecost Sequence and by reading the epistles of Paul and the Acts of the Apostles recounting the wonderful work of the Spirit in the early Christians. They also had read David Wilkerson's *The Cross and the Switchblade*, the story of remarkable conversions among New York gang members with whom Wilkerson had prayed for the Spirit's outpouring. Shortly before the retreat, some of the Duquesne students joined a faculty member in praying with Pentecostal Christians at a nearby home.

At the weekend retreat, several students prayed explicitly for a renewal of the graces of their confirmation. As they did so, they experienced a whole new outpouring of the Spirit into their hearts. This gift, called by many the "baptism in the Holy Spirit," filled them with a new love for Jesus as their Lord and Savior, an intimacy with the Father, and closeness to the Holy Spirit as a person. They experienced a profound peace and joy, as well as love for others, and a deepened thirst for Scripture and the sacraments. New desires filled their hearts, including a hunger to live as the early Christians did, as a community united in the Holy Spirit, with "one heart and soul" in the Lord (Acts 4:32). Many experienced a new depth and freedom in their prayer, including "praying in tongues"—a gift, as we shall see in chapter nine, of non-discursive prayer expressing our surrender to the Holy Spirit. The Charismatic Renewal spread from these few students and faculty members at Duquesne University to other students and faculty at other universities, including Notre Dame University at South Bend, Indiana; Ann Arbor, Michigan; Loyola University, New Orleans; and many other places throughout the world.

For various reasons, many Christians have reacted with caution to these "Pentecostal outpourings" among Protestants and Catholics alike. Skeptics point to other centuries in the Church's history that have witnessed heresies centered on the Holy Spirit. The early Church, for example, dealt with the heresy of Montanism, focused on enthusiasm in the Holy Spirit. Preaching that the end of the world was near, Montanists called others to a radical conversion, a rigid discipline, and a community life centered on ecstatic experience of the Holy Spirit. After joining this movement, the early Christian writer Tertullian began to oppose the "hierarchical Church" of the bishops with his Montanist "Church of the Spirit." In the Middle Ages, too, a heresy

---

[65] Bermejo, *Spirit of Life*, 375.

centered on the Spirit led Joachim of Flora, a Calabrian abbot, to prophesy the impending end of the world. Identifying Francis of Assisi as the eschatological sign of this imminent end, Joachim considered his times to be the new and final epoch for the Church, represented by people filled with the Spirit. According to Joachim, this new age of the Spirit replaced that of the Father symbolized in the Hebrew Scriptures, and that of the Son represented by the hierarchical Church. The ideas that influenced Joachim continued to make an impact on people after him, and reappeared in writers such as Kant, Hegel, Schelling, and Marx.[66]

Notwithstanding this caution and even fear of the Charismatic Renewal among some Christians, hundreds of thousands throughout the world have experienced the "baptism in the Holy Spirit"[67] (see Acts 1:5). This term refers to a "release" or "renewal" of the graces of the Spirit which all of us are meant to experience through the sacraments of initiation: "Let the Spirit fill you" (Eph 5:18). As Kilian McDonnell and George Montague emphasize, "baptism in the Spirit" describes what the early Christians actually experienced in their sacramental baptism.[68] This is the grace to which the Vatican II renewed Rite of Christian Initiation invites us, the full experience of the Holy Spirit's power, love, and joy offered to us through the sacraments of initiation today.

Obviously, those baptized as infants could not consciously experience the full effects of the Holy Spirit's outpouring. But the sacrament of confirmation can be the graced event in which persons say their *yes* to the Lord and experience the full release of the Holy Spirit's power and presence in their lives. Regretfully, many of those baptized or confirmed as adolescents or adults are not always prepared to expect these wonderful effects as the graces of these sacraments. This is one reason that a growing number of bishops, priests, and lay people working to implement the renewed rites of baptism and confirmation are enlisting the help of those involved in the Charismatic Renewal. Through these and other means of renewal, more and more Christians are experiencing the release of the Holy Spirit's presence and power bestowed on us through the sacraments of initiation.

For some people, this release of the graces of baptism and confirmation happens as an immediate effect of prayer for the "baptism in the Spirit." Some may experience a flood of joy, love, and peace, as well as the new freedom of praying in tongues. For others, this "release" of the

---

[66] Kasper, *God*, 208–9.
[67] The phrase is taken from Acts 1:5: "You will be baptized with the Holy Spirit."
[68] See note 64 above.

Spirit already received in the sacraments of baptism and confirmation may be hidden and gradual. In most instances, however, the effects of the "baptism in the Spirit," whether they are manifested in a sudden or gradual way, include knowing Jesus as Lord and Savior; closeness with the Father and the Holy Spirit; love for Scripture and the sacraments, especially the Eucharist; a deepened prayer life; and growth in love and service to others, especially the most vulnerable among us. Other effects are increasing freedom from sinful habits; deeper joy, peace, and good desires; and docility to the Holy Spirit. It is through such renewal of individual Christian lives that the entire Church constantly is reformed and made new. Indeed, this is the reason that the Church holds out to us all of her treasures—Scripture, sacraments, ministries, and way of life—that we may be opened to experience fully the Holy Spirit's presence and transforming power in our lives.[69]

The Spirit Giving New Life to the World

In his poem, "God's Grandeur," Gerard Manley Hopkins describes with special beauty this wonderful power of the Spirit to give ever new and fresh life to the whole world.[70] Hopkins' sentiments echo Karl Adam's lovely prayer adoring the Spirit as the "life of all that lives," the one through whom the entire cosmos has come into being and continues to flourish. By this Spirit, all of nature grows to its perfection in the glory of springtime: "This charming, irresistible burst of life which erupts in spite of all obstacles, this surprising triumph of nature that is springtime is your glorious presence O Holy Spirit!" Wherever we gaze on a luxuriant carpet of flowers along the edge of the road, or hear the gracious chirping of birds; wherever we encounter the clear look of a child, it is the Holy Spirit's overflowing love which we greet.[71]

This same Spirit is intimately at work in our world, in any culture or religion where good is found, and in our every effort and progress toward truth and goodness.[72] Living deep within and among us as our baptismal gift, the Holy Spirit continues to work miracles in every heart where the power of love and the fostering of life reign. We honor the Spirit of life in our care for the earth and its resources, and most of all in our protection of human life from conception to natural death. It is this Spirit of life whom we honor when we work against the forces

---

[69] Kasper, *God*, 228–29.

[70] Gerard Manley Hopkins, *The Major Poems*, ed. Walford Davies (New York: E.P. Dutton & Co., 1979) 64.

[71] Adam, *Christ Our Brother*, 151.

[72] GS 38.

of death in the world, laboring for the cause of peace and justice, working on behalf of the poor and helpless. Just as the created world itself is a manifestation of the Spirit, those surrendered to the Holy Spirit are called to become an ever more radiant "theophany," a living "theology" of the Spirit of life.[73] "Wherever reality reaches ecstatically beyond itself," in our desires and works for good, in the beauty of creation, and in every miracle that is the birth to new life, the Holy Spirit, giver of life, is at work, re-creating our hearts and our world.[74]

---

[73] *The Holy Spirit, Lord and Giver of Life,* prepared by the Theological-Historical Commission for the Great Jubilee of the Year 2000, trans. Agostino Bono (New York: Crossroad, 1997) 37, 47.

[74] Kasper, *God,* 229, 227. For further study of themes of this chapter, especially relating to the Spirit of life at work in the baptism of Jesus and in the sacramental baptism of Christians, see Kilian McDonnell, O.S.B., *The Baptism of Jesus in the Jordan* (Collegeville: The Liturgical Press, 1997). See also Raniero Cantalamessa, O.F.M. Cap., *The Holy Spirit in the Life of Jesus: The Mystery of Christ's Baptism,* trans. Alan Neame (Collegeville: The Liturgical Press, 1994).

4

SPIRIT OF LOVE

The Holy Spirit's loveliness shines in the beauty of creation, but it is even more radiant in the Trinity's dearest gift, loving and being loved. Through love we find our most precious way of knowing the Holy Spirit, the very person of love.

The Father's and Son's Mutual Love Is a Person

"God's love has been poured into our hearts through the Holy Spirit that has been given to us" (Rom 5:5). When Augustine reflected on these beautiful words of Paul, he found in our own experience of love an intimation of who the Holy Spirit is at the heart of the Trinity. We always experience a "threeness" in our love—we who love, our beloved, and the love between us.[1] In meditating on the scriptural texts that call the Holy Spirit the Spirit of both the Father and the Son, Augustine came to recognize the same insight that Hilary of Poitiers had pondered: the Holy Spirit is the Father's and Son's "embrace," their bond of love and "ineffable communion,"[2] proceeding eternally from them as the very person of their love.[3]

The contemporary theologian Heribert Mühlen reflects on this same insight when he considers how our love always involves an "I," a "Thou," and a "We." Our relationship of love, however, our "we," is not a living person. In contrast, the Father's and Son's love for one

---

[1] Augustine, *On the Trinity*, 8.10; trans. Stephen McKenna (New York: Fathers of the Church, 1954) 266.

[2] Ibid., 5.11.12; 15.17.27; McKenna, 190, 491.

[3] Ibid., 5.14.15; 15.26.47; McKenna, 193–94; 517–18.

another, their "We," is Someone, the Spirit who is the person of love.[4]
In Jesus' human love for his Father, we see unveiled this unfathomable
mystery that is the Trinity's inner life. Jesus, God the Word who has become flesh for us (John 1:14), is the one through whom the Father
shines and in whom the depths of eternal union between the Father
and Son are revealed. The Gospel of John contemplates with special
beauty the mystery of this Word who is forever turned toward the
Father's heart (John 1:1, 18), the mystery of the Father and Son who
live with one single life: "Whoever has seen me has seen the Father
. . . I am in the Father and the Father is in me . . . All that the Father
has is mine . . . the Father and I are one" (John 14:9, 10; 16:15; 10:30;
see also Matt 11:27). As we ponder scriptural texts such as these, we
begin to glimpse in prayer the profound intimacy with which the Son
exults in the Father's heart. There is no place in the Son that the Father
cannot enter, no place in the Father that is closed off to the Son. Distinct persons, they are yet the one same God, with the very same mind
and will. Forever they give themselves to one another, pouring out on
each other an infinite torrent of life and love, finding in each other their
perfect joy and satiation. And the very secret of their intimacy is their
living bond of love, the Holy Spirit.

When we ourselves love, we suffer from our powerlessness. Love
makes us long to be united with our beloved, to be one heart, one soul,
even one body with our dear one, but our desire can never be met by
the reality. There is always the mystery about the other which we cannot enter, always the helplessness of our being separate, simply because we are persons with our own minds and wills. But there is no
aloneness or separation between the Father and Son, only union which
is complete and without shadow. This very union is not only the oneness of the divine nature, but also the oneness of a divine person, the
Holy Spirit who is their living delight.

The joy we ourselves feel when we are united with a dear one can
only suggest this wonder of the Spirit who is the Father's and Son's
joyful love in person. Saints and mystics have struggled to find concepts and words to describe the indescribable, calling the Holy Spirit
the person of inexpressible enjoyment, unspeakable joy, enchanting
bliss, intoxicating perfume, and exquisite delight. Augustine tells us
that the Father's and Son's wondrous embrace is a person whose name
is joy: "Their love, delight, and happiness, if it can be expressed prop-
erly by any human word, is called Enjoyment. The Spirit is this sweet-

---

[4] Heribert Mühlen, *Der Heilige Geist als Person: in der Trinität bei der Inkarnation
und im Gnadenbund: Ich, du, wir,* 2nd ed. (Paderborn, 1966).

ness of the begetter and the begotten," inundating all of creation with immense liberality and abundance.[5] As the very "depths" of the Father's and Son's heart (1 Cor 2:10), the Holy Spirit is their indescribable communion and wondrous embrace, their intoxicating pleasure and love, their rapturous ecstasy and joy, their happiness and sweetness in person.[6]

Western mystics such as Bernard of Clairvaux and Thomas Aquinas were inspired to reflect on how the very name "Holy Spirit" alludes to the Spirit's identity as the person of love. As we have seen, the word "spirit" means "breath." Bernard of Clairvaux reminds us that one kind of gentle "breath" is the sigh of love. Lovers fall quiet in one another's presence, expressing the tenderness of their love with a sigh. This experience, so known to anyone who loves, gives us an intimation of who the Holy Spirit is at the heart of the Trinity. From all eternity, the Father's and Son's intimate "breath" and "sigh" of love is Someone. As Bernard of Clairvaux reflected on the scriptural verse, "O that you would kiss me with the kisses of your mouth" (Cant 1:2), he was inspired to call the Holy Spirit not only the Father and Son's sigh of love and sweet embrace, but also their most sweet and intimate "kiss" in person.[7]

Through reflecting on Romans 5:5, "God's love has been poured into our hearts through the Holy Spirit that has been given to us," Thomas Aquinas discovered what Augustine, Gregory the Great, and Bernard of Clairvaux had discerned, the beautiful name of the Holy Spirit as "Love."[8] Thomas also pondered the meaning of the word "spirit" not only as "breath" but also as "wind," suggesting love's force drawing us out of ourselves to our beloved. The Father and Son thus breathe forth the Holy Spirit as their eternal bond and impulse of love.[9] Love, however, is not only an impulse drawing us to our beloved, but also the tender way that our loved one dwells as a "seal" or "imprint" within us: "Set me as a seal upon your heart" (Cant 8:6). Our own experience of love in this way suggests for Thomas how the Holy Spirit also dwells and "rests" in the beloved Son as the Father's love for him in person.[10]

---

[5] Augustine, *On the Trinity*, 6.10.11; McKenna, 213–14.

[6] Ibid. Augustine uses the words *complexus* (embrace), as well as *perfruitione* and *usus* (enjoyment).

[7] Bernard of Clairvaux, *On the Song of Songs*, 8.2; trans. Kilian Walsh, O.C.S.O. (Kalamazoo, Mich.: Cistercian Publications, 1981) 2:46.

[8] Aquinas, ST, I, 37, 1.

[9] Ibid., I, 36, 1.

[10] Ibid., I, 36, 2, ad 4.

Bond of Friendship with the Trinity

Thomas Aquinas was touched also by the "torrential" nature of the Spirit's outpouring on us. Since it is "without measure" that the Father eternally gives the Spirit to the Son (John 3:34), God the Word is forever "breathing forth love," the very person of the Spirit.[11] Now, as risen Lord, Jesus possesses the Spirit without measure both in his divinity and humanity, and pours out the Spirit abundantly on us.[12] This Spirit is the Father's and Son's inmost heart as well as their ecstatic outpouring of love, given to be our inmost heart as well: "God's love has been *poured* into our hearts by the Holy Spirit that has been given to us" (Rom 5:5).

Through the Holy Spirit, the third divine person, the secret depths of the Trinity have been opened out to us, and have become overflowing love, infinitely close to us. This love poured into our hearts by the Spirit is not just any kind of love but the exquisite self-giving of friendship-love. The divine persons do not love us simply as creatures, then, but also as "equals" and intimate friends: "I have called you friends, because I have made known to you everything that I have heard from my Father" (John 15:15). As Aristotle stressed, our intimate friend is the other half of our soul, the one in whom we delight and for whose good we work as if it were our own. In company with Aristotle, Thomas Aquinas recognized that true friendship means equality, mutuality, and intimate communication, a sharing of our goods, our heart, and thoughts with our beloved friend, so that we say with our life: "All that is mine is yours" (see John 17:10). This is precisely the kind of love relationship which the Trinity has with us.[13]

Because of the Spirit of love within us, we are now God's home, and God is our home: "Those who love me will keep my word, and my Father will love them, and we will come to them and make our home with them" (John 14:23).[14] The Spirit by whom the Father and Son love each other from all eternity is bestowed on us as the one by whom they also love and dwell in us (John 17:26): "Those who abide in love abide in God, and God abides in them" (1 John 4:16).[15] And since love makes us freely belong to one another (Rom 12:5), through the Spirit of love the divine persons give themselves to "belong" to us, to be "pos-

---

[11] Ibid., I, 43, 5, ad 2.

[12] Aquinas, *Commentary on John* 3, lect 6.

[13] Aquinas, ST II–II, 23, 1–3; II–II, 27, 2.

[14] Ibid., 6, lect 8; CG IV, 21, 3 and 4.

[15] Aquinas, ST, I, 37, 2, ad 3. See also John of the Cross, *The Living Flame of Love*, 3.82; in *The Collected Works of St. John of the Cross*, trans. Kieran Kavanaugh, O.C.D., and Otilio Rodriquez, O.C.D. (Washington, D.C., ICS Publications, 1973) 642.

sessed" by us in the most intimate union possible.[16] This exquisite gift, intimate friendship with the divine persons, is a grace that we creatures could never imagine or gain for ourselves. The Spirit of love, however, has made the impossible possible for us. As we shall see, through the Holy Spirit, the Trinity's own love has been poured into our hearts so that we can now cherish the divine persons with the very same love with which they treasure us (Rom 5:5).[17]

Charity: The Spirit's Love Within Us

We read in 1 John 1:3 that we have been called to a "life together" with the Trinity and one another. Thomas Aquinas identifies this "life together" as the gift of charity, a created sharing in the Holy Spirit who makes us intimate friends of God (John 15:15).[18] To illumine how charity makes loving the Trinity easy and delightful for us, Thomas reflects on the natural inclinations we have been given to fulfill our purpose as human persons. In the depths of our being, the divine persons implant desires and attractions—to eat, to marry, to create new life, to protect our young—as a way of drawing us from within our own freedom to our fulfillment. For Thomas, the joy of these natural inclinations can only suggest the force of charity's sweetness attracting us freely to the Trinity. In friendship, we ourselves love our dear ones with ease and pleasure, and of our own free will. Our experience illumines how the Spirit's charity enables us to love the divine persons above all else, with an affection full of ease and joy.[19] We cherish the Trinity with a familiar love, as our heart's delight and infinitely "dear" to us. Charity thus makes intimate love for the Trinity not only possible but also easy and utterly delightful,[20] since our love for God comes not from ourselves (1 John 4:19) but from the Spirit of love within us (Rom 5.5).[21]

Our own experience of enjoying our loved ones helped Thomas to understand how the Spirit's love enables us also to delight in the divine persons. The Father and Son give us as their most precious gift their intimate love for each other. And just as they forever enjoy the Spirit as the sweetness of their love in person, they also give us this same Spirit not only to possess but also to enjoy.[22] The Spirit's love then

---

[16] Aquinas, ST, I, 38, 1.

[17] Ibid., II–II, 24, 2.

[18] Ibid., II–II, 25, 3.

[19] Ibid., I–II, 109, 3, ad 1; *On Charity*, a 1.

[20] Idem., ST, I–II, 26, 3; ST, II–II, 23, 6.

[21] Augustine, *On the Trinity*, 15.17.31; Burns, p. 192.

[22] Aquinas, ST, I, 43, 3.

draws us to delight in the divine persons for their own sake, just because they are so good.[23] Since nothing makes us happier than love, nothing delights us more than this charity uniting us to the Trinity and one another as a foretaste of heaven's joy.[24] Thomas reflected further on how, just as rain poured out from the sky covers the earth, charity floods our entire life with its torrents. Flowing in us as the root of all we do, charity is like a mother who conceives all the other virtues in us, turning them all to love: "Love is patient; love is kind . . ." (1 Cor 13:4).[25] By infusing them all with life, the Spirit's charity directs our every action to our one delightful goal of loving God and one another in God.[26]

Loving Others with the Trinity's Love

"Just as I have loved you, you also should love one another" (John 13:34). Because charity is a created sharing in the very person of love at the heart of the Trinity, the depths of love we are meant to have for one another in the Holy Spirit are inconceivable in merely human terms. The word "intimacy" comes from the Latin word *intimus*, meaning "deep within." The deeper the place within us that we are "knit fast" together, the more intimate our communion. Yet what is the deepest bond that unites us to our dear ones? It may be our own love for one another, for our children, or perhaps for beauty, art, or nature. Yet as wonderful as these gifts are, of themselves none of these bonds are enough to hold us together for a lifetime. We can love one another with a truly lasting love only when our bond of love is unbreakable. And God the Holy Spirit, the very person of love forever uniting the Father and Son, is this indestructible bond. Every other wonderful reason we have for loving our dear ones is meant to be permeated with the Spirit's charity, inspiring us to love what is of God in them, and precisely so that we and they may grow closer to God.[27] The Holy Spirit in this way inserts our love for one another into the depths of intimacy at the heart of the Trinity.

Jesus himself has asked his Father to give us the very same love which they have for one another from all eternity: May "the love with which you have loved me . . . be in them, and I in them" (John 17:26). This prayer of Jesus was answered fully at his resurrection when the

---

[23] Ibid., II–II, 28, 1.

[24] Aquinas, *Commentary on the Psalms*, Ps 50:6; *On Charity*, a 1; ST, II–II, 23, 2.

[25] Idem., *Commentary on Romans*, 5, lect 1; ST, II–II, 23, 8.

[26] Idem., ST, I–II, 65, 3; II–II, 23, 2.

[27] Idem., ST, II–II, 26, 7; *On Charity*, a 4.

risen Lord poured out upon us the Holy Spirit as his living glory (John 20:22) to be our bond of love with one another: "The glory that you have given me I have given them, so that they may be one, as we are one, that they may become completely one" (John 17:22-23).[28] The very same love that the Trinity has for us, then, is the love they have poured out on us to be our love for one another. This charity of the Spirit is the antithesis of all that is selfish and closed in on itself—our sin (Rom 8:2) and self-centeredness which Paul calls our "flesh" (Gal 5:17). In the Holy Spirit, we now can love our dear ones not as a possession nor as a means to fulfill our own needs, but for their own sake and good, dear to us as our own.[29]

This is love that redeems and matures us, love that we could never produce by ourselves. A friend once told me, "My marriage is saving me. I never knew how to give myself to another, but now I feel as if my heart is being broken open. And it is. Sometimes it hurts so much I want to cry; I feel the pain, and joy, of learning how to love." The world is filled with countless persons who, in the Holy Spirit's love, labor for their dear ones' good as if it were their own, permeating their homes and communities with this *agape* love at the heart of the Trinity. We ourselves may know especially striking examples of such love—a wife who tenderly nurses her paralyzed husband, a husband who cares for his bed-ridden wife, parents who cherish their child with down's syndrome or who adopt and love as their own a child with severe disabilities. We read of the father who could not swim but who died desperately trying to save his drowning child. Stories of love like this touch us because we all long to be treasured in this way, to be loved just for who we are, for our own sake and good, with a love that saves and heals us. This is precisely the difference between *eros*—love based simply on physical attraction—and *agape*, the Trinity's self-giving love, shown not only in the good times but also in the hard times as well. It is love given to one who may not always be physically attractive, love poured out on one who may be helpless, or even disfigured. This gift-love of the Spirit's charity opens our eyes to the soul of our loved one so that we can see his or her inner beauty, infinitely more attractive than mere physical appearance.

We know from experience that this kind of love does not come simply from our own resources. Because our freedom is wounded by original sin, we find it easy to center the world around ourselves. We hurt others and are hurt by others, even by those who should love us best, and it is easy for us to continue the pattern. The Spirit of love,

---

[28] Gregory of Nyssa, *Sermon Fifteen on the Song of Songs*; LH 390–91.

[29] Aquinas, *On Charity,* a 4; a 2, ad 6.

however, can make us feel so cherished that we blossom into secure persons, able to love ourselves and others with the divine persons' own friendship-love. Their love alone is *agape*, creating us not out of need but out of sheer abundance of love,[30] and pouring this very same love into our hearts at our baptism. Our love for one another in the Spirit takes us in this way to the very heart and depths of the Trinity. Wherever we, as husband and wife, parent and child, friend and friend are truly bound together in faithful gift-love, the Holy Spirit is at work, uniting us to the Trinity's love which draws us together and keeps us together. We can be faithful to one another because we have received into our hearts the one same Spirit[31] who unites the Father and Son as their own unbreakable bond of love.[32]

The Spirit Uniting Us in Friendship-Love

As the preceding insights suggest, we are created by the Trinity who is perfect gift-love, and we reach our fulfillment by receiving and returning to the divine persons and to one another not simply any kind of love, but the friendship-love at the very heart of the Trinity. It is the Spirit of love who enables us to do this by making us intimate friends of the Trinity, secure in our hearts, and able to extend the Trinity's friendship-love to others.[33] As we have seen, Thomas Aquinas stresses that true friends enflesh in their lives the words of Jesus, "All that is mine is yours" (see John 17:10); "I do not call you servants any longer . . . but I have called you friends, because I have made known to you everything that I have heard from my Father" (John 15:15). True friends thus share a "life together" through mutual self-giving for each other's good, and through sharing their hearts' secrets with one another.

We were created precisely for such friendship-love, but fear of rejection can keep us from opening our heart to those we love. In prayer, however, the Holy Spirit replaces our fear with growing trust, for the Spirit is the Father's and Son's unreserved openness to one another. No secret exists between them; there is nothing they want to hide, nothing they can hide, for they have the very same "heart," the Holy Spirit. It is this same Spirit of love who deepens our own security, trust, and willingness to share our life and heart with those dear to us. We learn to speak the truth in love, to praise and to help each other

---

[30] Idem., ST, I, 20, 2.

[31] Cyril of Alexandria, *Commentary on John*, 11.11; LH 380–81.

[32] Augustine, *Sermon Seventy-One*; in Yves Congar, O.P., *I Believe in the Holy Spirit*, trans. David Smith (New York: Seabury Press, 1983) 1:80.

[33] Aquinas, *On Charity*, a 7, ad 11; ST, II–II, 25, 4.

grow as unique persons. When a loved one compliments us, we gain from the Holy Spirit the gift of a glad and grateful heart. On the other hand, when a loved one speaks a difficult truth we need to hear, we are able to learn from the truth spoken to us in love. The Spirit of love in this way enables us to grow more secure and trusting in our friendships, and to communicate more deeply with those whom the Holy Spirit has given to us as beloved friends.

Often, through our very mistakes and heartaches, the Holy Spirit heals our selfishness or excessive dependence on others. By means of the pain that accompanies our loving not wisely or well, the Holy Spirit draws our heart to the Trinity's love that alone makes us fully secure and free. In prayer we experience the Trinity's closeness to us, as we ask the Father to care for us, the Lord to hold us close, and the Holy Spirit to heal our heart. We begin to discover that the complete security we seek from others we can receive only from God, and that the ultimate love story is not between man and woman, friend and friend, but between the divine persons and us. Since the divine persons alone love us with perfect gift-love, we grow to realize that we are given to one another as souls' companions, to help each other in our journey of love to God. As we become secure in the Spirit's love, we receive the grace to end relationships which the Holy Spirit has not given us, and to grow more self-giving in relationships which the Holy Spirit has given us. Learning by experience that our lasting loves are those formed by the Spirit, we begin not to grasp at others. Instead, we receive our friendships as gifts from the Spirit who chooses us for one another and who gives us to one another. By the Spirit's grace, we begin to foster only those friendships that enrich us because both we and our friends are in love most of all with God. Such self-giving love for the Lord and for one another is truly "spiritual" because it is love infused by the Holy Spirit.[34]

The Holy Spirit's tenderness also frees us to give ourselves and our loved ones the time and space we and they need to grow closer to the Trinity through prayer and to others through friendship. Because we draw our worth from the divine persons, we become fulfilled in our heart and free to encourage our dear ones' growth in their own gifts, knowing that we will have all the more to share with one another. Love "in the Holy Spirit" in this way inspires in us a deepening maturity in God and an openness to an ever wider circle of people.[35] The sweetest paradox of loving one another in the Holy Spirit, however, is

[34] Bernard, *On the Song of Songs*, 20.9; Walsh 2:155.
[35] Paul Hinnebusch, O.P., *Friendship in the Lord* (Notre Dame, Ind.: Ave Maria Press, 1974) 74.

that its joy allures us finally to the Trinity, whose love alone can satisfy our hearts completely. Our true friendships in this way flow from
the Trinity and lead us back to the Trinity. Just as praying with our
friends draws us also to spend time apart in prayer, our appreciation
of our loved ones allures us to worship the divine persons not only
because they are so good to us, but even more because they are goodness itself.

Our friendships in this way are drawn into the Father's and Son's
own union in the Holy Spirit, as an unending circle of love radiates
from the divine persons and draws us back to them. We begin to want
most of all that we and our loved ones grow closer to God, for "the
fullness of friendship is worship—not worship of one another, but
worship of the Lord, together."[36] The beautiful words of St. Francis de
Sales to St. Jane Frances de Chantal express this profound reason for
our being joined to one another in the Spirit of love: "I am ever yours
in Jesus Christ, and I marvel at this growth in affection. . . . Why do
we think God has willed to make one sole heart of our two, except that
this one heart might be extraordinarily bold, brave, spirited, constant
and loving in its Creator and in its Savior."[37]

The Holy Spirit's love in this way becomes the deepest bond uniting
us to our friends in an intimate sharing not only of material, intellec-
tual, and emotional goods but also of spiritual blessings. Thomas
Aquinas writes that just as the health of one part of our body contributes to the health of our whole body, we are meant to be generous
with both our material possessions and our spiritual blessings through
the intimate communion of the Spirit's charity.[38] By praying together
and sharing our love for the divine persons, we open not only our
heart but also our soul to our dear ones. This sharing of spiritual blessings profoundly deepens our communion in the Holy Spirit and binds
us even more closely to one another. Our mutual love in the Holy
Spirit in turn so increases our respect for ourselves and for our dear
ones that we refuse to be less for each other than we ought to be in
God, even if a loved one asks this diminishment of us for the sake of
love. Our love for the Trinity in this way greatly enriches our love for
one another by "knitting us together" in the Holy Spirit's own intimate
love (Col 2:2).

---

[36] Ibid., 116.

[37] *Letters to Persons in Religion,* trans. Henry B. Mackey (Westminster, Md.: Newman Press, 1943) 93–94; quoted in Hinnebusch, *Friendship,* 50.

[38] Aquinas, *Commentary on the Book of Sentences,* IV, d. 45, q 2, a 1, a 1. See Congar,
I Believe, 2:59-60.

Living Bond of Love in the Sacrament of Marriage

The love of those "knit together" in the Holy Spirit shines with unique beauty in spouses joined through the sacrament of marriage. The Holy Spirit who forms us in love calls certain members of the Church into a sacred communion with one another, an intimate, exclusive, and faithful self-giving that is a sharing in the very person of the Spirit. In the eastern rites, the celebration of sacramental marriage culminates in the priest's crowning of the bride and bridegroom. This action symbolizes the Holy Spirit's power transforming the spouses into "one flesh" through the sacrament of marriage, just as the Holy Spirit transforms the bread and wine into the Lord's body and blood in the Eucharist. The crowns thus symbolize the outpouring of the Spirit on the couple, just as the priest's gesture and prayer correspond to the invocation of the Spirit upon the bread and wine in the celebration of the Eucharist.[39]

Because only the Spirit of love can make two persons one heart and flesh in God, this same Spirit is the very soul of sacramental marriage. The Holy Spirit brings about an unbreakable bond between the couple so that the Spirit's own charity becomes their love for one another. The marriage of Christians, therefore, differs radically from the marriage of those who are not joined in the Lord Jesus. Because of our intimate union with him as members of his own body, those who live "in Christ" are also married "in Christ." The Holy Spirit's love binds Christian spouses together, so that their marriage shares in and reflects the intimate union between the Father and Jesus, and between Jesus and his Church.[40]

By their baptismal consecration, spouses belong to the Holy Spirit as individuals. But through the sacrament of marriage, they also are consecrated, set apart for a holy purpose, to belong to one another and to become "one flesh" in the Holy Spirit. As the sign of their complete self-giving, the couple's physical union consummates their consecration to one another in the Holy Spirit. The exclusivity of their physical union thus seals their sacrament in a total and permanent self-giving to one another, since, of its very nature, sexual union does not have a "transitory meaning." "In the bond of the Spirit, nuptial consummation and every act of sexual union thereafter means 'forever,' because this 'one flesh' is the temple of the Spirit [1 Cor 6:19] and can only cease to be 'one flesh' when death allows that temple to cease to be" (Gen 2:24; Matt 19:5; Mark 10:7).[41]

---

[39] Congar, *I Believe*, 3:269.

[40] Peter J. Elliott, *What God Has Joined: The Sacramentality of Marriage* (New York: Alba House, 1990) 146, 61, 63.

[41] Ibid., 153.

"In him . . . you were marked with the seal of the promised Holy Spirit . . . the pledge of our redemption" (Eph 1:13-14). Being "sealed" by the Spirit in baptism gives us a share in the priesthood of Jesus and therefore the power to be ministers of the Holy Spirit's grace to one another. Because of this baptismal "sealing" by the Spirit, spouses not only give the sacrament of marriage to each other, but also enter into this sacrament as an ecclesial vocation: they reproduce in their own marriage the "great mystery" of the Lord's spousal union with his Church:

> Husbands, love your wives, just as Christ loved the church and gave himself up for her . . . that she may be holy and without blemish. In the same way, husbands should love their wives as they do their own bodies. He who loves his wife loves himself. For no one ever hates his own body, but he nourishes and tenderly cares for it, just as Christ does for the church, because we are members of his body. "For this reason a man will leave his father and mother and be joined to his wife, and the two will become one flesh." This is a great mystery, and I am applying it to Christ and the church (Eph 5:25-32).

In the mystery of sacramental marriage, Jesus himself abides in the couple's life together. They are so "permeated" by Christ's own Spirit that they are "consecrated" for the sacred responsibilities of their vocation. Through their sacramental marriage, they are completely "penetrated with the Spirit of Christ."[42] Like every work of the Holy Spirit, therefore, the grace of sacramental marriage is the grace of relationship forming us as self-giving persons. Couples joined in this sacrament thus receive a transformed identity through the Holy Spirit in whom their love is sealed. Their life together in the Spirit of love forms their living prayer: "Set us as a seal upon your heart" (see Cant 8:6). As their union in the Holy Spirit deepens, they become a true "conjugal community," with the Lord himself as the "hidden Treasure" of their marriage.[43] Through their consecration to one another in the Holy Spirit, they learn to pray for the Spirit's love to make them holy together, to become the source of their unbreakable love and union, and to radiate from them to others.

Heart and Soul of Christian Families

Just as the divine persons generously open the circle of their love by creating us, the married love of Christian couples is intended to bear

---

[42] GS 48.
[43] Elliott, *What God Has Joined,* 138.

fruit in children as the "supreme gift of marriage." Spouses have the privilege of creating, in the Holy Spirit, the infinitely rich blessing of Christian families.[44] The Constitution on the Church tells us that these families become, as it were, "domestic churches,"[45] enabling the covenant of love between Christian spouses to build up the entire Church. If, as we shall see, the Holy Spirit is the very soul of the Church, and the Christian family is a "domestic Church," the Holy Spirit is also the soul of the Christian family. We are called, therefore, to ask the Spirit of love who consecrates us as Christian spouses to consecrate also our family life, to dwell in our hearts and home as its very life, its heart, and its soul. The Spirit who is the very "heart" of the family that is the Trinity is meant in this way to be the very "heart" of our Christian families as well. Deep spiritual riches are meant to be nurtured in Christian homes, with the Holy Spirit as the fountain of love flowing to them from the Church, and overflowing from them to the Church and world.

This profound vision of married and family life draws us to take seriously our call to reverse by our own lives the growing number of divorces, broken homes, and latch-key children. We can do this by consciously choosing the Holy Spirit as the inmost heart of our own family. To live in the Holy Spirit's power and love means consciously inviting the Holy Spirit to transform the way we live and relate to one another. Those of us who are parents will pray to have in our hearts the Holy Spirit's own love for our children. In this way we will be able to give our children the affection that they need and deserve, and will be inspired to work not simply for their material good, but most of all for their deepest emotional and spiritual good. In our use of time, energy, and money in raising our children, increasingly we will make every decision about our married and family life only after prayer to the Holy Spirit to guide us. Such prayer to the Spirit of love will lead us to discover, for example, that our children need and want our time, affection, and spiritual riches far more than the material possessions with which we may feel impelled to provide them, often at the cost of a real life together as a family.

One dimension of the spiritual riches that we are called by the Holy Spirit to give our children is the security of knowing that they are never alone, never uncared for. We help them to realize that even when we as parents cannot always be with them, the divine persons hold them close at every second. In a special way, the Holy Spirit dwells within them as their intimate friend, consoler, and beloved guide.

[44] GS 50.
[45] LG 11.

Catherine Marshall remarks that part of her own experience of the Holy Spirit's love was the sense of the Holy Spirit holding her close in the way a tender mother holds her child to her heart.[46] This image, as Marshall notes, can be especially consoling to children, for whom the word "mom" is meant to convey the sense of being held, protected, and cherished even in the most profound distress. Like the dearest mother, the Holy Spirit who knows and feels our every hurt not only comforts but also heals us in the depths of our heart where no one else can reach. In one of her own beautiful images for the Holy Spirit, Catherine of Siena pictures the Holy Spirit as a mother nursing us at the breast of God's own love. Clothing us, nurturing us more sweetly than the dearest mother or father could, the Holy Spirit holds us tenderly at God's breast. There we drink the milk of great contentment, and experience the Holy Spirit "nursing" our souls and "little bodies in every situation."[47]

Through our own closeness to the Holy Spirit, we who are parents also help our children by our courage in saying "no" to what is not for their spiritual good, teaching them to call upon the Holy Spirit as their intimate guide in every decision. Our prayer for our children in this way helps them to grow into persons capable of making wise decisions based on their own prayer for the Holy Spirit's guidance. We also pray for the grace to model by our own example deeply spiritual and not simply material values. Asking the Holy Spirit to be the heart of our home includes praying as a family for growing faith, hope, love, and trust in the divine persons. Experience quickly teaches us that anxiety and worry, especially about material needs, can wound the security of our life together. If our children see in us an unbounded trust in the Father's providential care for our every need, they can gain from us a spiritual heritage far more valuable than any material possession. This unshakable sense of being loved, treasured, and cared for not simply by our finite parental love but even more by the Trinity's infinite love will give our children a self-esteem and inner security that do not depend completely on external validation. Our own dependence on the Holy Spirit to heal our every hurt, to comfort us when we are discouraged, to strengthen us when we are anxious, and to give us joy when we are sad, will become for our children the gift that "keeps on giving," taking root in their very souls, where the Spirit of love intimately dwells.

---

[46] Catherine Marshall, *The Helper* (New York: Avon Books, 1978) 110–13.

[47] Catherine of Siena, *The Dialogue*, #151; trans. Suzanne Noffke, O.P. (New York: Paulist Press, 1980) 323.

The Spirit's Charity Expanding Our Love

"The whole group of those who believed were of one heart and soul . . . everything they owned was held in common . . . there was not a needy person among them" (Acts 4:32, 34). Our communion with one another in the Holy Spirit's love includes a sharing of goods not only with our family but also with the needy among us (Heb 13:16, Acts 2:44): "How does God's love abide in anyone who has the world's goods and sees a brother or sister in need and yet refuses help?" (1 John 3:17). Sharing our spiritual and material possessions with one another is an indispensable way we express our union in the Holy Spirit—a union that far surpasses ties of blood, familial love, or nationality. This is one reason that our Christian vocation to help the poor had such striking ecclesial importance for Paul (2 Cor 8:3-4, 9:12-13; Rom 12:13; 15:26-27). Because the Holy Spirit binds us together as one body in the Lord, the good of each of us in some way belongs to all of us. What is given by the Trinity to one of us is given for the sake of all of us, since "we are members of one another" (Rom 12:5).[48] The Spirit's charity thus inspires us to view others, especially the most weak, as another self. We learn to rejoice with others in their blessings and to help them in their need: "If one member suffers, all suffer together with it; if one member is honored, all rejoice together with it" (1 Cor 12:26).

Since the Spirit's charity gives us intimate friendship with the divine persons, we begin to give our love to everyone who belongs to the Trinity, even to those who have wronged us.[49] Thomas Aquinas uses the image of a powerful furnace which proves to be all the stronger in radiating its heat to what is distant from it. The deeper our love for the Trinity, the more our love extends to those who are furthest from us, even our enemies. Thomas notes that while we love our friends not only for God's sake, but also because of their own goodness and closeness to us, our beloved God is the only reason we can love our enemies.[50] Because the Holy Spirit's own love makes possible and easy for us what is impossible to our own power, we can grow to love even those who hate us, giving them our tender affection precisely because they belong to God.[51]

The one same Holy Spirit dwelling in our hearts binds us in a strong and tender communion that keeps us close even to dear ones who may

---

[48] Aquinas, ST, II–II, 32, 5.

[49] Ibid., II–II, 25, 8–9.

[50] Ibid., II–II, 27, 7.

[51] Ibid., II–II, 25, 8; *On Charity*, a 8, ad 13; *On the Religious Life*, 14.

be geographically far away. This same Spirit can bind us in love also to those we have never met.[52] The fifth-century bishop, Paulinus of Nola, describes this wonderful grace in a letter to another bishop, Alypius, with whom he became close friends through their correspondence. The affection and closeness of their communion made Paulinus feel that he already had known Alypius for a long time as a friend: "I seem to be remembering your affectionate heart rather than meeting it the first time." Such a devoted friendship comes only from God who, from all eternity, joins us in a love that anticipates even our knowing one another. The Holy Spirit who gives us the same desires for good and unity in faith thus chooses us for one another and opens our hearts to each other before we meet. Paulinus, who only recently had become a Christian, tells Alypius that he wants him to know everything about him, since the Holy Spirit always inspires affectionate love for God and one another. Paulinus concludes by saying that he has sent Alypius a loaf of bread symbolizing their unity of faith in the Trinity, the source of all their closeness.[53] Another saint, the second-century Ignatius, bishop of Antioch, wrote to the Ephesian community of this same closeness which is the Holy Spirit's own sweet gift: "In a short time I have entered into a familiarity with your bishop that is the work . . . of the Spirit."[54]

This Spirit-anointed love which we are called to give one another, even to the most weak and despised, is a gift like that bestowed on martyrs, who have drawn from the Holy Spirit the grace to die with love and joy.[55] To live every day of our own life in self-giving love to our families and communities is also a miracle which the Spirit of love wants to work in our hearts. Tertullian's beautiful words to those who awaited martyrdom speak to us today in our own circumstances. Tertullian urges his friends not to grieve the Holy Spirit (Eph 4:30) who accompanies us in our every trial, and remains with us when we refuse to be divided. In this way we will cherish the Spirit's charity and peace among us, and bestow its fragrance on others.[56]

"Make love your goal" (see 1 Cor 14:1). Scripture assures us that growing in this charity of the Spirit is our life's one great task: "Love the Lord your God with all your heart, and with all your soul, and with all your mind . . . love your neighbor as yourself"; "owe no one anything, except to love one another" (Matt 22:37, 39; Rom 13:8). Paul

---

[52] Augustine, *On Baptism*, 6.4.6; in Burns and Fagan, *Holy Spirit*, 171.

[53] St. Paulinus of Nola, *Letter Three: To Alypius*; LH, 1603–4.

[54] Ignatius of Antioch, *Letter to the Ephesians*; LH 128.

[55] Cyril of Jerusalem, *Catechetical Lectures*, 16.21; NPNF 2.7, 121.

[56] Tertullian, *To the Martyrs*, 1; in Burns and Fagan, *Holy Spirit*, 48–49.

tells us that, in the end, nothing else matters but the Holy Spirit's love in our hearts. Whatever else we may have, without this love, we are nothing at all (1 Cor 13:2). At our death, we will take no possessions or honors with us. Our greatness will be measured not by the money or power we have amassed, but rather by the love that fills our soul. The most unknown person with a heart full of love will be infinitely greater than the most powerful person with an empty heart.[57] This greatness can begin for us even now, for through the love poured into our hearts by the Spirit of love, we can become "the width, height and beauty of heaven itself."[58]

---

[57] Bernard of Clairvaux, *On the Song of Songs*, 27.10; Walsh, 3:83.
[58] Ibid., 27.11; Walsh, 3:84.

5

HOLY SPIRIT AT THE
HEART OF THE CHURCH

The Church as Communion in the Spirit

The Holy Spirit unites us to our dear ones, but even more wondrous is the bond which the Holy Spirit creates among us as Church, transforming many diverse peoples into the one body of Christ. Joining us with other believers in our families, our local churches, and throughout the world, the Holy Spirit forms us as Church into a "communion of communions" that enfleshes the Trinity's own rich distinction within profound union.[1]

The Greek word for Church, *ekklesia*, denotes a "gathering." Scriptural authors pondered the meaning of this "gathering" through varied images suggesting the profound mystery that is the Church: the body of Christ (1 Cor 12:12-27), the Lord's bride (Eph 5:31-32); God's holy temple (1 Cor 3:16-17; 6:19; 2 Cor 6:16); and the new people of God (1 Pet 2:9-10) reborn from water and the Holy Spirit (1 Pet 1:23, John 3:5-6). One central image used by scriptural authors, especially Paul and Luke, is that of *koinonia:* "The whole company of those who believed were of one heart and soul"; they "had all things in common" and "devoted themselves to the apostles' teaching and fellowship [*koinonia*], to the breaking of the bread and the prayers" (Acts 4:32; 2:44, 42). The word *koinonia*—"intimate sharing, participation, communion with"—is central to both Paul's and Luke's vision of the Church created by the Spirit at Pentecost. Because we exist as *ekklesia*

---

[1] LG 4.

only in the one Body of Christ formed by the Spirit of love, the Church is an "intimate sharing" in or "communion" with the Trinity and one another in the Holy Spirit (2 Cor 13:14).

As the living bond of love between the Father and Son, the Spirit is also the living communion among us, bringing us into existence as Church and keeping us united as Church. Only the Spirit's love can so fasten us to one another that our uniqueness is enhanced rather than destroyed by our union. Those whose own union with a dear one has deepened with time know that a true oneness of heart and soul is a sheer gift of God's grace. So many relationships end in broken hearts and lives that, even for people who love one another, a lasting union is nothing less than miraculous. Regardless of how much we love another, we remain separate individuals, with our own minds, wills, temperaments, and ideas. Even ties of blood and nationality, of love and affection, are not enough to make two people one—to say nothing of making millions of people one.

But this is precisely the miracle of the Church born at Pentecost: diverse peoples from all over the world become "one heart and soul" in the Lord (Acts 4:32). Luke's account of Pentecost in Acts 2:1-42 gives us a remarkable portrait of the divisive sin of Babel being reversed by the Spirit of love who forms us as Church. Sin makes us complete strangers and even enemies of one another. Human selfishness since the beginning of time has resulted in hatred and divisions, as well as the inability to communicate with or understand one another, all symbolized by the alienation of Babel. Our estrangement from one another, however, was reversed miraculously at Pentecost. By the Holy Spirit's power, disciples from many diverse peoples were made one heart and soul in God, singing praises to God in different languages inspired by the same Spirit of love. The Holy Spirit in this way accomplished the miracle of converting warring nations into loving members of the same family.[2] Total strangers were filled with the one fire of the Spirit's own love. Enemies became not only friends, not only members of the same family, but even members of the very same Body of Christ. At Pentecost, then, the Church was created as "communion in the Holy Spirit." Irenaeus was so struck by this mystery of the Holy Spirit at the heart of the Church that he wrote, "Where the Church is, there is also the Spirit of God, and where the Spirit of God is, there is the Church and all grace."[3]

---

[2] Irenaeus, *Against the Heresies*, 3.17.2; in J. Patout Burns and Gerald M. Fagin, eds., *The Holy Spirit* (Wilmington: Michael Glazier, Inc., 1984) 34.

[3] Ibid., 3.24.1; Burns and Fagan, *Holy Spirit*, 36.

As we have seen, Luke suggests the profound contrast between the division of Babel and the miracle of the Church's union effected at Pentecost. On the other hand, a wonderful parallel exists between the Genesis account of creation and the birth of the Church in the Spirit's loving breath on Pentecost. At the very beginning of the first "week" depicted in Genesis 1:31–2:3, creation flowered into being through the breath of God who hovered over the water. So, too, on that other "first" day of the week recounted in the Gospel of John—the day of the resurrection—Jesus breathed on the apostles the breath of the Holy Spirit. The Church, the new creation, was formed in the Spirit of the risen Lord Jesus and is continually born anew in the loving breath of this same Spirit who gathers the People of God into the one Body of Christ.[4]

Our own body lives not only because it is joined to our head but also because it draws its life-force from the invisible soul permeating our body. Our experience suggests how the risen Lord is head of the Church, and the Holy Spirit is its "soul," the person of love enabling us to live as members of the one body of Christ.[5] Just as a limb severed from our own body cannot live, we ourselves cannot live cut off from Christ's body, the Church. We truly live in this body, however, when we foster charity, love the truth, strive for unity, and draw our life from the Holy Spirit,[6] who is the very heart of our meaning as Church. This Spirit is the source of our union with one another in the apostles' teaching, the Eucharistic communion, and prayer (Acts 2:42).[7] Dwelling in us as in a temple (1 Cor 3:16; 6:19), the Holy Spirit unites and guides us as Church into the fullness of truth.[8] The same Spirit who fills the humanity of Christ, head of the Church, in this way also unites us in love as members of Christ's body. As the very source of the Church's unity, the Holy Spirit joins us intimately to one another in a marvelous communion.[9]

The phrase "communion of saints," used in the "Apostles Creed" dating from approximately 400 A.D., is one ancient term used to express this intimate union which the Holy Spirit creates among believers.

---

[4] F. X. Durrwell, *Holy Spirit of God: An Essay in Biblical Theology*, trans. Sr. Benedict Davies, O.S.U. (London: Geoffrey Chapman, 1983) 60.

[5] Augustine, *Sermons 341, 276,* and *268;* Pope Pius XII, *Mystici Corporis*, n. 69; LG 8.

[6] John of Fécamp; in Yolande Arsène-Henry, *Les plus beaux textes sur le Saint-Esprit*, rev. ed. (Paris: Lethielleux, 1968) 192.

[7] LG 13.

[8] LG 8.

[9] UR 2. See also LG 13.

Though we live in many lands and nations, the Holy Spirit unites us so intimately with one another that we share, through our faith and love, "one heart and soul" (Acts 4:32).[10] We have seen that the biblical Greek word, *koinonia*, translated by the Latin word *communio*, means participation, sharing, "communion with." Scripture tells us that in the communion of the Holy Spirit we have received the precious gift of intimate union with the Father, Jesus, and one another (1 John 1:3, 6-7; 1 Cor 1:9; 2 Cor 13:14).

In pondering scriptural texts such as these, Cyril of Jerusalem reflects on how we are bound to one another in a profound "commingling" of heart and soul given by the Spirit.[11] Cyril of Alexandria adds that our union with one another is the clearest sign of the Holy Spirit's presence among us as Church:[12] "There is one body and one Spirit . . . [make] every effort to maintain the unity of the Spirit in the bond of peace" (Eph 4:4, 3). Augustine contemplated our intimate communion not only with one another but also with the Father and Son as a gift bestowed on us through the person who is common to them, their Holy Spirit of love.[13]

Insights such as these suggest that the "communion of saints" means an intimate "sharing" that is inseparably twofold: we share first of all in the good things of the community, most especially in the Holy Spirit whom we receive in baptism, and in the Lord's body and blood which we receive in the Eucharist. But these blessings come to us through still another intimate sharing, our *koinonia* or communion with the other members of Christ's body, the "holy ones" sanctified by the Holy Spirit. Our unity as Church means that all of us cleave to one another, and together we cleave to the one Holy Spirit and the one Christ in the Eucharist, for there is "one body and one Spirit" (Eph 4:4).[14]

Augustine tells us that we can know this Spirit is at work within us if we have love for the Church spread throughout the world. We cannot love simply the neighbor we see, therefore, since we have many brothers and sisters whom we do not see and to whom we also are joined in the Spirit's unity.[15] As Thomas Aquinas meditated on this mystery of the "communion of saints," he understood that the Holy

---

[10] LG 13.

[11] Cyril of Jerusalem, *Catechetical Lectures,* 17.21; NPNF 2.7, 129.

[12] Cyril of Alexandria, *Commentary on John,* 11.11; LH 380–81.

[13] Augustine, *Sermon Seventy-One;* in Yves Congar, O.P., *I Believe in the Holy Spirit,* trans. David Smith (New York: Seabury Press, 1983) 1:80.

[14] Gregory of Nyssa, *Sermon Fifteen on the Song of Songs;* LH, 390–91.

[15] Augustine, *Sixth Homily on the First Epistle of John,* 10; Burns and Fagan, *Holy Spirit,* 174.

Spirit's love binds us so closely even to those we have never met that we share in all of the good done in the world.[16] Our intimate union in the Spirit becomes manifest especially in our practice of baptizing babies. Infants cannot yet believe with their own faith; but because their baptism gives them the Holy Spirit, they are united to their families and the entire Church in the Spirit of love. These little ones share in the faith of their families and of the whole Church through their "communion" with the spiritual goods we have in the Holy Spirit.[17] Thomas drew these insights from Augustine who considered how babies brought for baptism are carried not only in their parents and godparents' arms, but also in the arms of the whole company of believers. By the Spirit's charity filling the community, babies also share in the outpouring of the Spirit who is present both in the people offering the child and in the child who is baptized.[18]

F. X. Durrwell comments that the Spirit's love within believers binds them in some way even to those who may not yet believe but who can be touched by the Spirit's love flowing from believers. Pondering the depths of the Trinity's love given to us in the Holy Spirit, Durrwell asks whether anyone's refusal to love can be stronger finally than the boundless love of the Spirit. To be lost, one would have to be so much an enemy of love that no one could remain attached to that person. Yet can anyone be lost if another person, rooted in Christ, is bound to him or her in the Holy Spirit's love? Can anyone loved by a believer be far from Christ or the Church which, through its members' love, is close even to those who do not yet believe? Even if it might seem that some people are bereft of anyone to love them, in the Spirit's love, not only those who are believers on earth but also the saints in heaven are joined to these seemingly abandoned people. The saints thus give themselves not only to us but also to them as their brothers and sisters in the Spirit.[19]

A Eucharistic "Communion of Communions"

Since the Church is "communion in the Holy Spirit," we become Church most deeply as we celebrate the sacraments, through which the Spirit comes to us today.[20] Eastern Christians have always invoked the Holy Spirit in each sacrament, emphasizing that it is the Spirit who

---

[16] Aquinas, *Sermons on the Creed*, a. 10.

[17] Idem., ST, III, 68, 9, ad 2.

[18] Augustine, *Letter Ninety-Eight, to Boniface*, 2, 5; Burns and Fagan, *Holy Spirit*, 172, 173.

[19] Durrwell, *Holy Spirit*, 81, 82.

[20] LG 50.

baptizes, who forgives, and whose power transforms bread and wine into the body and blood of Christ. Vatican II has helped us to reclaim also in the West this awareness of the Holy Spirit forming us as Church through our sacramental celebrations, especially of baptism and the Eucharist, which constitute us as local churches and unite us in a Eucharistic "communion of communions."

Scripture itself assures us that we live fully in the *koinonia* of the Church only as members of baptismal-Eucharistic communities. First of all, we are born as members of the Church through *koinonia* with the Spirit whom we receive in baptism. By the one same Spirit we are baptized into one body and "drink of one Spirit" (1 Cor 12:13), becoming "partakers of the Holy Spirit" (see Heb 6:4). This unity which the Spirit gives us in baptism cannot be separated from the Eucharist which makes us one body of the Lord. The cup of blessing is "a sharing *(koinonia)* in the blood of Christ," and the bread that we break is "a sharing in the body of Christ." We who are many, therefore, "are one body, for we all partake of the one bread" (1 Cor 10:16-17). Paul uses the same word, *koinonia,* for our "communion" in the Holy Spirit: "The grace of the Lord Jesus Christ, the love of God, and the communion of the Holy Spirit be with all of you" (2 Cor 13:14). Our *koinonia* or communion with the Trinity through baptism and the Eucharist, therefore, is the very same *koinonia* uniting us to one another as Church: May [you] have "fellowship *[koinonia]* with us; and our fellowship is with the Father and with his Son Jesus Christ" (1 John 1:3).

Our intimate union or "commingling" with the Trinity and with one another in this way has two inseparable causes: our communion with the one Holy Spirit in baptism, and our communion with the one Christ in the Eucharist.[21] We were baptized into one body in the one Spirit (1 Cor 12:13) who is the source of our union with one another.[22] We also are made one through feeding on the Lord's body and blood in the Eucharist, the sacrament from which the Church draws its very life.[23]

The Eucharist, Sacrament of the Spirit

We have already reflected in chapter 3 on the Holy Spirit's intimate relation to us through baptism, the sacrament which founds the Church as *koinonia* in the Spirit. In this chapter we ponder the mystery of the Spirit's relation to us through the Eucharist, the sacrament which feeds our unity as the one body of Christ. The eastern rites have always

[21] Cyril of Alexandria, *Commentary on John,* 11.11; LH 380–81.
[22] LG 7.
[23] SC 10; LG 11.

stressed the intimate relationship between the Eucharist and the Holy Spirit, by whose power Christ was raised from the dead and through whom his death and resurrection are made present to us today. One key way that eastern Churches express this intimate connection is through the Eucharistic *"epiklesis,"* a prayer invoking the Spirit upon the bread and wine to change them into Christ's body and blood. The Spirit is also invoked upon the people so that they, too, may be changed by the same Spirit. In the Liturgy of St. John Chrysostom, for example, the priest prays for the outpouring of the Spirit upon the people as well as the bread and wine, so that both may be changed by the transforming power of the Holy Spirit.[24] The priest also proclaims: "Holy Things for the Holy": the holy body and blood of Christ will be received by those who themselves are sanctified by the Holy Spirit within them.

The fourth-century bishop St. Cyril of Jerusalem, describing the use of the *epiklesis* in his own church community, stresses that the Holy Spirit is invoked upon the gifts after the people themselves have been "sanctified" or made holy by "spiritual" hymns, for all that the Spirit touches is transformed and made holy.[25] The *epiklesis*, spoken in the plural in the eastern churches, indicates that the whole community together with the priest invokes the Spirit upon the bread and wine. While maintaining the irreducible distinction between ordained priesthood and the priesthood of all the baptized, the eastern liturgies thus continue to make clear the intimate union between the community and priest in celebrating the Divine Liturgy as one *ekklesia.*[26]

Eastern writers also focus on the Holy Spirit at the heart of the Eucharist by picturing the Spirit as the fire "baking" the bread, transforming it into the Lord's body and blood. A loaf of bread is made by mixing many grains of wheat with water and baking it in the fire's heat. So, too, the Spirit's fire in the Eucharist transforms into the one body of Christ many peoples already made one through the Spirit's baptismal waters. Syrian Christians, in particular, have a strong tradition of associating this fire of the Spirit with the Eucharist. Ephrem the Syrian writes that the Lord has filled the Eucharist with himself and with the Holy Spirit. When we feed on the Eucharist, then, we also feed on the Holy Spirit, for the Eucharistic bread has been "kneaded and baked" with the Spirit's fire, and the Eucharistic wine has been mixed with "fire and the Holy Spirit."[27] In his hymns, Ephrem writes with special tenderness about the Spirit's fire at the heart of the Eucharist. Just as

[24] Congar, *I Believe*, 3:233.
[25] Cyril of Jerusalem, *Catechetical Lectures*, 23.7; NPNF 2.7, 154.
[26] Congar, *I Believe*, 3:236.
[27] Ephrem, *Sermons for Holy Saturday*, 4, 4; Congar, *I Believe*, 3:262.

"fire and the Spirit" filled Mary's womb at the incarnation and the Jordan River at Jesus' baptism, "fire and the Spirit" fill the waters of our baptism as well as the Eucharistic bread and wine.[28]

In company with eastern Church Fathers, Thomas Aquinas also stressed that the Eucharist and the Holy Spirit are the twofold cause of our unity, for there is only "one body and one Spirit" (Eph 4:4). When we receive the Eucharist with faith, we "commune" with and share not only in the Lord's body and blood but also in the Holy Spirit who unites us to Christ and his body, the Church.[29] Although this key insight often was lost in western theology after Aquinas, it is being regained through the liturgical renewal initiated by Vatican Council II. Our Eucharistic prayers again proclaim the intimate relation between the Holy Spirit and the Eucharist in causing our unity as Church. The Third Eucharistic Prayer asks that, just as we are fed by the Lord's body and blood, we may be filled also with his Holy Spirit and become "one body and one Spirit" in the Lord. The Fourth Eucharistic Prayer invokes the same Spirit upon the Eucharistic bread and wine, that all who share in it may become the one body of Christ, filled with the Holy Spirit.[30] The inseparability of the Spirit and the Eucharist in uniting us is also evident in the Second Eucharistic Prayer as it asks the Spirit to fill not only the Eucharistic gifts but also our own hearts with love.

As Cardinal Suenens remarked, this love is the very reason why the Church gathered for the Eucharist prays for the Spirit's coming.[31] Because Jesus died for us through love alone, during the Eucharistic celebration of his death and resurrection we ask the Spirit of love who inspired Jesus' death to fill us with love and to unite us "in the bond of peace" (Eph 4:3). The Holy Spirit thus gives us the power to live the love we celebrate in the Eucharist.[32]

Local Churches United with the Apostolic Church

The same Spirit who unites us as members of local Eucharistic communities into a universal communion also joins us backward through time to the apostolic Church itself. Our "horizontal" communion in the Spirit with the Church throughout the world is thus inseparable from

---

[28] Idem., *Hymns on Faith* 10, 17; in Sebastian Brock, *The Harp of the Spirit* (London: Fellowship of St. Alban and St. Sergius, 1983) 16.

[29] Aquinas, *Commentary on John* 6, lect. 7; Congar, *I Believe*, 3:262.

[30] The Fourth Eucharistic Prayer quotes Hippolytus, *The Apostolic Tradition*, 4. See Burns and Fagan, *Holy Spirit*, 64.

[31] Léon Joseph Cardinal Suenens, *A New Pentecost?*, trans. Francis Martin (New York: Crossroad Seabury, 1975) 36.

[32] St. Fulgentius of Ruspe, *Against Fabian*, 28. 16–19; LH 673–74.

a "vertical" communion through our ordained bishops with the apostolic Church. We have reflected on our baptismal-Eucharistic communion which unites all the faithful throughout the world in the communion of the Holy Spirit.[33] Not only the Lord but also the entire Church is present when the Eucharist is licitly celebrated in local communities, regardless of how small or poor,[34] for it is in these local church communities that the universal Church exists[35] and is "actualized."[36] Since, however, the whole Church is present in these churches where the Eucharist is celebrated, so, too, is the apostolic Church. Baptism and Eucharist, the twofold cause of our unity, are thus inseparable from the sacrament of orders, through which the Holy Spirit unites each local church with the apostolic church. For the Holy Spirit lavished on the apostles (Acts 1:8, 2:4; John 20:22) has been passed on to the apostles' successors by the laying on of hands (1 Tim 4:14, 2 Tim 1:6-7). Through the Spirit's anointing poured out in the sacrament of ordination today, bishops, as successors of the apostles, act in the place of Christ and assume his own work as teacher, shepherd, and priest.[37] In each legitimately constituted local church, therefore, not only the universal Church but also the apostolic Church is present.[38]

Our communion with the apostolic Church is made actual in this way through each church's bishop, ordained into the apostolic ministry through the Holy Spirit's power. Ignatius of Antioch pictures us as closely knit to our bishop as the bishop is knit to Jesus, and as Jesus himself is united to the Father.[39] Where the bishop is, therefore, there, too, are his local church, Christ, and the whole Church.[40] Indeed, the union of a bishop with his church community is so deep and exclusive that it shares in the marriage union of Jesus with his Church. Just as Jesus is the only Bridegroom of the Church, the bishop who makes visible the presence of Jesus presiding over his community, is, in some profound way, espoused to his community. Futhermore, the Spirit creates such a deep bond of union between a bishop and his community that there can be only one bishop for each local church.[41]

[33] LG 13; LG 9.

[34] LG 26.

[35] LG 23.

[36] Karl Rahner, "The Episcopate and the Primacy," in Karl Rahner and Joseph Ratzinger, *The Episcopate and the Primacy, Quaestiones Disputatae* 4 (New York: Herder and Herder, 1962) 23, 26.

[37] LG 21.

[38] J. M. R. Tillard, *Eglise d'Eglises: L'écclésiologie de communion* (Paris: Cerf, 1987) 240.

[39] Ignatius of Antioch, *Epistle to the Ephesians*, 5.

[40] Idem., *Letter to the Smyrnians*, 8.2.

[41] Tillard, *Eglise*, 247, 249.

Each bishop, however, truly presides at the Eucharist of his local church only in communion with other bishops and their churches. As Cyprian emphasizes, episcopal ordination is ordination into an order that is "one and undivided,"[42] since the communion of bishops with one another is a concrete way that the Holy Spirit makes visible the entire Church's unity. Every bishop, then, presides over the Eucharist of his local church as the one whose central ministry is to guard its union with the apostolic Church founded on Jesus, and with the entire Church united in a "communion of communions."[43]

The Constitution on the Church summarizes this intimate relation between each bishop, his local community, the entire Church, and the apostolic Church, by reflecting on every bishop's call to be the "visible source and foundation of unity" in his own local church.[44] Bishops, then, have the ministry of fostering not only the unity of their own local churches, but also that of the entire Church. Within this charge given to every bishop, the bishop of Rome is entrusted by the risen Lord with a special ministry. Because he presides over the Church of Rome—the Church of Peter and Paul, and the city of their witness through martyrdom to the risen Lord—the bishop of Rome has the unifying ministry of supporting and fostering each bishop's ministry and of guarding the unity and communion of the entire Church.[45] With each bishop representing his own local church, all of the bishops, united with the bishop of Rome as visible guardian of ecclesial communion, represent the universal Church in the Spirit's bond of peace and love.[46]

The Spirit's Gifts to Build Up the Church

In the one body of the Church, the Holy Spirit gives gifts of service not only to those called to ordained ministry, but also to every member of the Church as a way of enriching the Church's unity in the Spirit:

> There are varieties of gifts, but the same Spirit. . . . To each is given the manifestation of the Spirit for the common good. To one is given through the Spirit the utterance of wisdom, and to another the utterance of knowledge. . . . All these are activated by one and the same Spirit, who allots to each one individually just as the Spirit

[42] Cyprian, *On the Unity of the Church*, 5.
[43] See Tillard, *Eglise*, 323, 325, 328.
[44] LG 23; VC 376.
[45] DS 3050, 3061; Tillard, *Eglise*, 333, 341.
[46] LG 23.

chooses. . . . In the one Spirit we were all baptized into one body—Jews or Greeks, slaves or free—and we were all made to drink of one Spirit (1 Cor 12:4, 7-8, 11, 13).

The Holy Spirit who is gift in person thus gives not only to bishops but also to each one of us special gifts to enrich the Church's growth in love (Eph 4:11-12, 16; 1 Cor 12:4).[47] The Vatican II document on *The Apostolate of the Laity* reflects on the Spirit who makes us holy not only through the sacraments but also through the special gifts of each one of us (1 Cor 12:7). As we have seen, the Spirit gives "hierarchical gifts" to those called to ordained ministry, but the same Spirit distributes "charismatic" gifts not only for ordained but also for non-ordained service in the Church.[48] Both kinds of gifts are essential for the Church's growth in love because each of us is an indispensable member of the Body. Inspired by the freedom of the Spirit (John 3:8), and in communion with our ordained leaders, we are called to use our gifts for the Church's upbuilding and the good of humanity.[49]

The one Spirit in this way produces many wonderful results, filling one of us with wisdom and another with prophecy. Always one and yet different in each of us, the Spirit gives the gift of compassion to one, a special gift of patience to another, and justice or temperance to still others.[50] Reflecting on John 4:14, "The water that I will give will become in them a spring of water gushing up to eternal life," Cyril of Jerusalem compares the one rain that nourishes life in all of creation with the one Spirit who fosters many diverse gifts in us. The showers pour from the heavens, and yet this one rain gives life to myriads of different species, becoming white in the lily, red in the rose, and purple in the violet. The one same rain forms the life of the palm tree and the vine, adapting itself to the make-up of everything that receives it. This lovely image helps us to see that just as the Spirit hovered over the waters to create marvelously different forms of life (Gen 1:1-31), the same Spirit hovers over us today, lavishing unique gifts on each of us as the Spirit desires (1 Cor 12:4-11).[51]

In every good gift and grace, then, the Spirit is present as the whole in its parts; all of the Trinity's blessings come to us in this Spirit who is the Kingdom of God in person (Luke 17:21).[52] When we receive everything

---

[47] Basil the Great, *On the Holy Spirit*, 26.61; NPNF 2.8, 38; LH 91.

[48] See LG 4.

[49] AA 3.

[50] Cyril of Jerusalem, *Catechetical Lectures*, 16.12; NPNF 2.7, 118.

[51] Ibid.

[52] Basil, *On the Holy Spirit*, 26.61; NPNF 2.8, 38.

good in our life as the Spirit's own gift to us, we begin to accomplish marvels we could never do on our own. Thomas Aquinas, for example, produced theological and philosophical works he knew surpassed his own powers. All that he taught and wrote he attributed to the Holy Spirit's anointing.[53] Without schooling, Catherine of Siena also was given by the same Spirit the gift to write with such theological depth that she has been named one of only three women "Doctors of the Church."

Beyond and deeper than specific gifts such as these, however, the Holy Spirit gives us our very vocations as a means of building up the Church in love. The Spirit calls some of us to marriage, others to the single life, and still others to religious life in community. In this way the Spirit shines in us like a single light with millions of rays of varied colors and brilliance.[54] Those called by the Spirit to the priesthood or religious life, for example, are meant to witness to the deep longings in every human heart for the joys of heaven. The same Spirit invites others to dedicate themselves to the married or single life and to witness to God through their professions and work in the world. In this way, Christ himself is active today in our hearts through the power of his Holy Spirit, giving life to our efforts to bring greater love and peace to our world.[55]

This ecclesial meaning of our life-call is central in our understanding of how precious each of us is, and how irreplaceable we are in contributing to the Church's growth in love. Baptized in the Spirit's power, we are confirmed in this same Spirit's anointing and united more closely to the Church. Every one of us has been chosen and given a true vocation in the Church; every one of us has been anointed by the Spirit to witness to the Lord by our lives and words.[56] We are called, therefore, not simply to find a job, or to work only to make money. Rather, we are urged to pray for the Spirit's guidance to discern our vocation, and to view our work as a means of building up the Church and world. In a special way, the sacraments of initiation, matrimony, and orders give us the Holy Spirit's power to live and to carry out our life-work as Christians in a different way, as a path of love that proclaims Christ in all that we do. All of our prayer and apostolic endeavors, our married and family life, our work and recreation, when they are undertaken in the Holy Spirit's anointing, become a sacrifice of love and praise to the Trinity.[57]

---

[53] Aquinas, *Commentary on 1 Thessalonians* 4:1. See Mary Ann Fatula, O.P., *Thomas Aquinas, Preacher and Friend* (Collegeville: The Liturgical Press, 1993) 120–21; 191.

[54] Cyril of Jerusalem, *Catechetical Lectures*, 16.22; NPNF 2.7, 121.

[55] GS 38.

[56] LG 11.

[57] LG 34.

The Holy Spirit and Mary

Vatican Council II invites us to behold in Mary, the mother of Jesus and his first disciple, the one who is also mother of the Church and our own beloved mother as well (John 19:27). It is she who is our supreme example of loving docility to the Holy Spirit in our own vocations. The Constitution on the Church recalls how Scripture itself intimately associates Mary with the Holy Spirit: "The Holy Spirit will come upon you, and the power of the Most High will overshadow you; therefore the child to be born will be holy" (Luke 1:35). The Holy Spirit who is love and uncreated gift in person made her heart a complete "yes" to God the Word's unreserved self-gift to us,[58] and brought about the incarnation as an act of perfect love for us.[59] Mary's faith and love enabled her to be the mother completely surrendered to her Son and to the Father's plan of love for our salvation. By the Holy Spirit's overshadowing, therefore, she gave birth to Jesus not only physically but even more deeply through her obedience and loving faith.[60]

To prepare her for this most marvelous of vocations in the Church, bringing Jesus to the world, the Holy Spirit who fashioned Mary also made her holy, free from all sin.[61] "Like a trousseau for a heavenly wedding," marvelous graces were lavished on this woman the Father chose to be the spouse of the Holy Spirit and Mother of Jesus, the Word made flesh. It is because all of her graces are the Spirit's gift to her that Mary is called not only the "Temple of the Lord" but also the "Sanctuary of the Holy Spirit."[62] After uniting herself with Jesus in every second of his life, Mary also implored upon the Church the gift of the Spirit who had already overshadowed her in the Annunciation. She was present, then, at the very birth of the Church at Pentecost: the apostles "were constantly devoting themselves to prayers together with certain women, including Mary the Mother of Jesus" (Acts 1:14).[63]

After Pentecost, Mary continued to live a life of ardent love inspired by the Spirit of love. Finally, at her death, the Holy Spirit transformed her body, taking her to heaven through the grace we call her Assumption. Now in heaven's glory, Mary is still intimately united to the Holy

---

[58] John Paul II, *Dominum et Vivificantem: Lord and Giver of Life*, #50. Encyclical on The Holy Spirit in the Life of the Church and the World, May 30, 1986 (Washington, D.C.: United States Catholic Conference, 1986) 95.

[59] Ibid., #51, 97.

[60] LG 56.

[61] Ibid.

[62] Michael O'Carroll, C.S.Sp., *Veni Creator Spiritus: A Theological Encyclopedia of the Holy Spirit* (Collegeville: The Liturgical Press, 1990) 181.

[63] LG 59.

Spirit, helping us who are her dear children, sisters and brothers of her Son, Jesus.[64] Catherine of Siena writes that such love took hold of Mary's heart that if Jesus had had no other way to ascend the cross, Mary would have bent over her own body and offered herself as the step by which her beloved Son could be crucified for us.[65] And the Spirit who filled her with such unbounded love for her Son, Jesus, now continues to fill her motherly heart with intense love for us who are members of her Son's body.[66]

The same Spirit who fills Mary with love for us also inspires our love for her.[67] As our mother she helps us to grow in love for the Lord, so that, by the Spirit's power, the entire Church grows in faith, hope, and love. Moreover, in union with Mary, the Church itself also becomes our mother through preaching and baptism, bringing forth children conceived and brought to birth by the Spirit of God.[68] As Mary cares for us and leads us to Jesus, she continues even now to depend completely on the Holy Spirit's anointing. Interceding for us as our mother, Mary prepares us to receive the Spirit by her own prayer and docility to the Spirit. In our surrender to this same Spirit as members of the Church, we are helped and inspired by the ardent love of Mary, our mother, and Mother of the Church.[69]

Echoing these insights of Vatican II, Pope Paul VI wrote in an especially beautiful way about Mary's intimate communion with the Holy Spirit in the Spirit's work of making us holy members of the Church. The International Marian Congress held in Rome on May 18–21, 1975, had adopted as its theme, "The Holy Spirit and Mary." To honor this Congress, Paul VI chose as his papal legate, Cardinal Suenens, patron of both the Legion of Mary and the Charismatic Renewal. In his official letter to Suenens, Paul VI recalled how, by an influence both "very powerful and very sweet," the Holy Spirit perfectly adapted Mary's entire person, with all of her gifts and energies, for her mission as Mother of the Church. Through the love which the Holy Spirit ceaselessly inspires in her, Mary continues to care tenderly for us, helping us to grow holy as members of her Son's body, the Church she loves so much.[70]

---

[64] LG 62.

[65] *Letter 144* (Dupré Theseider 34) to Monna Pavola; Mary Ann Fatula, O.P., *Catherine of Siena's Way*, rev. ed. (Collegeville: The Liturgical Press, 1990) 195.

[66] Pope Paul VI, *E con sentimenti;* in O'Carroll, *Veni Creator Spiritus,* 181.

[67] LG 53.

[68] LG 64. See also LG 13.

[69] LG 65.

[70] O'Carroll, *Veni Creator Spiritus,* 181.

The Spirit Converting and Uniting Us as Church

As we have seen, the Spirit who filled Mary and who unceasingly fills the Church dwells, not in division, but in a union of minds and hearts, since charity makes each one's good the good of all. The tragic divisions in Christ's Church, therefore, not only scandalize the world but also sin gravely against the Lord's own will for his Church: "I ask . . . that they may all be one. As you, Father, are in me and I am in you, may they also be one in us, so that the world may believe that you have sent me" (John 17:20, 21). The Vatican II Decree on Ecumenism contemplates how the Holy Spirit permeates the entire Church as the body of Christ, effecting a wondrous communion among us and joining us so intimately to one another that the Holy Spirit is the very source of our unity. This same Spirit of love is inspiring among Christians of all denominations a great hunger today for the unity of Christ's Church, inspiring us to make "every effort to maintain the unity of the Spirit in the bond of peace" (Eph 4:3).[71]

We draw courage from the truth that in spite of and deeper than our visible differences, we are intimately united in the Holy Spirit with Christians of other denominations, for the same Spirit within us is at work in them, giving them holiness, graces, and manifold gifts.[72] This is why the Decree on Ecumenism urges us as members of the Catholic Church to take the initiative in ecumenical labors. We are asked to join with persons of other religious communions to go forward boldly, placing no obstacles in the way of the Father's loving providence and the Holy Spirit's inspiration. Because we cannot possibly achieve Church unity through our own efforts alone, we are urged to place all of our hope in Christ's prayer for the Church, in the Father's tender love for us, and in the Holy Spirit's power within and among us.[73] Since true ecumenism requires a change of heart in each of us, we also are urged to pray that the Spirit who ceaselessly renews the Church (Eph 4:23) may continually convert us, giving us a spirit of generous service to our brothers and sisters in other religious communions.[74]

It is a source of great hope for us that the Holy Spirit is constantly at work to reform the Church, making it always new and young again.[75] The Spirit is renewing family life through means such as Marriage

---

[71] UR 2; UR 1.

[72] LG 15.

[73] UR 24.

[74] UR 7, 8.

[75] Vladimir Lossky, *The Mystical Theology of the Eastern Church* (New York: St. Vladimir's Seminary Press, 1976) 178.

Encounter and Cursillo, and reinvigorating the spiritual life of parish members through programs such as Renew, the Charismatic Renewal, and most especially the implementation of the Rite of Christian Initiation of Adults. Means of renewal such as these all contribute to the Church's goal of carrying out Christ's own work under the Holy Spirit's guidance.[76]

Augustine stresses that this Spirit joins us to one another in ecclesial communion to proclaim Jesus "not by loud noises but by love."[77] Another early Christian writer reminds us there is more than one way to "speak in tongues" as the apostles did. The Spirit's presence was manifested by the apostles' proclamation in countless languages. Yet even more wonderful than the "gift of tongues" is the gift of love in our hearts. If someone points out that we have received the Spirit and asks us if we speak in tongues, we should answer that we do, because we belong to Christ's body, the Church, which speaks in all languages. The apostles themselves were transformed into fresh "wineskins" holding the "new wine" of the Spirit. Their speaking in tongues was above all a wonderful foreshadowing of the future Church spread throughout the whole world, the Church that would speak, through its diverse members, the tongue of every race and nation.[78]

As the Breath of God who fills every living being (Wis 12:1; Ps 104:28-30; Job 34:14-15), the Holy Spirit is constantly active not only in the Church but also in our world today, in the hopes, desires, and spiritual longing felt by all people. Wherever people love unselfishly, and share in any movement towards greater justice, peace, and truth in the world, the same Spirit at work in the Church is also at work beyond the boundaries of the visible Church.[79] Even many pagans, Irenaeus tells us, have salvation written in their hearts by the Spirit of love (2 Cor 3:3).[80] It is this Spirit who impels us as Church to pray and to labor that the entire world may become the "Temple of the Holy Spirit." For this is the purpose of the Church of Christ here on earth, to bring all of humanity, with its manifold gifts and blessings, back to Christ its head in the unity of the Spirit of love.[81]

---

[76] GS 3.

[77] Augustine, *Sixth Homily on the First Epistle of John*, 13; Burns and Fagan, *Holy Spirit*, 176.

[78] *Sermon Eight of a Sixth Century African Writer;* LH 401–2.

[79] GS 26, 38; UR 3; Walter Kasper, *The God of Jesus Christ*, trans. Matthew J. O'Connell (New York: Crossroad, 1986) 229.

[80] Irenaeus, *Against the Heresies*, 3.4.2; Burns and Fagan, *Holy Spirit*, 33.

[81] LG 13; Walter Kasper, *God*, 203.

6

CONTEMPORARY THEOLOGICAL APPROACHES TO THE HOLY SPIRIT

Our reflections on the Holy Spirit's presence in the Church lead us to consider contemporary insights on the Spirit in light of our theme of closeness with the Holy Spirit, giver of the Trinity's life and joy. As the preceding chapters have emphasized, one key way that we are called to deepen our life in the Spirit is through reflecting on theological insights that are both faithful to Christian tradition and open to the future of a Church and world always being made new by this same Spirit. Contemporary pneumatologies in this way invite both our reflection and critical assessment.

Contemporary Pneumatology: Historical Background

We begin by outlining the historical backdrop to contemporary emphases in pneumatologies. As we have seen, early Christian thinkers, especially those of the East, permeated their homilies, commentaries on Scripture, baptismal instructions, and theological writings with a profound sense of the Holy Spirit present and active in the life of the Church. Even now, centuries later, eastern Christian churches continue this focus on the centrality of the Holy Spirit in the Christian life.

For many reasons, the same has not always been true for western Christianity. After the tragic schism between East and West in 1054 A.D., the western Church lost contact with many sources in eastern Christianity that would have fostered a sense of the Holy Spirit's central role. After the plague that decimated Europe in the fourteenth century, monasteries and the ranks of the clergy often were populated with ignorant and unworthy candidates. The sacraments not infrequently became empty ritual, divorced from the Spirit-filled proclaiming of the Word essential to their reality. Because of these and other weaknesses, the Church that was meant to be the community of God's people animated by the Holy Spirit became in some places an institution whose leaders were guided by the desire for power and wealth rather than the Holy Spirit. The Protestant reformation of the sixteenth century was an inevitable result. Reformers such as Martin Luther and John Calvin stressed the enlivening role of the Holy Spirit within believers in contrast to the corruption and seemingly empty ritualism of the Catholic Church.

During the sixteenth to the first part of the twentieth century, Catholic writers who were steeped in the Scriptures, patristic writings, and liturgical texts preserved a focus on the Holy Spirit that often was lost to the Roman Catholic Church as a whole. Mystics especially kept alive this awareness of the centrality of the Holy Spirit in the lives of Christians. The sixteenth century Carmelite, John of the Cross, for example, both experienced and wrote about intimacy with the Holy Spirit as the "living Flame of Love" in the hearts of those surrendered to God. Writers such as the seventeeth-century Jesuit Louis Lallemant also stressed the need for docility to the Holy Spirit as the essence of the spiritual life.

During the nineteenth century, theologians such as Matthias Scheeben, Cardinal John Henry Newman, and Cardinal Henry Edward Manning—the latter two both converts from Anglicanism—maintained this focus on the Holy Spirit at the heart of the Church.[1] On May 9, 1897, Pope Leo XIII published an encyclical on the Holy Spirit, *Divinum Illud Munus*, in which he spoke of the Holy Spirit as the "soul" of the Church, a theme drawn from Augustine.[2] Leo XIII expressed his regret that there were so many in the Catholic Church who, "like the disciples at Ephesus," could say, "We have not even heard that there is a Holy Spirit" (Acts 19:2). In his encyclical, the pope stressed Aquinas' insight that the Holy Spirit is the divine person who reveals the depths of the Trinity to us: "The lover is not content with a superficial knowledge of the beloved, but strives to enquire intimately into all that pertains to the beloved, and so to penetrate into the beloved's very soul. So it is said of the Holy Spirit, who is the love of

---

[1] Manning's key works on the Holy Spirit are *The Temporal Mission of the Holy Ghost* and *The Internal Mission of the Holy Ghost.*

[2] Augustine, *Sermons* 268, 276, and 341. See also Pope Pius XII, *Mystici Corporis,* 69, and LG 7.

God, that the Spirit searches even the depths of God" (1 Cor 2:10).[3] Leo XIII encouraged Catholics to develop a renewed devotion to the Holy Spirit, and urged priests and teachers to help others to "know and love the Holy Spirit." Pope Pius XII later stressed this same theme of the Holy Spirit as the "soul of the Church" in his 1943 encyclical on the Church as the Mystical Body of Christ *(Mystici Corporis)*.

In the years preceding Vatican II, held from 1962–1965, twentieth-century writers such as Dom Columba Marmion, O.S.B., Yves Congar, O.P., Louis Bouyer, and Archbishop Luis Martinez of Mexico, whose own lives were fed by the study of Scripture, liturgy, and the Fathers of the Church, continued to emphasize the central role of the Holy Spirit in the Church. These very writings helped to prepare the way for the remarkable event of the Second Vatican Council. In 1958, Pope John XXIII was elected, it seems, as a harmless "interim" pope. Soon after, he astounded everyone by announcing that he would convoke an ecumenical council in order to fling open the windows of the Church to the refreshing wind of the Holy Spirit. He urged prayer for the outpouring of the Holy Spirit in a "new Pentecost" on the entire Church through this council. In announcing the council, Pope John used themes and even the very words of writers such as Dom Columba Marmion who had stressed the central place of the Holy Spirit in Christian life. Echoing Marmion's own words, Pope John urged all Catholics to pray this prayer invoking the Holy Spirit upon the Council: "Renew your marvelous works in this our time as by a new Pentecost!"[4]

Although the documents of Vatican Council II are not as permeated by a pneumatology as council observers such as the Orthodox Nikos Nissiotis and others urged, they do call the Church to a renewed and deepened awareness of the Spirit in the Christian life. In the Constitution on the Church, for example, we read that the whole people of God and not simply the clergy are "anointed" by the Holy Spirit through their baptism. As we have seen, the Holy Spirit pervades the Church and accomplishes a profound communion among us, distributing to all believers various gifts and ministries to build up the body of Christ.[5] Every member of the Church is meant to be permeated with the Spirit. Not only clergy but also lay people are urged to live every dimension of their existence, including their married and family life,

---

[3] Aquinas, ST, I–II, 28, 2.

[4] Marmion had written, for example, "Perfect in us an ever-new Pentecost" (*Christ in His Mysteries*, ch. 17, introduction; quoted in Charles Dollen, *Fire of Love: An Anthology of Abbot Marmion's Published Writings on the Holy Spirit* [London: Sands & Co., 1964] 33).

[5] LG 12, 13.

their daily tasks and recreation in the anointing and power of the Holy Spirit.[6]

The Constitution on the Sacred Liturgy in a special way emphasizes the key role of the Holy Spirit in the Church. Since the liturgy is the "summit" and source of the Church's life, we can grow most deeply in the life of the Spirit precisely through our sacramental celebrations.[7] By means of the invocation of the Spirit on the sacramental elements, earthly realities such as water and oil, and bread and wine are transformed to mediate the Holy Spirit's presence and power. But the renewed liturgical rites stress, too, that the Holy Spirit is invoked also upon the Church community celebrating the sacraments, so that our own hearts and lives may be transformed as well.

Church leaders such as Cardinal Léon Suenens of Belgium recognized not only this liturgical renewal but also the Catholic Charismatic Renewal awakened at the University of Duquesne in 1967 as a sign of the "new Pentecost" implored by John XXIII. In an address to the First International Charismatic Congress held in Rome in May, 1975, Pope Paul VI publicly acknowledged the Charismatic Renewal as a gift of the Holy Spirit in and to the Church. The pope drew attention to how informed involvement in the Charismatic Renewal fosters conversion to the risen Lord; personal experience of the closeness and power of the Holy Spirit; intimacy with the triune God; renewed desire for Scripture, the sacraments, and prayer; deeper understanding of the mysteries of the faith; and loving communion with and service to others.[8] Several years later, Pope John Paul II also publicly endorsed the Catholic Charismatic Renewal in an address to the Sixth International Charismatic Congress.[9]

The Spirit Drawing the Church into the Future

"What is the greatest need of the Church today?" As we have seen, Pope Paul VI, Pope John XXIII's successor, responded to this urgent question with these words: "The Holy Spirit." It is the Spirit who is the font of the Church's life and holiness, the source of her comfort and strength, her unity and gifts, her song and her joy.[10] On June 6, 1973, less than a year after he spoke these words, Pope Paul VI called the whole Church to deepened study of and submission to the Holy Spirit

[6] LG 34.

[7] SC 10; LG 50.

[8] *L'Osservatore Romano,* May 19–20, 1975.

[9] See Luis M. Bermejo, S.J., *The Spirit of Life: The Holy Spirit in the Life of the Christian* (Chicago: Loyola University Press, 1989) 376.

[10] *L'Osservatore Romano,* November 30, 1972.

as the indispensable fulfillment of all that Vatican II had begun. On Pentecost, 1986, Pope John Paul II, recalling these very words of Paul VI, issued the encyclical *Dominum et Vivificantem* ("Lord and Giver of Life"), solemnly placing the Church under the guidance of the Holy Spirit in preparation for the third millennium. In doing so, Pope John Paul II quoted and made his own the call of Pope Paul VI to the entire Church,[11] that the christology and ecclesiology of Vatican II must be followed by a "new study of and devotion to the Holy Spirit, precisely as the indispensable complement of the teaching of the Council."[12]

This emphasis of Popes John XXIII, Paul VI, and John Paul II on the importance of the Holy Spirit in the Church reflects what is happening in the "grass roots" of the Church today. The liturgical, theological, and pastoral renewal fostered by Vatican II continues to inspire Catholics to draw close to the Holy Spirit. The growing implementation of the renewed Rite of Christian Initiation of Adults (RCIA), in which the Holy Spirit's role is recognized as fundamental, is becoming an increasing force of renewal in the Catholic Church. In addition, the conciliar affirmation of the vocation of all the baptized to use the gifts bestowed on them by the Spirit to build up the body of Christ is fostering the growing involvement of lay people in varied ministries in the Church. The Holy Spirit continues to inspire Church reform and renewal through such means as the Charismatic Renewal, Scripture and prayer groups, parish renewal programs, Marriage Encounter, and Cursillo.

Impelled by their own experience of the Holy Spirit in their lives, an increasing number of contemporary Catholic theologians, including Cardinals Léon Suenens, Yves Congar, O.P., and Hans Urs Von Balthasar; Bishop Walter Kasper; Louis Bouyer, Heribert Mühlen, J. M. R. Tillard, O.P., Kilian McDonnell, O.S.B., George Montague, S.M., Francis A. Sullivan, S.J., Francis Martin, Edward O'Connor, C.S.C., and Luis Bermejo, S.J., have encouraged through their scholarship a deepened realization of the Christian life as life in the power and anointing of the Holy Spirit. Theologians such as Kilian McDonnell and George Montague, in particular, have shown that early Christian experience of the initiation rites resulted in an outpouring of the Holy Spirit's presence, power, and charisms which those in the Charismatic Renewal now call "baptism in the Holy Spirit."[13]

[11] Ibid., June 7, 1973.

[12] Pope John Paul II, *Dominum et Vivificantem: Lord and Giver of Life*, #2. Encyclical on The Holy Spirit in the Life of the Church and the World, May 30, 1986 (Washington, D.C.: United States Catholic Conference, 1986) 5.

[13] Kilian McDonnell, O.S.B., and George T. Montague, S.M., *Christian Initiation and Baptism in the Holy Spirit: Evidence from the First Eight Centuries* (Collegeville: The Liturgical Press, 1991).

Vatican II also has encouraged in Catholics a new ecumenical awareness of Church unity as a mandate of Jesus which must not be ignored.
A growing focus on the Holy Spirit has fostered in the Catholic Church
a deepened commitment to work for the Church's unity, a gift which
only the Spirit can give us, in the bond of peace (Eph 4:3). And since
the Spirit's gifts also are available outside the visible structure of the
Catholic Church,[14] the marvels which the Holy Spirit accomplishes in
other Christian communions and in other religions are recognized as
gifts, too, for the Catholic Church. Vatican Council II thus has opened
the Church to a global perspective by affirming that the Holy Spirit is
at work wherever people pursue the tasks of goodness and truth that
make life more human.[15] The reclaiming of the Holy Spirit's central
role in the Church has served also to relate Catholic belief and life even
more closely to contemporary issues of a global nature. Before Vatican
II, writings on the Holy Spirit often stressed the activity of the Spirit in
the individual "souls" of Christians. In the diverse historical, cultural,
and social contexts of today, however, writings on the Holy Spirit include a focus on the Holy Spirit as immanent Creator who forms communities of equals and who inspires life-giving activity related to
social justice, ecumenical, feminist, and ecological concerns.

Contemporary Approaches in Pneumatology

Having reflected briefly on the historical backdrop to a growing
Catholic awareness of the Holy Spirit in Christian life, we turn now to
consider representative approaches in contemporary pneumatology.
Varying concerns have given birth to pneumatologies developed from
different perspectives: biblical, historical, Trinitarian, liturgical, spiritual,
ecumenical, cosmic, feminist, and liberation theologies, to name a few.
For our purposes, we outline representative pneumatologies in the light
of our theme of intimate friendship with the Holy Spirit, giver of joy.

The first theologian we consider, Karl Rahner, S.J., did not focus in a
systematic way on pneumatology. As thoughtful critics point out, his
rich theological synthesis lacks a sustained focus on the person of the
Holy Spirit.[16] However, because his approach has had much impact on
other contemporary theologians who do develop explicit pneumatologies, we begin our reflections with an outline of Rahner's Trinitarian
theology. In his book, *The Trinity,* Rahner intended to encourage in

---

[14] UR 3.

[15] GS 38.

[16] See, for example, the comments of William J. Hill, O.P. in *The Three-Personed
God: The Trinity as a Mystery of Salvation* (Washington, D.C.: The Catholic University
of America Press, 1982) 139.

readers a deepened awareness of the Trinity not as an abstract theory but as the God who is the "mystery of salvation." Rahner develops the following proposition as the basis of achieving this purpose and of showing that every mystery of faith must be infused by Trinitarian doctrine: "The 'economic' Trinity is the 'immanent' Trinity and the 'immanent' Trinity is the 'economic' Trinity."[17] By this dictum Rahner stresses that what the Trinity does for us (the economic Trinity) is identical with who the Trinity is in the inner divine life (immanent Trinity).

In company with the reformed theologian Karl Barth, Rahner advocated avoiding the word "person" in referring to the Father, Son, and Spirit. He feared that the term could be misunderstood as implying three centers of consciousness in God, and in this way encourage tritheism, belief in three different gods rather than in three divine persons who are the one same God. To underline clearly God's unity, Rahner advocated using the phrase "three modes" or "manners of subsistence" instead of "three persons" in speaking of the Father, Son and Holy Spirit. He urges us to envision the Trinity as one God relating to us in a "threefold manner."[18] In emphasizing this "threefold manner" of the one God's relating to us, Rahner so focuses on the "monarchy" of the Father that he also seems to identify the essence of God with the one person who is the Father.[19] The Father is the first "mode of subsisting" who is the principle of self-communication and self-mediation. The Word and the Spirit are the aspects of the self-communication of this one God who seems to be identified with the Father. Rahner reflects on the Word, the second "manner of subsistence," as origin, history, offer, and knowledge. He views the Spirit, the third "mode of subsistence," in terms of future, transcendence, acceptance, and love.[20]

In assessing Rahner's Trinitarian approach, theologians such as Walter Kasper, William J. Hill, O.P., and Jürgen Moltmann have stressed that the vast majority of Christians today have little or no awareness of God as Trinity. The Christian faith today, therefore, is threatened not by tritheism but rather by a modalism which views the divine persons simply as different names, manifestations, or "modes" of a God who is only one person. These theologians consider Rahner's Trinitarian theology to be modalistic not in conscious intent but in effect.[21]

[17] *The Trinity*, trans. Joseph Donceel (New York: Seabury Press, 1969) 21, 22.

[18] Ibid., 113, 35.

[19] Catherine Mowry LaCugna, *God for Us: The Trinity and Christian Life* (New York: HarperSanFrancisco, 1991) 253.

[20] Rahner, *The Trinity*, 91, 93.

[21] See Walter Kasper, *The God of Jesus Christ*, trans. Matthew J. O'Connell (New York: Crossroad, 1986) 288; Jurgen Moltmann, *The Trinity and the Kingdom*, trans. Margaret Kohl (London and New York: SCM, 1981) 144.

Other contemporary theologies, presenting variations of what can seem to be a modalistic imaging of God, are subject to the same critique. Elizabeth Johnson, for example, argues in her book, *She Who Is*, that we need to envision and speak of the mystery of God with female images and metaphors in order to free women from a subordination imposed by a patriarchal imaging of God. In service of her project, Johnson adopts "She Who Is" as the female metaphor for the mystery of the God she envisions as feminine "Sophia" or "Wisdom," source of life and relationship.[22]

Johnson is convinced that when people speak of "God" they most often refer to the Spirit, Sophia's active presence in the world, creating, transforming, empowering, and drawing us to solidarity, especially with the suffering.[23] Johnson criticizes theological approaches that associate women with the Spirit through attributing "feminine traits" to the Spirit; this practice subordinates women to men by reducing their identity to limited roles such as mothering or service.[24] In contrast, we need to model our relationships on Sophia, in whose "inner relatedness" there is no subordination. Sophia herself is "unknowable mother of all." Jesus, who is "Sophia's child and prophet," is "Sophia herself personally pitching her tent in the flesh of humanity." Finally, Sophia also "forever unfurls as distinct self-bestowing Spirit."[25] Not only is woman the image of this Sophia, but Sophia herself is the image of woman: naming God as the feminine "Sophia" "points to the mystery of triune Holy Wisdom as *imago feminae*" (the image of woman). According to Johnson, what is modeled in this re-creation of Trinitarian doctrine is "the life-giving power of women."[26] Thoughtful critics rightly ask how possible it is to recognize in such an approach the Trinity of divine persons worshipped in Christian faith.[27]

Other pneumatologies focus on the Spirit as the "anonymous" bond between the Father, Son, and us. In *The Spirit of Love*, for example, Brian Gaybba agrees with Rahner's thesis that the divine persons are "distinct ways in which the entire divine nature exists." Gaybba recognizes the Spirit as a "distinct personality" whose identity is to be the "anonymous" or "faceless" way in which Jesus and the Father make

[22] *She Who Is: The Mystery of God in Feminist Theological Discourse* (New York: Crossroad, 1992) 127.

[23] Ibid., 131, 146; 133–41.

[24] Johnson, *She Who Is*, 51–53, 143–44.

[25] Ibid., 215, 214.

[26] Ibid., 215.

[27] See, for example, Robin Darling Young, "She Who Is: Who Is She?" *The Thomist* 58 (1994) 323–33.

themselves present to us. According to Gaybba, we do not experience the Holy Spirit as a divine person with a unique personal identity. Rather, the Spirit is the very person of love, and love "has no identity of its own" except to be unity. This is the reason "why the Spirit is experienced as the presence of Father and Son, and not as a person with a clear and distinct identity."[28]

Gaybba considers it a kind of "distortion" to give our attention to the Spirit as we do to the Father and Son. Rather, our prayer to the Spirit should always be prayer asking that the Spirit draw us closer to Jesus, the Father, and one another. Gaybba concludes that the Spirit is the way in which we experience the Father's and Son's presence. Just as the Spirit has no other "face" than to be the Father's and Son's presence to one another, so, too, the Spirit's only "revelatory role" is to make them known to us and to unite us in love to them.[29]

Kilian McDonnell's work on early Christian initiation and baptism in the Spirit focuses on the Holy Spirit as a divine person whose power, gifts, and personal presence we are meant to experience.[30] In an earlier article McDonnell also stresses the centrality of the Holy Spirit in Christian doctrine, and maintains that the missions of the Son and Spirit are inseparable and of equal importance. However, the Spirit's "hiddenness" accounts for the "elusive quality" of all that we know and say about the Holy Spirit.[31] McDonnell agrees with Gabriel Marcel's insistence that we treat mystery as a presence which we cannot grasp through objective knowledge. The Holy Spirit is not meant to be the "object" of our theological reflection, then, but rather the "means" for our knowing Jesus: Jesus is the "'what' of theology, the Spirit is the 'how.'" The Spirit is thus the "interpretative perspective" for the whole of theology and the means of our knowing the Father and Jesus.[32] McDonnell in this way embraces Barth's conviction that the Spirit is our "light," and "contact with" the Father and Son, our means of knowing about them. We are meant to focus on theology "in" the Spirit, rather than theology about the Spirit,[33] since the Holy Spirit

[28] *The Spirit of Love: Theology of the Holy Spirit* (London: Geoffrey Chapman, 1987) 123, 137, 136.

[29] Ibid., 138, 139.

[30] Kilian McDonnell, O.S.B., and George Montague, S.M., *Christian Initiation and Baptism in the Holy Spirit: Evidence from the First Eight Centuries* (Collegeville: The Liturgical Press, 1991).

[31] Ibid., 224.

[32] "A Trinitarian Theology of the Holy Spirit?" *Theological Studies* 46 (1985) 215, 226.

[33] Ibid., 216–17, 223, 219.

pervades the whole of Christian experience, doctrine, and theological reflection.[34]

In contrast to these "modalistic" and "binitarian" approaches, other pneumatologies rightly encourage believers to grow in explicit knowledge of and friendship with the person of the Holy Spirit. We consider first several Trinitarian pneumatologies that encourage this closeness through imaging the Spirit as the divine person with "feminine" attributes.

Donald Gelpi urges believers to draw close to the person of the Holy Spirit by relating to the Spirit as our "Divine Mother." Reflecting on Bernard Lonergan's theology of conversion, he advocates using the biblical image of "God's Breath" to speak of the Spirit, for the word "breath" is closer to the meaning of the Hebrew word for Spirit, *ruah.* Gelpi then employs the Jungian "archetype of the feminine in its positive, transforming aspects" as the key image for Holy Breath.[35] Reflecting on the imagery of the early Christian writer, Victorinus, Gelpi refers to "Holy Breath" as our "Mother." Gelpi concludes that the era of the Divine Mother in its eschatological fullness will begin when Christians follow the example of Jesus and give women equal status with men, allowing all of their gifts to thrive in the Church and world.[36]

In *The Spirit in the World,* Gelpi maintains that Christians perceive the Holy Spirit or the "Breath of God" as a divine person, but do not have an image helping them to draw close to the Holy Spirit in a personal way. Since we naturally think of persons as inseparable from gender, we tend to imagine "Holy Breath" as either male or female. Scripture, tradition, and the "archetypal structure of the human psyche" all encourage our envisioning the Holy Spirit as feminine. After reflecting on the Spirit as God's Breath breathing on Israel, on Jesus, on the Church, and on the world, Gelpi develops a final chapter on the "feminine face of God." He stresses the importance of developing a closeness to the Holy Spirit, and is convinced that this intimacy can be deepened if we imagine "Holy Breath" as our own "Mama." The Spirit is the one who conceives divine life in us and who, like a loving mother, nurtures us to the fullness of risen life in Christ.[37] When we call the "Holy Breath" our "Divine Mother" and think of the Trinity in familial terms, we also image the love which should be at the

---

[34] McDonnell, "A Trinitarian Theology," 213.

[35] Donald L. Gelpi, S. J., *The Divine Mother: A Trinitarian Theology of the Holy Spirit* (Lanham, Md.: University Press of America, 1984) 9, 11, 215.

[36] Ibid., 217–18, 235.

[37] *The Spirit in the World* (Wilmington: Michael Glazier, 1988) 108–12, 113, 114.

heart of Christian families. The Holy Spirit, our "divine Mother" thus works among us to heal the injustices that divide us.[38]

In another Trinitarian approach, Yves Congar develops a pneumatology from the perspective of an historical theologian devoted to fostering ecumenism and to illumining the role of tradition in the Church. In his three volume study, *I Believe in the Holy Spirit,* Congar reflects on the theology of the Spirit as it is developed in Scripture and the major thinkers of the Christian tradition until the Reformation. He also stresses the role of the Holy Spirit at the heart of the Church and of the sacraments, especially the Eucharist and confirmation. Congar shows his sensitivity to Orthodox concerns by acknowledging the unilateral nature of the *filioque*'s addition to the Creed in the West. Advocating Roman Catholic suppression of the *filioque* in the Creed as a gesture of humility and ecumenical sensitivity, he also urges Orthodox Churches to recognize that professing belief in the *filioque* is not heretical.[39] Along with his profound knowledge of and commitment to the tradition of the Church, Congar also manifests his openness to current theological insights. In his chapter on "Motherhood in God, Femininity of the Holy Spirit," for example, Congar encourages a growing closeness to the Holy Spirit through recognizing the Holy Spirit's tender, maternal role in our Christian life.[40]

In his study, *Holy Spirit of God: An Essay in Biblical Theology,* F. X. Durrwell focuses on Christ's paschal mystery, the source of the Spirit's outpouring on the world, for Christ's death has given us communion with the Spirit.[41] Stressing that we can speak of the Spirit's infinitely rich person only in paradoxes, as simultaneously God's humility and glory, Durrwell also reflects on the Spirit's maternal role in our lives. In doing so, he develops the theme of the Spirit as the divine "Womb" in whom we are all born to eternal life. Biblical symbols as well as the Church's baptismal waters intimate that the Holy Spirit plays a maternal role for us. Early Christians sometimes thought of the baptismal font, the place where catechumens were given new birth in the Spirit, as a symbol of the Church's motherly role. So, too, the Holy Spirit is not only like a mother for us but also like a "womb" in which we are nurtured to the fullness of life.[42]

---

[38] Ibid., 114.

[39] Yves Congar, O.P., *I Believe in the Holy Spirit,* trans. David Smith (New York: Seabury Press, 1983) 3:206.

[40] Congar, *I Believe,* 3:157, 161.

[41] F. X. Durrwell, *Holy Spirit of God,* trans. Sr. Benedict Davies, O.S.U. (London: Geoffrey Chapman, 1983) 137.

[42] Ibid., 158, 152, 155.

For Durrwell, the maternal role of the Spirit also shows that the Holy Spirit is the humility of God in person. Like a mother who fosters only life, the Holy Spirit works only for our welfare and good. Durrwell's emphasis on the Spirit's maternal tenderness leads him to ponder the role of the Holy Spirit as our comforter who completely transforms our experience of death. In the motherly Spirit, our relationships with our loved ones are only deepened by death, since the Spirit transforms the isolation of our suffering and death into the most profound communion. It is the Holy Spirit who accomplishes this beautiful transformation because the Spirit is the very person of the Lord's Easter joy.[43]

Adopting still another approach, Walter Kasper develops a "pneumatological Christology" that emphasizes both the "uniqueness and the universality of Jesus Christ." In *Jesus the Christ,* Kasper stresses that while Jesus is the revelation of the freedom of God's love, the Holy Spirit is the outpouring or effusion of the Father's and Son's freedom in love. Kasper points out that in western theology, the Spirit is viewed as the mutual love of Father and Son, their inmost mystery and the most hidden person of the Trinity. In the person of the Spirit, the inner Trinitarian circle of love appears to be closed. Kasper comments that this western approach seems to have removed the Trinity from salvation history and turned the Trinity into theory. In eastern Trinitarian doctrine, however, the Holy Spirit is viewed as the overflow of the Trinity's love made visible in Jesus: as the Son reveals the Father, the Spirit reveals the Son. The Spirit is, "as it were, God's outermost and uttermost" through whom "God acts in creation and history."[44]

Kasper further reflects on the Father's eternal giving of himself in love to the Son; in the Spirit, this love is communicated outside the Trinity. In the same Spirit, however, an inverse movement also occurs. By permeating Jesus' humanity, the Holy Spirit opens it to serve as a perfect "receptacle for God's self-communication." In Jesus' total self-giving to the Father and to us even unto death, the Spirit is outpoured, so that Jesus' death and resurrection are the source of Pentecost.[45] We can identify the Holy Spirit, therefore, as God's "innermost" and "outermost"; in this Spirit, the inmost mystery of God's being—the freedom of God's love—is poured outward. The Holy Spirit in this way is God's love and freedom in person.[46] The Spirit's continuing work is "to universalize the reality of Jesus Christ," that is, to incor-

---

[43] Ibid., 143–59; 122, 123.
[44] Walter Kasper, *Jesus the Christ* (New York: Paulist Press, 1977) 257, 258.
[45] Ibid., 250, 251, 252.
[46] Ibid., 250, 258.

porate all of us into the new creation the Holy Spirit accomplished in Jesus.[47]

In *The God of Jesus Christ*, Kasper stresses that theology "itself is a spirit-ual process, something done in the Holy Spirit" who is the very person of God's "ecstasy," "abundance," and "overflow of love and grace" to us.[48] Focusing on the unique personal identity of the Holy Spirit, Kasper stresses that the Spirit's freedom expressed in scriptural texts such as 2 Corinthians 3:17 shows that the Holy Spirit is not an impersonal reality but the personal giver of all of the Trinity's gifts. What is at stake in an approach that does not view the Spirit as a unique divine person is the very reality of salvation, which is sharing in God's life through Jesus and in the Holy Spirit.[49] With regard to the *filioque*, Kasper advocates an approach that encourages an ecumenical freedom of unity in diversity. Both East and West, however, need to respect one another's theological traditions as legitimate, because a hasty elimination of the *filioque* from the Creed could leave serious theological problems unfaced.[50]

Pneumatology, Ecclesiology, and Spirituality

Heribert Mühlen has devoted his life to promoting theological understanding of the personal identity of the Holy Spirit in the Trinity and in the community of the Church. In a first ground-breaking work, *Der Heilige Geist als Person: Ich-Du-Wir*, Mühlen reflects on the Spirit as "one person in two persons," in the Father and the Son. In a second key work, on the Spirit in the Church, *Una Mystica Persona*, Mühlen ponders the identity of the Spirit as "one Person in many persons," in Christ and believers. In both works, Mühlen also develops a theology of the Son's and Spirit's "personal causality," and reflects on the Spirit's "mission" of anointing Jesus. He examines the continuation of this mission in the Spirit's anointing of us through grace.

In *Der Heilige Geist als Person*, Mühlen contemplates the "I-Thou" and "We" sayings of Jesus in the Gospel of John, statements which refer to Jesus' relation to the Father. Following these considerations, Mühlen suggests that the Holy Spirit is the "We" in person between the Father and Son, the utter "nearness" of their personal relationship within the Trinity. So, too, in the covenant of grace, the Spirit has a direct, unmediated "person to person" relation with us. According to

---

[47] Ibid., 256.

[48] Walter Kasper, *The God of Jesus Christ*, trans. Matthew J. O'Connell (New York: Crossroad, 1986) 224, 226.

[49] Ibid., 210–13.

[50] Ibid., 221, 222.

Mühlen, it is the unique personal property of the Spirit that we have a direct relation with the Spirit, and it is only through the Spirit that we have an intimate relation with the Father and the Son.[51]

Mühlen's second key work, *Una Mystica Persona,* presents his insights on the Church as the continuation in salvation history of the Spirit's anointing of Jesus.[52] Within the Trinity, the Spirit is the divine person who unites the persons of the Father and Son. As the one same divine person in Jesus and in us, the Spirit transcends time, joining us to the historical Jesus through the Word in Scripture and tradition, and through the apostolic succession in the ordained ministry. The Holy Spirit is intimately present now in the Church to enable us also to share in Jesus' anointing by the Spirit. The Father's and Son's "personal action" in eternally breathing forth their Spirit of love is thus continued in the economy of salvation by Christ's "personal causality" of pouring out upon us this same Spirit.[53]

Mühlen further reflects on the Spirit, the eternal "We" between the Father and Son, as the divine person at the heart of the Church's social structure. The Church is the visible "sacrament" of the invisible Spirit of Christ. Through union with Jesus, "Bearer of the Spirit," the entire community of the Church is now also the "Bearer of the Spirit." The Holy Spirit is not only one person in many persons, therefore, but also one person in many churches, drawing us to that ecclesial unity that reflects the Trinitarian unity.[54]

An event of momentous personal impact for Mühlen occurred when, after months of reflection, he joined the Catholic Charismatic Renewal. Of this grace he commented that for years his knowledge of the Holy Spirit had been a "head" knowledge. After entering the Charismatic Renewal, however, he experienced the Holy Spirit fulfilling his deepest longings and transforming his life. "For fifteen years I have known the Holy Spirit with my head, but now I also know him with my heart, and wish the same joy for you."[55]

Mühlen in recent years has stressed the importance of personal experience of the Holy Spirit's presence and power in our lives. In *The Spirit of Life: The Holy Spirit in the Life of the Christian,* Luis Bermejo, S.J.,

---

[51] Heribert Mühlen, *Der Heilige Geist als Person: Ich-Du-Wir,* 2nd ed. (Paderborn, 1966) 168, 329.

[52] French translation: *L'Esprit dans l'Eglise,* trans. A. Liefooghe, M. Massart, R. Virrion (Paris: Cerf, 1969) 1:292.

[53] Ibid., 246, 361, 393.

[54] Ibid., 2:94, 97, 16.

[55] Ralph Martin, "An Interview with Fr. Heribert Mühlen, Theologian of the Holy Spirit," *New Covenant* (July 1974) 6.

contributes to this emphasis by reflecting on the Holy Spirit intimately at work in the Christian's entire self, body as well as soul. According to Bermejo, growing in the spiritual life is our ever deepening permeation with the Holy Spirit. Drawing from Johannine writings, Bermejo stresses that we are meant to have an intimate friendship with each divine person. Psychologically, however, we cannot direct equal attention to all three persons at any given moment. In addition, we grow close to each divine person at different times in our life and according to our spiritual needs.[56] We are meant to have a special closeness with the Holy Spirit, an intimacy so profound that our longing for completion by union with another is fulfilled in the person of the Spirit. Pointing out that Paul, especially, speaks of our relation to the Spirit in terms that are unique for the Spirit, Bermejo stresses that we are meant not only to believe in the Holy Spirit but also to feel and experience the Spirit deep within us. Our very baptism gives us the grace to grow from a vague sense of the Holy Spirit to an explicit, intimate experience of the Spirit giving us a peace and joy that are a foretaste of heaven.[57]

The seven gifts of the Spirit are the means of our becoming more docile to the Holy Spirit as well as permeated by the Spirit's anointing. Yet it is not simply our heart or soul but our human totality, including the materiality of our body, in which the Spirit intimately dwells. Bermejo stresses that the Holy Spirit takes possession of our entire self, including our affections and sexuality. The intensity of prayer sometimes may even have an effect on our body, such as the instinctive inclination to close our eyes and to rest without words in prayer inspired by the Holy Spirit.[58] Bermejo concludes that the Spirit's intimacy with us is so profound, filling us with so much contentment, that being possessed by the Holy Spirit is our deepest fulfillment as human persons.[59]

"Holistic Pneumatology": The Spirit, "Wellspring of Life"

Bermejo's pneumatology focuses on the profound inner life we gain through giving ourselves in reciprocal love to the Holy Spirit. In a complementary approach, Jürgen Moltmann develops a rich contemporary pneumatology that focuses also on the cosmic work of the Holy Spirit in creation. In *The Spirit of Life: A Universal Affirmation*,[60] Moltmann stresses both the "inner" and the "outer" life of Christians called

[56] Luis Bermejo, S.J., *The Spirit of Life* (Chicago: Loyola University Press, 1989) 114, 115.

[57] Ibid., 239.

[58] Ibid., 83, 243–50.

[59] Ibid., 207, 211, 217.

[60] Trans. Margaret Kohl (London: SCM Press, 1992).

in the Spirit of life to nurture life in the world. At the heart of Moltmann's pneumatology is the conviction that we are meant to know and love not only the Father and Son but also the Holy Spirit in the intimacy of a mutual self-giving that is our deepest fulfillment. Because Moltmann provides us with an especially rich synthesis, we conclude this chapter with a more detailed summary of his key insights.

Moltmann begins by critiquing as modalistic the pneumatologies of writers such as Karl Rahner, Karl Barth, and Hendrik Berkhof, for whom the Holy Spirit seems to be only "the mode of efficacy of the one God." Convinced that it matters profoundly whether our pneumatology has a Trinitarian or unitarian starting point, Moltmann develops in *The Spirit of Life* an explicitly Trinitarian pneumatology.[61] His own experience of living through the ravages of World War II drew him to realize that spirituality inspired by the Holy Spirit is ultimately a love for life, "a new delight in living in the joy of God." He therefore felt called to develop a "holistic" pneumatology which focuses on the Holy Spirit as the "wellspring of life" in creation.[62]

In an age in which the forces of death grow stronger daily, the Spirit who is the "life-giver" intensifies our commitment to life, and gives us the power to live a holy life, that is, a whole, healthy, complete life. Moltmann urges us to reverence the earth as "God's beloved creation," and to live in harmony with all in an interdependent "life together." Most importantly, he urges us to resist actively all that destroys life, especially human life, in the world.[63] Moltmann agrees that "Christianity learns from the feminist movement" that the patriarchal sins against women are sins also against the Spirit. However, the feminist movement can learn from Christianity not to focus simply on the rights of women but on the "rebirth of all the living."[64]

From within his Trinitarian perspective, Moltmann focuses on the unique personhood of the Holy Spirit through reflecting on metaphors for the Spirit such as Lord, mother, energy, fire, love, tempest, light, water, and fertility. He reflects on how the mother carrying her child within her and giving life to her child, is the "archetypal image" for the Spirit who is *vita vivificans* (life giving life). We thus live "in" the Spirit, who is all around us. Moltmann stresses that the Holy Spirit is not simply the "light" in whom we know the Father and Son, and not simply the bond or "link" between the Father and Son and us. Rather, in the Holy Spirit's light, we can also know and come close to the very per-

[61] Ibid., 13, 217, 14.
[62] Ibid., 178, 35.
[63] Ibid., 177–78, 175, 97, 171, 173.
[64] Ibid., 241.

son of the Holy Spirit: "In your light we see light" (Ps 36:9). Since early times, Christian tradition has addressed prayers to the person of the Spirit in the Eucharistic *epikleses* and in prayers such as the Pentecost hymns, speaking directly to the Spirit and asking the Spirit to come down upon us and fill us.[65]

The activity and effects of the Holy Spirit in us are distinct from those of the Father and Son, but Moltmann stresses that we cannot know intimately the person of the Spirit simply by considering what the Spirit does for us. In our closest relationships, we do not cherish our dear ones because of what they do for us but rather because of who they are in the depths of their own goodness as persons. "What we revere and love for itself, rests for us in itself and exists in itself even without us."[66] In true self-giving love, we worship the Trinity for the Trinity's own sake.

Moltmann contrasts this "doxological" worship of the Trinity with Rahner's "monarchical" approach, in which the Spirit seems to be "nothing other than the efficacy of the Son and Father." Furthermore, Moltmann critiques Rahner's dictum that the economic Trinity is the immanent Trinity "and vice versa"—that what God does for us is identical with who God is. In this approach of Rahner and of others influenced by him, Moltmann notes, there seems to be no "immanent Trinity" at all, but only a "functional" Trinity, only a "God for us."[67] Moltmann therefore agrees with Congar: the economic Trinity does reveal the immanent Trinity—but *not entirely*. Congar himself notes, "There is always a limit. . . . The infinite and divine manner in which the perfections that we attribute to God are accomplished elude us to a very great extent. This should make us cautious in saying 'and vice versa.'"[68]

According to Moltmann, a "monarchical" concept of the Trinity leads us to a perception of the "historical" Trinity who creates and redeems us: the Father acts through the Son in the Spirit. Salvation thus begins in the Father, is given to us in Jesus, and is consummated in the Spirit. Furthermore, through experiencing the Trinity's graced presence in our lives, we are meant to move beyond these "monarchical" and "historical" perceptions of the Trinity to a "Eucharistic" or thanks-filled perception, since the experience of grace cannot help inspiring

---

[65] Ibid., 269–70, 286–87.

[66] Ibid., 285–89, 290.

[67] Ibid., 291, 292. For an example of this approach critiqued by Moltmann, see Catherine Mowry LaCugna, *God for Us: The Trinity and Christian Life* (New York: HarperSanFrancisco, 1991).

[68] Congar, *I Believe*, 3:16; Moltmann, *The Spirit of Life*, 344, n. 42.

our gratitude. Reversing the monarchical movement, "Father, Son, Spirit," the "Eucharistic" Trinity is experienced in the order, "Spirit, Son, Father." Thanksgiving to the Trinity, however, leads us even further to our true goal, "Trinitarian doxology" in which we glorify the divine persons for their own sake. In the prayer of adoration, "Glory be to the Father and to the Son and to the Holy Spirit," we recognize that the divine persons are not only intimately near to us but also infinitely "other." We pass beyond self-centered love to glorify the divine persons for who they are and not simply for who they are for us.[69] We come to know the Spirit's deepest identity, therefore, not simply in relation to us but in the Spirit's relationship to the other divine persons. Noting that the unilateral insertion of the *filioque* in the Creed has placed the Spirit in an apparently subordinate place in the Trinity, Moltmann urges the deletion of the *filioque* from the Creed.[70]

Moltmann concludes that we are called to glorify, together with the Father and the Son, the very person of the Holy Spirit. Such adoration of the Spirit for the Spirit's own sake is the fruit of love drawing our gaze from the gifts of our beloved to rejoice in the very person of our beloved. The Holy Spirit is not simply another name for "God's" "creative activity" or "nearness," for such an identification reduces the person of the Holy Spirit to a function of a uni-personal God. Furthermore, it is true that the Spirit of love joins us to the Father and Son and to one another. But in the reciprocity of selfless love which is our highest call and deepest fulfillment, we recognize that far from being simply the anonymous bond and "link" between the Father and Son and us, the Holy Spirit is also "the be-wondered" "Other," the boundless source of unending wonderment for us. We are thus meant to pray not only "in" the Spirit but also "to" the Spirit as beloved other, whom we will one day see "face to face" in the ecstasy of unending mutual gift-love.[71]

As we have seen, explicitly Trinitarian pneumatologies offer us profound insights which can help us to develop a deepening friendship with the Holy Spirit. In the following chapters we turn now to reflect on growing close to the Holy Spirit who heals and teaches us, who inspires our prayer, and who leads us to heaven's joy.

---

[69] *The Spirit of Life*, 299–300; 305, 302, 304.
[70] Ibid., 298, 293, 71.
[71] Ibid., 301, 302, 304, 305.

7

Spirit of Healing

Spirit of Love, Our Comfort and Healing

In the Sequence for the Mass of Pentecost, we ask the Holy Spirit to heal our every wound. Physicians and health professionals can diagnose our symptoms, pointing us to the path of healing, but only the Spirit of love can reach down to mend the broken places of our heart and soul. Luke's parable of the Good Samaritan tells of someone who needs this kind of healing (Luke 10:29-37). A person falls among thieves who rob and beat him. Several people pass by as he lies helpless, but a Samaritan has pity on him, tenderly washing him and binding up his wounds. Because the victim's healing will take some time, the Samaritan entrusts him to another person who nurses him to full health. Early Christian writers such as Irenaeus found in this story a symbol of the Lord giving us the Holy Spirit as the tender healer of our every wound.[1] We ourselves fall victim to inner thieves—physical pain, emotional and spiritual wounds—which steal away our peace and joy. The Lord himself, however, brings us the healing we cannot give ourselves. Bernard of Clairvaux tells us that Jesus has come to us as the "anointed" one, full of healing mercy for us all: "The Spirit of the Lord is upon me, because he has anointed me" (Luke 4:18). The Father has anointed Jesus with the Holy Spirit so that he might bestow on us this same Spirit as the living ointment to heal our every wound (Ps 45:7).[2] The Lord has bandaged our sores through his death

[1] Irenaeus, *Against the Heresies*, 3.17.3; in J. Patout Burns and Gerald M. Fagin, eds., *The Holy Spirit* (Wilmington: Michael Glazier, Inc., 1984) 35–36.

[2] Bernard of Clairvaux, *On the Song of Songs*, 16.13; in *The Works of Bernard of Clairvaux*, trans. Kilian Walsh, O.C.S.O. (Kalamazoo, Mich.: Cistercian Publications, 1971) 2:123.

on the cross and then entrusted us, his dear ones, to his own Spirit as our healer.

Cyril of Jerusalem reflects on fire penetrating iron as a symbol of the Holy Spirit's gentle warmth healing us from deep within our being. Fire makes iron glow so brightly that the iron itself seems to become fire. But if a mere physical reality can permeate and work unhindered in another object, how much more can the Holy Spirit enter into the inmost recesses of our soul to cherish the unloved places in us and to heal us with the love that only God can give.[3] Basil the Great gives us another beautiful image by comparing the Holy Spirit to the sun shining down on us its warmth. The sun's rays light up the vast lands and seas of the entire earth and yet benefit each of us as though we were the only one. So, too, the Holy Spirit is present to each of us as though no one else existed.[4] And just as parents' affection mends their children's hurts, the Holy Spirit's love comforts and heals our emotional, spiritual, and physical pain. Commenting on the Johannine word for the Holy Spirit, "Paraclete"—"Advocate" or "Counselor"—(John 14:26), Irenaeus tells us that Jesus has poured out on us his own Spirit as our comforter.[5] Cyril of Jerusalem adds that persons such as Susanna (Dan 13:1-54) have been saved even from death by this helper, the Spirit who makes us holy.[6] Coming only to save and heal us, our comforter dwells in us in a way that is most gentle and sweet, most fragrant and consoling.[7] It is this Spirit who breathes into us healing peace for our mind, heart, and soul.[8]

The Spirit Who Cares for the Poor

Both the Hebrew and Christian Scriptures tell us of the infinitely gracious God who is near to the weak, who is close to the poor (1 Sam 2:1-10; Luke 1:46-55). Luke describes Mary herself as crying out in joy that God "has looked with favor on the lowliness of his servant" and has "filled the hungry with good things" (Luke 1:48, 53). In a special way, the Holy Spirit who is gift and grace in person is also unbounded riches for the needy, the one who is in love with the poor. We have seen that the Holy Spirit's name is Gift, and a gift by its very nature is freely bestowed, not because we deserve it but precisely because in our need we do not deserve it. This is why the Pentecost Sequence invokes the

---

[3] Cyril of Jerusalem, *Catechetical Lectures,* 17.14; NPNF 2.7, 128.

[4] *On the Holy Spirit,* 9.22; NPNF 2.8, 15; LH 394–95.

[5] *Against the Heresies,* 3.17.3; in Burns and Fagin, *Holy Spirit,* 35.

[6] *Catechetical Lectures,* 16.31; NPNF 2.7, 123.

[7] Ibid., 16.16; NPNF 2.7, 119.

[8] Ambrose, *The Mysteries,* 11; LH 495.

Holy Spirit as "Father of the Poor"; the Spirit comes not to those who are worthy—since no one is worthy of God's unmerited gift—but rather to those who are full of need.

With Mary, the saints show us that our weakness is not a cause for discouragement, therefore, but rather for joy, since our very need draws to us the Holy Spirit who is helper of the poor. St. Therese of Lisieux, for example, surrendered herself to the Lord and had a great desire to suffer for him magnanimously. But in her last agony she often felt that she suffered not with a great, courageous heart, but with a small, impatient heart. Far from becoming disheartened, however, she experienced her frailty as a precious grace.[9] Trusting that the more vulnerable she was, the more irresistibly the Holy Spirit's power was drawn into her heart, she learned to say with Paul, "I will all the more gladly boast of my weaknesses, that the power of Christ may dwell in me . . . for whenever I am weak, then I am strong" (2 Cor 12:9, 10).

In his own helplessness Soren Kierkegaard would pray to the Holy Spirit, confident that the Spirit chooses to dwell in the unworthy in order to transform their hearts into a beautiful dwelling for God.[10] In one of his poems, Gerard Manley Hopkins also pleads for God's help in his weakness by asking for the Lord's rain on the dry roots of his soul.[11] For each one of us also, the Holy Spirit is the living "dew," the healing "rain" for whom the parched earth of our hearts cries out.[12] Bernard of Clairvaux reminds us that we are faithful only with the Holy Spirit's help, and we fall miserably without it—yet "never fatally," for we are always held by the hand. If we humbly ask for the grace to rise again, our very faults can become a blessing for us, keeping us totally dependent on God. Even holy people experience their weakness. Since the Holy Spirit never comes to us empty-handed, however, all of us have the power for our healing deep within us.[13] We need only to persevere in asking the Holy Spirit to heal us, and our prayer will always be answered, often in a far deeper way than we could have imagined. Even in difficult times our heart will be consoled, and the Holy Spirit's healing peace will fill our soul.

---

[9] See *St. Thérèse of Lisieux: Her Last Conversations*, trans. John Clarke, O.C.D. (Washington, D.C.: ICS Publications, 1977) 116, #3; 83, #6; 193, #1; 143, #4; 145, #3; 153, #4, #7.

[10] See Yves Congar, O.P., *I Believe in the Holy Spirit*, trans. David Smith (New York: Seabury Press, 1983) 3:150.

[11] Gerard Manley Hopkins, *The Major Poems*, ed. Walford Davies (New York: E. P. Dutton & Co., 1979) 104

[12] Irenaeus, *Against the Heresies*, 3.17.3; LH 404.

[13] Bernard of Clairvaux, *On the Song of Songs*, 17.2; Walsh, 2:127.

The paradox of God's mercy is that often the Spirit works most deeply within us at the lowest points of our life. It is at these times that the Holy Spirit can give us the gift of a humble, honest heart as the first step in our healing. St. John of the Cross comments that often we want to be freed of our weakness immediately. Yet if our faults were removed quickly we could become proud, relying on our own supposed strength instead of on God. Wonderful graces, then, can come to us in our weakness that are denied to those too proud to ask for help.[14] When we are helpless, giving up our defenses and concerns about appearing strong and good, the Holy Spirit can become strength within us, healing and freeing us in ways that we could never accomplish ourselves.

The Spirit Filling Us with Good Desires

Paul tells us that without the Holy Spirit, our existence is mere "flesh" whose painful "works" are strife, anger, jealousy, dissensions, envy, drunkenness, carousing, enmity, immorality (Gal 5:19-21). These sinful works bring us heartache, not joy. Yet the Holy Spirit can transform even the unpeace of our sin into the first step of our healing. Augustine, for example, was chained to sexual sin for many years. The good God, however, allowed his sin to become so unbearable to him that he longed to be free of his pain and to taste God's sweetness. He found, however, that he could not rely on his own weak efforts but only on God's strength. He began to pray for chastity, then, not as a virtue his own power could achieve but rather as a gift from the Holy Spirit. And the Spirit who inspired his prayer also answered it. Augustine found that his unchaste desires were being replaced by desire for the infinitely sweeter delights of the Spirit's chastity.

In this way Augustine discovered by experience that we are freely drawn only by what delights us. Just as the body has its delights, so too, does our inmost soul. If we show a green branch to sheep, they will follow us. If we hold out a treat to children, they will run to us. We are all attracted by love, by "ties of the heart."[15] Augustine himself found that when our heart is free, we choose what is good not through fear but through delight. We may exercise each day, for example, not because we are afraid of sickness but because exercising makes us feel good. So, too, we are drawn to virtue by the delight we experience in

---

[14] John of the Cross, *Dark Night of the Soul*, 1.2.5; 1.2.7; in *The Collected Works of St. John of the Cross*, trans. Kieran Kavanaugh, O.C.D., and Otilio Rodriguez, O.C.D. (Washington, D.C.: ICS Publications, 1973) 300, 301.

[15] Augustine, *Commentary on John*, tract. 26; LH 679, 680.

being and doing good.[16] But even our very desire for virtue comes only from the Spirit who is both healing power and delight within us.[17]

When, by God's grace, we ourselves want to be free of our sin, the Holy Spirit begins to purify our desires, just as the same Spirit transformed Augustine's desires.[18] Like Augustine, we begin to tire of sin's pain and to want to live virtuously. But even then we find that we are weak; we have good desires and discover that we are faithless. Yet the Holy Spirit seeps into the secret recesses of our heart to love into wholeness what has been unloved in us. As we give ourselves to the Spirit of love and joy within us, our sinful desires begin to give way to a greater longing for God. The Holy Spirit inspires us with good thoughts, with desires for a more pure and generous life, a more loving and truthful life. Strengthened by the Holy Spirit who alone can heal us, we learn not to rely on ourselves in our weakness, and to ask for the Spirit's strength in our daily struggles. This Spirit who is the friend of the poor is also the call within us for better things,[19] protecting us from harm, caring for our needs,[20] inspiring our good desires, and giving us the love to carry them out.[21] What our own efforts and resolutions could not achieve, then, we begin to enjoy as a precious gift from the Spirit who defends us and fights for us.[22] Cyril of Jerusalem reminds us that the Holy Spirit has converted countless persons throughout the ages, inspiring even very worldly people to scorn not only sin but even wealth and rank for the sake of God's love.[23]

Our Pardon and Peace in the Sacrament of Reconciliation

The Holy Spirit who has accomplished these wonders for others wants to work the same miracle of love for us: "When you send forth your spirit, they are created" (Ps 104:30).[24] No sin or destructive habit of ours, and no inner wound which causes them, can be greater than the Holy Spirit's power to heal us. Scripture tells us that Jesus himself healed and freed others through the Holy Spirit filling his humanity (Matt 12:28). And Jesus continues to heal us today, first of all through

[16] Idem., *Letter 145*, 5; Burns and Fagan, *Holy Spirit*, 179.

[17] Idem., *On Rebuke and Grace*, 12.38; Burns and Fagan, *Holy Spirit*, 183.

[18] Novatian, *Treatise Concerning the Trinity*, 29; Burns and Fagan, *Holy Spirit*, 78.

[19] Paul Claudel, *Hymne de la Pentecôte*; in Yolande Arsène-Henry, ed., *Les plus beaux textes sur le Saint-Esprit*, rev. ed. (Paris: Lethielleux, 1968) 310.

[20] William of Saint-Thierry, *The Contemplation of God*, 11; LH 50.

[21] Augustine, *On Rebuke and Grace*, 12.38; Burns and Fagan, *Holy Spirit*, 183.

[22] Cyril of Jerusalem, *Catechetical Lectures*, 21.4; NPNF 2.7, 150.

[23] Ibid., 16.19; NPNF 2.7, 120.

[24] Cyril of Alexandria, *Commentary on John*, 10; LH 398.

the Spirit-filled sacraments of his Body, the Church. At every Eucharist we take seriously the Lord's great desire to heal us as we pray, "Lord, I am not worthy to receive you, but only say the word and I shall be healed." The very first sacrament of our healing, then, is the Eucharist, the summit and goal of every other sacrament because it contains Jesus himself, who comes to heal us with his Spirit's fire of love.

In a special way the sacrament of reconciliation also brings us healing for our sin. The new rite for this sacrament assures us that the Holy Spirit has been given to us for the forgiveness of sins. We read, too, in the Gospel of John that the risen Lord "breathed" on the apostles, saying to them, "Receive the Holy Spirit. If you forgive the sins of any, they are forgiven" (John 20:22-23). The formula of absolution used by priests today makes present this very mystery. Just as the Lord Jesus poured out the Spirit on the apostles for the ministry of forgiveness, the same Lord comes to us in the sacrament of reconciliation to fill us with the Spirit who ministers to us pardon and peace. Because the Spirit of love fills us with healing peace, both priests and penitents are urged by the new rite to prepare for reconciliation by praying for the Holy Spirit's love and enlightenment. In order that this healing sacrament may take root in our entire life, priests, especially, are urged to ask the Holy Spirit's help to discern their penitents' deepest needs.[25]

In *The Healing Power of the Sacraments*, Jim McManus, C.SS.R. encourages priests to pray with penitents explicitly for inner healing of the wounds at the source of their sins, so that they will experience not only the Lord's pardon but also his peace. Many times, our sins are the symptoms of inner hurts which become apparent when we think of areas of our past or present life for which we cannot praise God.[26] As we shall see, inner healing takes place through prayer to experience the Trinity's intimate love freeing us from hurts, damaged self-image, bitterness, and unforgiveness. McManus comments that priests sometimes feel such compassion for penitents struggling with sin, especially sexual sins committed through weakness, that instead of asking the Holy Spirit's healing for the root cause of the sin, they assure penitents that what they are doing is not sin. From his own experience as a priest, however, McManus has learned that this approach, far from freeing people, only leads them into deeper servitude. "Jesus does not want us to rationalize away the sinful habits which burden people, but to free them from those habits through healing prayer."[27] Because our

---

[25] *Introduction to the New Rite of the Sacrament of Reconciliation*, #15.

[26] Jim McManus, C.SS.R., *The Healing Power of the Sacraments* (Notre Dame, Ind.: Ave Maria Press, 1984) 45.

[27] Ibid., 42, 52.

sins often are the symptoms of a wounded heart, we need to bring the wound and not merely the sin to this healing sacrament. The Holy Spirit who is both infinite power and unbounded delight then can fill the deprived places of our heart that hunger for love but seek it in ways that cannot satisfy us. The Spirit of love in this way not only forgives us but also frees us from the sin that our unaided efforts cannot overcome.[28]

The Spirit Freeing Us

"Where the Spirit of the Lord is, there is freedom" (2 Cor 3:17). The Spirit of love comes especially to release us from the bonds that tie us to the past, to our own mistakes and failures, to our inner wounds, and to bitterness at those who may have caused them. One of the Spirit's most powerful ways of freeing us is through breaking the chains that bind us to someone we cannot forgive. Basil tells us that all sins are forgiven by the Holy Spirit,[29] and the liturgy itself calls the Holy Spirit God's pardon and forgiveness.[30] We also read these beautiful words in Ephesians: "Do not grieve the Holy Spirit of God, with which you were marked with a seal for the day of redemption. Put away from you all bitterness . . . be kind to one another, tenderhearted, forgiving one another, as God in Christ has forgiven you" (Eph 4:30-32). The Holy Spirit enables us to feel so treasured by the divine persons that in the contentment of their love we grow rich enough to ask forgiveness of those we have hurt and to forgive those who have hurt us. We find ourselves being healed of inner wounds as we pray in words as simple as these: "Lord, reach deep into my being with your Holy Spirit's healing love in the places where I am most wounded, where I feel most hurt, and where I most need you. Holy Spirit of love, heal my heart and soul, my mind and body. Free me and those you have given me from all chains of the evil one. Fill us with your own love, peace, and joy." Gradually, and even sometimes instantaneously, we will feel so loved by God that our anger will be changed into pity for those who have wounded us. We will begin to feel cherished with the Trinity's own tender love that far outweighs any hurt we have suffered, and our pain will be transformed into freedom from a bitter heart.

Death itself is powerless before this Spirit of love who transcends all time. The Holy Spirit can bring to us our loved ones who have died, allowing us to speak with them, to forgive them, and to feel their love

---

[28] Ibid., 51.

[29] Basil the Great, *On the Holy Spirit*, 19.49; NPNF 2.8, 31.

[30] Prayer over the Gifts, 7th Saturday of Easter.

and forgiveness of us. For example, grieving women who cannot forgive themselves for having had an abortion can find forgiveness through the sacrament of reconciliation. This healing, however, is greatly intensified if it is joined with prayer to experience the unborn child's love and forgiveness for his or her mother and father.

Prayer for the Holy Spirit's healing can free us not only from unbearable burdens of guilt but also from unbearable burdens of loneliness. One man whose mother had died when he was three years old had suffered from depression for years without being able to identify its cause or to be freed from its grip. During prayer for inner healing, he asked Mary to hold him close as her child. As he did so, he felt the tenderness of Mary as his own mother, and experienced her giving him also his earthly mother to cherish him and hold him close. In this precious grace, he felt a great loneliness lifted from him.[31] Healing experiences such as these show us that, in the Spirit of love, those who have died can be present to us in their risen existence and enable us to enjoy a true communion as well as loving communication with them. In this way, Jesus himself comforts us with the Holy Spirit's healing love and turns our grief into peace and joy.[32]

Our prayer for the Holy Spirit's healing can and often should include the powerful practice which the Church holds out to us at the Easter Vigil. Along with the catechumens, the entire community is asked to "renounce Satan and all his pomps and works." The Gospels show that Jesus himself freed others by commanding demons to depart from them (Mark 9:17-29; Matt 12:22-28; Luke 8:26-39).[33] In union with Jesus, Christians since early times have included in the Church's initiation rites the ministry of freeing catechumens through commands to evil spirits to depart from them. We, too, can be held in bondage by evil spirits who steal our freedom and joy, plaguing us through fears, anxiety, depression, and addictions.

Physicians and counselors can help us to identify these bondages, but God the Holy Spirit, our true healer, can free us from them. Jim McManus writes that in his own priestly ministry he has witnessed numerous times the Holy Spirit's power at work through the sacraments and prayer, freeing people from burdens of guilt, anxiety, depression, and addictions, including homosexual urges and actions. In company with countless other believers, he has seen the tremendous freeing power of commanding evil spirits to depart in the name of

---

[31] Barbara Leahy Shlemon, *Healing the Hidden Self* (Notre Dame, Ind.: Ave Maria Press, 1982) 66–67.

[32] Ibid., 90, 91.

[33] See also Mark 5:1-20, 6:13, 7:24-30, 9:17-29; Matt 8:28-34; Luke 11:14-23.

Jesus. He urges us to bring our own burdens and addictions, as well as those of our loved ones, to the healing, freeing power of the Lord Jesus and his Spirit.[34] Our prayer to the Holy Spirit, therefore, can and often should include this "prayer of deliverance," a command to evil spirits who may be stealing from us or our loved ones the Holy Spirit's joy and peace: "Be gone, evil spirits of (depression, fear, addiction to . . .), in the name of Jesus Christ. I renounce you. Most Holy Spirit, possess me, fill me and my loved ones with your joy and peace." Through prayer such as this we ask the Holy Spirit to dwell in us as our healer and to rebuild the crumbling house of our soul.[35] I myself have witnessed countless times the power of this prayer in the lives of my students, even those who begin to pray it with little or no expectation of results. We have found this command to be so beneficial that we regularly include it as part of our prayer as we begin each class: "All demons of fear, depression, anxiety, and addiction, be gone from us in the name of Jesus. Sweet Holy Spirit of love, fill us with your peace and joy." Even students who do not identify themselves initially as religious persons attest to the power of this prayer by their own experience.

Another way that the Holy Spirit wants to free us is through releasing us from the effects of bondage to hurt or sin which other members of our family, including our parents, grandparents, and other ancestors, may have suffered. We know from experience that one person's suffering or unfreedom always has consequences for other family members—not only those living but also those yet to be born. Because we are "members one of another" (Rom 12:5), Paul's words in 1 Corinthians 12:26 take on special meaning in this context: "If one member suffers, all suffer together with it." The scars of emotional deprivations, abuse, or addictions which we ourselves suffer always take their toll on those related to us, especially our children, who then suffer wounds which affect how they will relate to their own children. Many people, however, have experienced the Holy Spirit's great power to free them and family members from scars of sins or wounds suffered by relatives, living and dead. In *Healing Your Family Tree*, Fr. John Hampsch urges us to experience for ourselves this freeing grace of the Holy Spirit, working in an especially powerful way when we assist at a Eucharistic Celebration offered explicitly for this purpose.[36]

---

[34] McManus, *Healing Power*, 97–98.

[35] Symeon the New Theologian, *Hymn Forty-Four*; in *Hymns of Divine Love*, intro. and trans., George Maloney, S.J. (Denville, N.J.: Dimension Books, 1975) 228.

[36] John Hampsch, *Healing Your Family Tree* (Huntington, Ind.: Our Sunday Visitor, 1989).

Our Inner Healer

As the new Rite for the sacrament of reconciliation suggests, the Spirit who makes all things new brings us not only forgiveness and freedom from individual and familial sin, but also healing for the inner wounds which cause this sin. We suffer physical damage when deprived of oxygen for too long, but our hearts, too, are damaged when we fail to receive the love and affection the Trinity has intended for us. Even when forgotten by our conscious memory, inner hurts can steal from us our baptismal joy. Someone else may have gained the attention we longed to receive, or become the chosen one while we were ignored. A person we loved may have mistreated or abused us. A dear one may have died, or walked out of our life. Hurts like these can grow into inner wounds whose pain seeps even into our body. We may try untold remedies for our pain, but with little or no results, since our suffering stems from wounds which only God can heal.

Often these wounds are not the result of others' malicious intentions. When we are vulnerable, however, even small hurts can take on enormous proportions. A mother's pain or anxiety, for example, or a father's rejection or absence can affect even their unborn infant, who needs to bond with both father and mother for security and emotional wholeness. Yet regardless of how overwhelming or apparently insignificant our hurts, the Spirit of love can take us back to past events that have caused these hurts. In the Holy Spirit's power we can experience now what we could not feel then, the warmth of Jesus' love, and the tenderness of the Father's arms around us, protecting us and absorbing every hurt for us. Jesus himself was held in his Father's loving arms even as he was beaten and crucified for us. Precisely because he has suffered for us every hurt we could experience, he can fill us with the Holy Spirit's healing even in the most tragic areas of our lives, changing our pain into healing and the assurance of being loved and cherished.

Through prayer for inner healing, the Holy Spirit who transcends time can take us back not only to our recent past but also to our youth, infancy, and even to our time in the womb, touching with infinite love the roots of wounds we may not even consciously remember. Children can push hurtful experiences into their unconscious selves, in this way protecting themselves from feeling pain that seems too overwhelming. The distress that we could not bear as an infant or child, however, can make itself felt later in adulthood through symptoms such as anxiety, depression, addiction, and sin.[37] Barbara Leahy Shlemon, a delivery

---

[37] Shlemon, *Healing the Hidden Self*, 44, 35, 19.

room nurse for ten years, has prayed with many people suffering from inexplicable fears, guilt, or depression. She has witnessed the power of the Holy Spirit freeing these persons when they would pray for healing during the time when they were developing in their mothers' wombs. Shlemon encourages us to ask the Holy Spirit to heal any deprivations that we ourselves may have experienced, beginning at the very moment of our conception. We simply ask the Lord Jesus, who transcends all time, to go back with us to our pre-natal development, and to meet all of our needs, surrounding us with the warmth of his Spirit's love, and healing any fears or deprivations that we may have experienced while in the womb.[38]

Because even the process of being born can be traumatic for the infant, the Holy Spirit may inspire us also to pray for inner healing of wounds that may have occurred during our birth. We ask the Lord to breathe his Spirit of love and life into our entire being, and to let us be born into his own sweet arms, where we are held with infinite love and cherishing. As we experience Jesus giving us to our mother and father, we ask Jesus to bond us to them with a perfect sense of security in being loved by them, and to heal any trauma or deprivations of love and acceptance that we may have experienced at this time.[39]

Every child needs to be tenderly touched, held, cuddled, caressed. Dramatic changes can take place in persons deprived of the tenderness they needed as children when they ask Jesus to give them his own mother to cradle them in her arms. Persons who pray in this way often feel a tremendous sense of comfort and security filling their heart, as well as a sense of finally "belonging" and being totally accepted. The Holy Spirit may inspire us, also, to rest in the arms of Mary, our dear Mother, and to ask Jesus and our beloved Father to hold us close, to fill with their infinite love any wounds or deprivations we may have experienced as an infant or child, especially feelings of being abandoned, unprotected, lonely, or uncared for.[40]

We cannot grow without opening our heart, trusting and reaching out to love others; but if we do not learn to trust as children, it will be difficult for us as adults to trust even those we love. Jesus, however, can touch the broken places within us with the comforting love of his heart and give us the Holy Spirit to heal our distrust. One reason for being unable to trust others can stem from hurts we may have suffered at the hands of those who should have protected and cherished us. Shlemon recounts praying with a woman whose alcoholic father had

[38] Ibid., 31, 39–40.
[39] Ibid., 52–53.
[40] Ibid., 66–67; 70–71.

beaten both her and her mother. A profound inner healing occurred when the woman prayed for healing of the time when she had been in the womb. She experienced Jesus surrounding her with his protective love, standing between her mother and her abusive father, and receiving the blows in place of her mother. The passage from Isaiah 53:5, "through his wounds we are healed," came to her mind, flooding her heart with grateful tears. She realized that Jesus submitted himself to physical beatings and abuse of every kind during his passion so that he could absorb our pain and heal it with his love.[41] Those who have been emotionally, physically, or sexually abused can ask the Holy Spirit for this same kind of healing through prayer such as the following: "Lord Jesus, heal any wounds of abuse I may have suffered, whether physical, verbal, emotional, or sexual. Let me feel your tender touch cherishing me, making me feel clean and whole, loved and infinitely precious."

Another area of inner healing may be needed by those who have been adopted. Regardless of how much they are loved by the parents they know, they can sometimes suffer from an unexplainable emptiness or depression. One person who prayed for this healing asked Jesus to bring his birth parents to him in his heart's sight. As he did so, the Holy Spirit filled the emptiness inside him with the sense of how loved he was. He felt his birth parents tell him that they loved him, and that their love was always with him. Resting in the embrace of his Abba, of Jesus, and of his mother Mary, he felt bathed in peace, his depression washed away by the Holy Spirit, the best of comforters.[42]

The Spirit and Physical Healing

As we learn to ask continually for the Holy Spirit's healing within us, we begin to realize the intimate connection between spiritual, emotional, and physical healing. The infinitely good God wants to free us from the destructive forces of evil, including the physical evils of suffering and illness. The Gospels place great emphasis on the power of Jesus to heal us physically, and the risen Lord continues to give us the Holy Spirit's healing through the sacraments and our prayer for one another. In *The Prayer that Heals: Praying for Healing in the Family*,[43] Francis MacNutt stresses that, more often than we realize, the Trinity wants to heal our emotional, spiritual, and physical sufferings not only through the sacraments but also through our prayer for

---

[41] Ibid., 113, 121, 36, 90.
[42] Ibid., 64.
[43] Notre Dame, Ind.: Ave Maria Press, 1981.

one another. It is true that suffering cannot be completely eradicated from our world, for it is intertwined with the mystery of our human condition damaged by sin. But spontaneous prayer spoken aloud by those who love one another, simple prayer shared by married couples, families, and friends, is a wonderful way that the Lord Jesus continues to bring us the Holy Spirit's healing for our emotional, spiritual, and physical needs. In his own ministry of healing, MacNutt has found that spouses, families, and friends often miss this wonderful opportunity of praying with one another for healing. We ourselves would be amazed at the emotional, spiritual, and physical healings that we and our loved ones could experience if we would simply pray with each other.[44]

When we do pray for physical, emotional, and spiritual healing, we need only to use our own words, speaking to the divine persons as our dearest friends who want us to be well and whole. We may find it difficult at first to pray aloud in our own words even with our loved ones. But we do not need many or complicated sentiments; our prayer can be simply, "Lord, please heal my spouse, my child, my parent, my loved one, my friend." We discover by experience that an added gift of this prayer with one another is the grace of growing close not only to the Trinity but also to one another. Holding the sick person's hand or putting our hand on his or her shoulder or forehead is also a powerful means of conveying the Holy Spirit's healing through one another. Jesus continues to heal us today through loving touch, just as the Gospels depict Jesus himself healing others through his touch.

In a special way, the Holy Spirit comes to heal us in the sacrament of the anointing of the sick. It is significant that this sacrament also employs not only soothing oil but also the comforting touch of the priest, family, and community. Through this sacrament, the Spirit of healing comes to bring us consolation and healing, often for our physical illness, and always for our emotional and spiritual pain. In the blessing of oil used for this sacrament, the bishop prays that the Spirit, our comforter, helper, and "friend," may come upon the oil, so that those anointed with it may grow strong and well in every part of their being. The Introduction to the New Rite for celebrating this sacrament also tells us that the Holy Spirit's healing grace is poured out upon the sick so that their entire person may be strengthened, comforted, and healed of anxiety about death. The Holy Spirit in this way comes to heal not only our physical pain but also our fear and guilt, our anxieties and depression. The assembled family and community unite with the priest to support their sick and to pray for this healing within them. As

[44] Ibid., 13.

family members and other persons in the community join in the sacramental invocation of the Spirit's healing upon their beloved sick, they help and encourage them to offer themselves completely to the Trinity's loving care for their lives.

Both in this sacrament and in our prayer for physical healing it is important to ask the Holy Spirit to guide our prayer, since it may be the Trinity's plan of love to heal our sick loved ones spiritually and emotionally but not necessarily physically. In these instances, the Lord wants to fill both us and our loved one with the Holy Spirit's own peace. This sacrament invokes the Holy Spirit's deep inner healing not only upon our sick, therefore, but also upon us, their families, so that we, too, may share in the Holy Spirit's comfort and grace. Even if our dear one is being prepared for the loving encounter with the Lord that is death, we can convey the Holy Spirit's healing peace by our prayer and comforting touch, and draw untold good from the most painful experiences. The Spirit who cannot die thus gives us healing power over the forces of death itself.[45]

The Spirit Transforming Us

As we have seen, early Christians experienced miracles happening through the Holy Spirit whom they received in their baptism. Enemies became friends, strangers were transformed into sons and daughters, and people centered on worldly concerns began to value what is truly important in life.[46] This same Spirit is joy for us today, the power in virtuous people to do good, the chastity of those who are chaste, the strength of those who are martyred.[47] If we call upon the Holy Spirit's power in our own lives, we will see in ourselves and loved ones the same miracles of love that have healed and transformed the saints. Samuel, for example, assured Saul, "The spirit of the Lord will possess you, and you will . . . be turned into another person" (1 Sam 10:6). Gregory Nazianzen reminds us that this most wise and loving Spirit took possession of the shepherd David, made him a psalmist who subdued evil spirits by his song, and then proclaimed him king. The Spirit also possessed Amos, the goatherd and scraper of sycamore trees, and made him a prophet. This same Spirit dwelt in the apostles, speaking in them as they proclaimed the Lord, changing them from cowards into martyrs, so that they loved Christ with all of their hearts and faced their murderers unafraid. The Spirit took possession of fishermen and

---

[45] Symeon the New Theologian, *Hymn Forty-Four;* Maloney, *Hymns of Divine Love,* 231.

[46] Asterius of Amasea, *Sermon Thirteen;* LH 240.

[47] Novatian, *Treatise Concerning the Trinity,* 29; Burns and Fagan, *Holy Spirit,* 79.

made them catch the whole world in the nets of Christ: "Look at Peter and Andrew and the Sons of Thunder," Gregory comments; the apostles began as timid cowards and ended by "thundering the things of the Spirit!"[48]

The apostle Paul's own life was turned completely around by this Spirit of love; he was transformed from a hater of Jesus into a man passionately in love with him. Paul promises that, as we ourselves behold the Lord with unveiled faces, we, too, are "being transformed into the same image from one degree of glory to another; for this comes from the Lord, the Spirit" (2 Cor 3:18).[49] In a beautiful prayer to the Holy Spirit, the eastern saint Symeon the New Theologian praises the Holy Spirit for wounding him with healing love, restoring his health, and transforming his life.[50] In the Spirit of love, we, too, can grow strong and bear fruit, repaying the Lord's kindness to us with our own self-giving love toward others.

The Holy Spirit gains for us all good things, forgiving, healing, and freeing us, working miracles for us, driving out demons, and even now raising us to new life.[51] Basil the Great thinks of how tarnished silver, after it is polished, shines with new brilliance. When the Holy Spirit fills us, we ourselves become like this, full of light, and beautiful channels of grace for others.[52] Cyril of Jerusalem offers us another image for the Holy Spirit's healing power when he considers how a dry tree, when watered, springs to life again and blossoms with new branches. The Holy Spirit is the living fountain who waters what has become dry in us, making us blossom with new life.[53] In this Spirit we find our faithful friend and advocate, the living "dew of God," who will not allow us to be destroyed or made fruitless.[54] Possessed by this Spirit we have received in our baptism, we have real power within us to grow in virtue and to become strong against all evil.[55]

Through our intimate baptismal communion with the Holy Spirit, we ourselves can become "persons of the Spirit." Our whole being can be transformed, completely filled with the Spirit who raises our hearts to God, leads the weak by the hand, and brings to perfection those

---

[48] Gregory Nazianzen, *Sermon Forty-One: On Pentecost*, 14; Burns and Fagan, *Holy Spirit*, 134.

[49] Cyril of Alexandria, *Commentary on John*, 10; LH 398.

[50] *Hymn Twenty-Four*; Maloney, *Hymns of Divine Love*, 131.

[51] Basil, *On the Holy Spirit*, 19.49; NPNF 2.8, 31.

[52] Ibid., 9.23; NPNF 2.8, 15; LH 395.

[53] Cyril of Jerusalem, *Catechetical Lectures*, 16.2; NPNF 2.7, 118.

[54] Irenaeus, *Against the Heresies*, 3.17.3; Burns and Fagan, *Holy Spirit*, 35–36.

[55] Cyril of Alexandria, *Commentary on John*, 10; LH 398.

advancing on the way.[56] This Spirit is the cool fountain for our dryness, the warm hearth for our cold hearts, the sweet fire that cleanses and heals us. In one of his prayers to the Holy Spirit, Cardinal Newman adores the Holy Spirit as the one who turns sinners into saints.[57] St. Leo the Great urges us to pray that we ourselves may experience this same miracle of grace, for the Spirit of love wants to accomplish in each one of us marvels more wonderful than the heavens.[58]

[56] Basil, *On the Holy Spirit*, 9.23; NPNF 2.8, 15.
[57] John Henry Newman, *Meditations and Devotions* (London: Longmans, Green and Co., 1953) 310.
[58] Leo the Great, *Sermon Seven: On the Nativity*, 7.2.6; LH 178.

8

OUR INNER TEACHER

Our Soul's Anointing

The Lord has given us the Holy Spirit not only as our healer but also as our teacher to anoint our minds with the truth that sets us free (John 8:32). The lovely word "anointing" suggests the comfort we feel when a soothing balm is spread on our sun-burnt skin, or the consolation we experience when a loved one's tenderness fills our heart. The Holy Spirit, more interior to us than we are to ourselves, is our inner teacher and soul's "anointing": "His anointing teaches you about all things and is true" (1 John 2:27; see 1 Cor 2:10-12). No other teacher can be with us at every moment, and no external teacher, regardless of how close to us, can live within us to open our soul to the healing truth. The Holy Spirit, however, dwells deep in our heart not as a transient guest but as our beloved teacher who will never leave us: "I will ask the Father and he will give you another Advocate to be with you forever. This is the Spirit of truth" who "abides with you" and "will be in you" to guide you "into all the truth" (John 14:16, 17; 16:13).

Commenting on insights of Augustine, the Orthodox theologian Vladimir Lossky stresses that only the Holy Spirit, our interior teacher, truly teaches us. If this living anointing does not speak within us, we learn nothing, for where the Holy Spirit is absent, words of an external teacher bombard our ears to no avail.[1] We know how futile our own words can be when we long to speak truth that a loved one needs to hear. The most beautiful sentences spoken by the most eloquent

---

[1] Vladimir Lossky, *Orthodox Theology: An Introduction,* trans. Ian and Ihita Kesarcodi-Watson (New York: St. Vladimir's Seminary Press, 1978) 18.

preacher cannot open closed minds or change hardened hearts. Paul himself realized this: "I planted, Apollos watered, but God gave the growth" (1 Cor 3:6). We grasp the truth, then, only when the Spirit of truth speaks it in our heart.[2] And, unlike our unaided words, the Holy Spirit's anointing causes miracles to happen.

Light for Our Minds

In the Pentecost Sequence we ask the Holy Spirit, the very person of light, to shine in our hearts and to fill our inmost being. Surely the medieval author of this liturgical poem was inspired by the psalmist's words, "In your light we see light" (Ps 36:9). Church Fathers such as Cyril of Jerusalem interpreted this passage as referring to the Holy Spirit, the living light through whom we know the truth that sets us free. We sometimes refer to our own power of reason as an inner light that enables us to "see" the truth. If this light of our own intelligence is lacking, no amount of external teaching can make us understand created realities. Yet to know God and the things of God, we need an even more wonderful light, the Holy Spirit's baptismal anointing, which enables us to know through faith the truth of God and our precious identity in God.[3] It was for this very reason that early Christians called baptism, *photismos,* "enlightenment."

Basil the Great uses the example of a darkened room that is suddenly flooded with sunshine. In a room without light, we cannot see the true value of things; we could trample on gold and not know it. But when sunshine fills the room, we begin to see everything clearly. Our experience helps us to understand how the Holy Spirit gives us an inner light, enabling us to know through faith the truth that we could not recognize without it.[4] Just as we see created realities with created light, we "see" Jesus and the Father through the uncreated light who is the Holy Spirit (1 Cor 12:3).[5] The Spirit becomes the living light for our minds,[6] our true teacher illumining us about the things of God.[7]

---

[2] Aquinas, *Commentary on 1 Corinthians,* 2:13; Paul Claudel, *Hymne de la Pentecôte;* in Yolande Arsène-Henry, ed., *Les plus beaux textes sur le Saint-Esprit,* rev. ed. (Paris: Lethielleux, 1968) 309.

[3] Cyril of Jerusalem, *Catechetical Lectures,* 16.16; NPNF 2.7, 119.

[4] Basil, *On the Holy Spirit,* 16.38; NPNF 2.8, 24.

[5] Ibid., 26.64; NPNF 2.8, 40.

[6] Hilary of Poitiers, *On the Trinity,* 2.1.35; LH 400.

[7] Cyril of Jerusalem, *Catechetical Lectures,* 16.16; LH 393; John of the Cross, *Ascent of Mount Carmel,* 2.29.1; in *The Collected Works of St. John of the Cross,* trans. Kieran Kavanaugh, O.C.D., and Otilio Rodriguez, O.C.D.; (Washington, D.C.: ICS Publications, 1973) 204.

Symeon the New Theologian uses another beautiful image for the Holy Spirit as the "key" (Luke 11:52) who opens the riches of the Trinity's heart to us. The Father is our welcoming home, full of beauty and love; the Son is the door to our home (John 10:7, 9), and the Holy Spirit is the precious key. Without this key, the home remains locked for us. But with the key, the door is swung open so that we can enter, see, and possess the Trinity's infinite riches (Luke 24:45):[8] "What human being knows what is truly human except the human spirit that is within? So also no one comprehends what is truly God's except the Spirit of God. . . . These things God has revealed to us through the Spirit" who searches "even the depths of God" (1 Cor 2:11, 10).[9]

Spirit of Truth

The Holy Spirit teaches us first of all about Jesus, "in whom are hidden all the treasures of wisdom and knowledge" (Col 2:3), for Jesus is the very person of truth (John 1:14; 8:12).[10] The Hebrew word for truth, *'emeth*, comes from the word *'aman*, to support, to be firm. *'Emeth* conveys the sense of being trustworthy, true to one's word; it is inseparable from *hesed*, God's loving kindness and the source of God's promises to us. God's truth, then, is God's fidelity to the promises of love God has made to us. As early Christians reflected on this meaning of truth in the Hebrew Scriptures, they began to recognize Jesus as the very person of truth (John 14:6) because he is the living "Yes" to every one of the Father's promises to us (2 Cor 1:20).

We ourselves cannot help thirsting for truth, since we have been created in the Word who is truth itself (Col 1:16). Just as our lungs were made to breathe, and our hearts were made to love, our minds were made to know truth. Thomas Aquinas reflects on how the Trinity, who is infinite be-ing itself, has made us who are limited creatures to grow rich through knowing truth. Truth, however, is not simply knowing opinions, facts, or mere information. On the contrary, it is the conformity between our knowledge and what really is. To know what someone has said, for example, is to know a fact, but not necessarily truth. Lies, illusions, and false opinions, regardless of how many hold these opinions, join us only to the emptiness of non-being. Truth, however, unites us with reality, not simply with ideas about reality. And the marvelous reality we are meant to know first of all is the incompre-

---

[8] Symeon the New Theologian, *Catecheses*, 33; in *Symeon the New Theologian: The Discourses*, trans. C. J. De Catanzaro (New York: Paulist Press, 1980) 341–42.

[9] Basil, *On the Holy Spirit*, 16.38; NPNF 2.8, 24.

[10] Ibid., 26.64; NPNF 2.8, 40.

hensible yet infinitely knowable and delightful mystery of God, the inexhaustible feast for our minds and hearts.[11] Since the Trinity is unbounded be-ing itself, such knowing of the divine persons' truth expands our souls without limit. In a special way, knowing truth means knowing Jesus, the very person of truth in whom all of creation has its origin and perfect fulfillment (Col 1:16). The Spirit of truth thus teaches us to know Jesus, to live in him, and to see the full meaning and splendor of all of reality in him.[12]

The Spirit Teaches Us Through Love

"I pray that the God of our Lord Jesus Christ, the Father of glory, may give you a spirit of wisdom and revelation as you come to know him, so that, with the eyes of your heart enlightened, you may know what is the hope to which he has called you" (Eph 1:17-18). When we love, we cannot help wanting to know more and more about our dear ones; we would like, if possible, to reach into and understand their very souls.[13] But we "see" and know them not simply with our bodily eyes or with our intellect alone, but far more with the eyes of our heart. This is a knowing of truth, of the reality of our dear ones, that only love can give us. Love unites us to our dear ones so that we live inside them; their eyes become our eyes by which we understand them and all of reality in a new way and from their perspective. This experience, so known to anyone who loves, helps us to understand that we will grasp the truth that we read or hear about God only when we love God. This is why it is the Spirit, the very person of love, who is the Spirit of truth, opening the eyes of our mind and heart to the truth. Our experience of knowing about our beloved through the eyes of love helps us to understand how the Spirit teaches us not only by enlightening our minds but also by inflaming our hearts. The Spirit of truth teaches us through love the meaning of God's Word, and enables us to respond with love to its words of love.[14]

One way that we ourselves express our love is through a tender kiss. As Bernard of Clairvaux reflected on the Lord's giving of the Spirit to his apostles, he interpreted the Lord's "breathing" the Spirit on them (John 21:22) as their receiving the tender "kiss" of his love. This Spirit

---

[11] Aquinas, ST, I, 16, aa. 1–6.

[12] *Catechism of the Catholic Church*, #2465–70 (Dubuque, Ia.: Brown-Roa, 1994) 591–92.

[13] Aquinas, ST, I–II, 28, 2.

[14] Bernard of Clairvaux, *On the Song of Songs*, 8.5; in *The Works of Bernard of Clairvaux*, trans. Kilian Walsh, O.C.S.O. (Kalamazoo, Mich.: Cistercian Publications, 1981) 2:48.

is the same "kiss" the Father eternally gives the Son by sharing with him all of the treasures of his being. Though no creature can fathom this wondrous embrace within the Trinity, the Father and Son so treasure us that they give us their intimate kiss to be our own: "Oh that you would kiss me with the kisses of your mouth" (Cant 1:2). The Holy Spirit, then, is the kiss of love whom the Lord now tenderly imparts to us as his spouse, the Church. And just as the beloved disciple rested on the heart of Jesus at the Last Supper, we now rest in the heart of Jesus. There we receive as his most precious kiss to us the same Spirit with whom the Father kisses him with unfathomable love: "I have called you friends, because I have made known to you everything that I have heard from my Father" (John 15:15).[15]

The Teaching Church and the Seven Gifts of the Spirit

This Spirit of truth is always the Spirit of love who teaches us not as isolated individuals but as members of the Church community, united in heart and soul with other believers. Jesus gives us the kiss of his Spirit by guiding us in the way of truth (John 16:13) through intimate communion with one another (Eph 4:3, 11-13). In a union that mirrors the profound oneness of the Trinity, the Holy Spirit knits us together in a *koinonia* shared through the breaking of the bread, prayer, and the apostles' teaching (Acts 2:42). The "internal" voice of the Spirit speaking the truth through love in our hearts thus is inseparable from the Spirit's "external" voice speaking the truth to us through the community, and preeminently in the inspired word of Scripture illumined by the Church's teaching.

The same Spirit who inspired the apostles' preaching and the scriptural authors' writing continues to teach us the freeing truth today through the preaching and teaching of bishops, the successors of the apostles.[16] To enable bishops to fulfill their great teaching task, the Holy Spirit lavishes on them at their ordination the "sure charism of truth." In preaching the Gospel and teaching God's Word, bishops thus hand on the apostolic tradition to us and serve as a means for the Holy Spirit's voice to speak the truth to us today.[17] In this way the living voice of the Spirit, the great teacher of the Church,[18] rings out in our world, leading us ever more deeply into the fullness of truth.[19]

---

[15] Ibid., 8.6., 8.7; Walsh, 2:50.
[16] LG 24, 25.
[17] DV 8.
[18] Cyril of Jerusalem, *Catechetical Lectures*, 16.19; 16.14; NPNF 2.7, 120, 119; DV 23.
[19] DV 8, 21.

Scripture, tradition, and the Church's authoritative teaching are each inspired in their own way by the Spirit of truth and love, and together they form the Church's one deposit of faith. Furthermore, the same Spirit who inspires their truth enables us to recognize and believe it as the Spirit's own voice speaking to us today.[20] As we give ourselves to the Holy Spirit, the Spirit strengthens our faith, enabling us to understand more deeply what we believe,[21] especially through prayerful study and contemplation (Luke 2:19, 51).

One key means of our recognizing the truth the Spirit teaches us through Scripture and the Church is our baptismal gift of the "sense of the faith" *(sensus fidei)*. This is an instinctive, supernatural sense of what does and does not belong to the faith we have received from the apostles. Vatican II tells us that the entire Church community receives from the Spirit this baptismal "anointing" (1 John 2:20, 27) which cannot err in matters of faith, and which is at work in us when the entire Church gives its universal consent in matters of faith and morals. This "sense of faith" inspires us first of all to accept the Scriptures as God's own Word,[22] and to receive the Church's authoritative teaching also as God's Word illuminating these Scriptures (1 Thess 2:13).

The Holy Spirit also gives us special baptismal gifts to help us understand and live the truth which the Spirit speaks to us through Scripture, the Church, and our own hearts. These gifts of the Spirit are those referred to in Isaiah 11:2-3: wisdom, understanding, knowledge, counsel, fortitude, and fear of the Lord. This last mentioned gift is translated twice in the Greek version of the Hebrew Scriptures as "piety" and "fear of the Lord," thus bringing the number of the gifts to seven. Thomas Aquinas reflects on our indispensable need for these gifts, habits which make us so receptive to the Spirit's inspiration that through them the very person of the Spirit teaches, leads, and guides us.

We consider here the gifts of wisdom, understanding, knowledge, and counsel, by which the Spirit anoints our minds to know God's truth more deeply and to live it more fully. We have seen that love is our best teacher, and that the most important truths are those which love teaches us.[23] At our baptism the Holy Spirit gives us first of all the gift of wisdom to perfect our love and enable us to know God and the things of God through loving union with them. Devoted parents need no prompting to embrace their children; they spontaneously reach out

---

[20] DV 9, 10.
[21] DV 5.
[22] LG 12, 13, 11.
[23] Aquinas, ST, II–II, 45, 2.

to hold their dear ones just because they love them. The Spirit's gift of wisdom, given to us through charity, is like this. Without effort and strain we have a certain "familiarity" with the things of God, recognizing instinctively what is of God and what is not.[24] By faith we say "yes" to what is proclaimed to us. Through wisdom, however, the Holy Spirit enlightens us to grasp the things of God through a "sweet knowing" inflamed by love, a profound knowing which intimately unites us to the Spirit of love.[25] The Holy Spirit thus gives us not only comfort and joy but also the gift of contemplating the truth as a fruit of the Trinity's friendship with us.[26]

The stronger the Spirit's light and fire within us, the more deeply we understand the things of God. Aquinas comments that to "understand" (*intelligere*) is to have an "intimate" knowing whereby we "read inwardly" (*intus legere*) what we know. There are myriads of dimensions "hidden within" every reality, and if we are blessed by God with a "keen" mind, we seem to penetrate to the very heart of things. When we understand something, we grasp in some intuitive way its very essence. The Spirit's gift of understanding is like this, an intimate knowing, making us pierce to the very heart of what we hear or read about God.[27]

While these gifts of wisdom and understanding enlighten us to know the wonderful truth of God more deeply, the Spirit's gift of knowledge enables us to discern truth from error about the created world. We have a humble, sure judgment about what we should believe about creation, a judgment we attain not through our own reasoning but through the Spirit's intuition within us. Finally, by the Spirit's gift of counsel we know intuitively what we should do in certain situations, in a way that perfects and far exceeds what our prudence alone could advise us to do. When we are prudent, our own good common sense leads us, but when we are inspired by the gift of counsel, the very person of the Spirit guides us in what we should do.[28]

Prayer and Study Anointed by the Spirit

"We speak of these things in words not taught by human wisdom but taught by the Spirit, interpreting spiritual things to those who are spiritual" (1 Cor 2:13). Using the gifts of the Spirit within us, each one

[24] Ibid., II–II, 9, 2, ad 1; II–II, 45, 2 and 4; I, 1, 6, ad 3.

[25] Ibid., II–II, 45, 1, ad 2; II–II, 45, 6, ad 2; I, 43, 5, ad 2 and 3.

[26] Aquinas, CG IV, 22, 3.

[27] Idem., ST, II–II, 8, 1; II–II, 8, 6, ad 1 and 2.

[28] Ibid., II–II, 9, 1, ad 1 and 2; II–II, 52, 1–2.

of us is called by our very baptism to contemplate and to proclaim the truth of Jesus in our life and words. The words of truth we speak, however, are meant to breathe forth love because they are anointed with the Spirit of love. Catherine of Siena tells us that since only the Holy Spirit enables us to see the truth (John 16:13), the same Spirit speaks through us when we speak the truth in love.[29]

Because we can give only what we have, the source for our words of truth about God must be prayer as well as profound study, especially of Scripture. In reflecting on the words, "In my meditation a fire shall flame forth" (see Ps 39:3), Augustine comments that we truly know Jesus only through the Holy Spirit's wisdom, a sweet knowing of the truth through love. Bernard of Clairvaux adds that if we try to study even Scripture without the condiment of the Spirit, we will find that the written letter alone cannot give life (2 Cor 3:6). If we study Scripture with hearts warmed by the Spirit's love, however, devotion will flow from our words as honey flows from the comb.[30]

In a special way, we who are preachers and teachers are called to speak God's truth as it is warmed with the Spirit's fire, helping others to experience more deeply the presence of Jesus in their hearts (Col 1:27-28). As we have seen, Bernard of Clairvaux calls the Holy Spirit the Father's and Son's sweet "kiss." Preachers and teachers especially are meant to know the sweetness of this "kiss" and to draw others to experience this exquisite kiss in their own lives. Thomas Aquinas stresses that the Word is forever "breathing forth" the love who is the Holy Spirit.[31] And just as the words of Jesus had power because they also breathed forth this Spirit of love, our own words of truth are meant to be a tender breathing of the Spirit of love on others.

Our words, however, will have real power for others only when we draw them from the Holy Spirit's anointing in our study and prayer. We know that intimate friendship includes sharing our hearts' secrets with one another. Our experience mirrors the profound mystery of the Holy Spirit who treats us as another self, revealing the secrets of God's heart to us through the most intimate friendship.[32] We learn by experience that the Spirit is the true teacher of any teacher, instructing us most of all by inspiring our love. And since we truly understand what we study only when the Spirit of love instructs us, our preparation for teaching, especially our study of God's Word, needs to be "winged" with the Spirit's love. As Bernard of Clairvaux stresses, "Flesh and blood

[29] *The Dialogue*, 26; trans. Suzanne Noffke, O.P. (New York: Paulist Press, 1980) 77.
[30] Bernard of Clairvaux, *On the Song of Songs*, 7.5; Walsh, 2:42.
[31] Aquinas, ST, I, 43, 5, ad 2.
[32] Idem., CG IV, 21, 5.

do not reveal these secrets but only the one who searches the depths of God, the Spirit of God" (1 Cor 2:10).[33]

When the Holy Spirit teaches us the mysteries of God's heart, we feel a joy that consoles and gladdens us,[34] for we were made by God to love to learn. When the light in our mind "clicks," and we finally "see" something we did not understand before, we cannot help smiling. This happens because we are an unlimited capacity to grow. Knowing truth gives us joy because it expands us, uniting us with more and more of the vast universe. Nothing, however, compares with the joy that is ours in understanding more deeply the secrets of God's heart. Every time the Holy Spirit allows us to know and proclaim God's truth more deeply, a new Pentecost happens.

Our Guide

"All who are led by the Spirit of God are children of God" (Rom 8:14). The above insights lead us to ponder our call as Christians not merely to have a devotion to the Holy Spirit but rather to be completely possessed by the Spirit as our teacher and guide in every aspect of our life.[35] One key way that the Holy Spirit guides us is through speaking to us in the "most secret core and sanctuary" of our conscience,[36] teaching us to distinguish good from evil, truth from falsehood. When we give ourselves to the Holy Spirit as our guide,[37] increasingly we are so drawn to do only what pleases the divine persons that whatever is contrary to their loving will begins to lose its attraction for us. In a special way, we become reluctant to "grieve the Holy Spirit" (Eph 4:30; see 1 Thess 5:19) who fills us with a deepening sensitivity to recognize and repent of our sin. Pope John Paul II interprets this repentance as a precious gift of the Spirit of truth to us, letting us share redemptively in the pain that our sin brings not only to others but also to the Trinity. The same Spirit who entered into Jesus' suffering, transforming it into redemptive love, thus enters into our regret over our sin and fills it with saving love. Just as the Father's grief over our sin is "translated" into the suffering of Jesus on the Cross, our own remorse for our sin is converted by the Holy Spirit into a healing

[33] Bernard of Clairvaux, *On the Song of Songs,* 22.2; Walsh, 3:15.

[34] Origen, *On First Principles,* 2.7.4; in J. Patout Burns and Gerald M. Fagin, eds., *The Holy Spirit* (Wilmington: Michael Glazier, Inc., 1984) 72.

[35] Aquinas, *Commentary on Romans* 8, lect 3.

[36] Pope John Paul II, *Dominum et Vivificantem,* #43; Encyclical on The Holy Spirit in the Life of the Church and the World, May 30, 1986 (Washington, D.C.: United States Catholic Conference, 1986) 85.

[37] John of the Cross, *Living Flame of Love,* 3.46; Kavanaugh and Rodríguez, 627.

love that attaches us to God.[38] The Holy Spirit in this way continually transforms our repentance into "a new beginning," an ever new "bestowal of grace and love."[39]

As we give ourselves to the Holy Spirit as our guide, our thoughts and actions become more and more one with God's,[40] for those united to God become "one spirit" with God (1 Cor 6:17). We begin to do everything only with the inspiration of the Holy Spirit, who guides us with the sweet skill of a "heaven-sent director."[41] The Spirit not only guides us in making decisions for the present, but also on some occasions enlightens us in a general way about future situations we may have to encounter.[42] The Holy Spirit gave Paul, for example, an intimation of what would happen to him in Jerusalem: "As a captive to the Spirit, I am on my way to Jerusalem, not knowing what will happen to me there, except that the Holy Spirit testifies to me in every city that imprisonment and persecutions are waiting for me" (Acts 20:22-23).

We ourselves need never fear the future nor where the Holy Spirit is taking us, for the Spirit of truth who knows the very depths of God (1 Cor 2:10) cannot lead us astray.[43] On the contrary, since the Holy Spirit is always the giver of new life, the creator of new persons, we discover by experience the marvels that happen when we allow the Holy Spirit to possess and lead us. As we draw our life from this Heart of love beating invisibly within us, our life becomes increasingly rich and sweet. We find our life truly beginning—a life full of sweetness, vigor, and wonderful surprises.

Because the Holy Spirit's plan for us is far more wonderful than anything we could arrange for ourselves, we will be secure in following wherever the Spirit leads us. As we trust in the Holy Spirit's guidance, we begin to see that the Trinity works out everything in our life for the best. We give to the Holy Spirit the fears and anxiety that plague us, and ask for deepening trust as well as courage to take the risks the Holy Spirit inspires in us. Prayer for the Holy Spirit's anointing begins to fill our heart not simply before important events but at every moment: "Most Holy Spirit, possess me. I yield myself and this situation

---

[38] Pope John Paul II, *Dominum et Vivificantem*, #45, 85.

[39] Ibid., #40, #39, #31; 73, 70, 55.

[40] John of the Cross, *Ascent of Mount Carmel*, 3.2.8; Kavanaugh and Rodriguez, 216–17.

[41] Bernard, *On the Song of Songs*, 17.2; Walsh, 2:127.

[42] John of the Cross, *Ascent of Mount Carmel*, 3.2.12; Kavanaugh and Rodriguez, 217.

[43] Bernard of Clairvaux, *On the Song of Songs*, 17.3; Walsh, 2:128.

to you. Lead me, guide me, anoint me with your sweet power." In the Spirit's love, we become more and more the persons we were meant by God to be, and discover by our own experience that those yielded to the Holy Spirit grow more vigorous, energetic, and creative. Gifts we did not know were ours begin to emerge under the Holy Spirit's leading, as we find ourselves accomplishing tasks we once thought beyond our talents.

In this way, the Holy Spirit increasingly opens the horizons of our lives to the Trinity's infinite perspective. Because the Holy Spirit has far more wonderful plans for us than our hearts could imagine, surrendering ourselves to the Holy Spirit's guidance becomes our truest freedom. Often we will not know where the Holy Spirit is leading us (John 3:8); the joy of a life guided by the Holy Spirit is that we cannot even imagine the possibilities. The poet Paul Claudel, who experienced in his own life this grace of being liberated by the Spirit of love, wrote that those surrendered to the Holy Spirit find peace. They do not argue; rather, with loving docility they do everything that the Spirit inspires them to do.[44] If we ourselves ask for the grace to be always open to the Holy Spirit's leading, we will be inspired to set our course to the open sea, and to let the sails of the Spirit take us where they will. As we grow more and more docile to this sweet Spirit of truth (John 13:52), we will discover for ourselves the wondrous joy of being led by the Spirit, our teacher and guide.

---

[44] Paul Claudel, *Hymne de la Pentecôte*; Arsène-Henry, *Les plus beaux textes*, 309.

9

Spirit of Prayer

At sacred times when we share our heart's secrets with a loved one, we realize that nothing on earth is more precious than the gift of intimacy. Through it we are healed and made whole; in its warmth we blossom into the person we were meant to be. Opening our heart to someone we love, we feel treasured in all that we are, and just for who we are. Such intimate communion with another cannot be forced; it is a gift bestowed and received in love. Prayer is this kind of intimacy. In prayer we experience the healing truth that we are never alone, for through the Spirit of love, the Trinity dwells within us, closer to us than we are to ourselves.

Both Luke and Paul stress this intimate relationship between prayer and the Holy Spirit's presence in our hearts. Luke recounts how, at Jesus' baptism by John, Jesus experienced the Holy Spirit descending upon him while he prayed (Luke 3:21-22). Mary and the apostles also received the outpouring of the Holy Spirit at Pentecost as they devoted themselves to prayer (Acts 1:14; 2:1-4). And Peter was inspired by the Holy Spirit to recognize Gentiles as full members of the Church only after he prayed (Acts 10:9, 19). Paul tells us that the Spirit's activity in our hearts during prayer is so profound that the Holy Spirit actually prays within us: "The Spirit helps us in our weakness; for we do not know how to pray as we ought," but the Spirit prays within us "with sighs too deep for words" (Rom 8:26).[1] In a special way, the very person of the Spirit becomes our desire, our prayer, and the very answer to our prayer.[2] When we enter into our hearts we do not find emptiness

---

[1] Gregory Nazianzen, *Fifth Theological Oration,* 12; NPNF 2.7, 321.

[2] Symeon the New Theologian, "Prayer to the Holy Spirit preceding the *Hymns,"* in George Maloney, S.J., *Hymns of Divine Love* (Denville, N.J.: Dimension Books, 1975) 9.

but rather contentment, for through the Holy Spirit, the Father and Son also live within us as our life and joy.

Prayer: Intimacy with the Trinity in the Spirit

We seem to pray most fervently when we want a favor from the Trinity, yet often we do not know the deepest meaning of our desire. When we ask for a specific blessing—a job, a healing, someone to love—our plea is in reality a longing for the Holy Spirit, who, as Luke assures us, is every good we could ever desire (Luke 11:13). The Holy Spirit prays in us by becoming within us a living desire deeper than even our own longings expressed in prayer.[3] Through drawing us to want specific blessings, the Holy Spirit allures us to want the best of all goods, the Trinity's love hidden in everything good that we can desire. The prayer of petition, so natural to our make-up as persons who are always desiring something, in this way leads us to the even deeper prayer that is intimacy with the divine persons.

Our own desires for good things in fact reflect the divine persons' desire for *us*, their longing to give us far more than the answer to our specific requests. This is why the Trinity often expands our desires by not fulfilling them immediately. Our waiting intensifies our plea, stretching our heart to hold more than we could imagine. For we were created to enjoy not simply the sweet gifts of God, but even more, the sweetness of God. Since we were meant to satisfy our thirst for intimacy at the very heart of God, the Spirit who is the sweetness of God in person draws us into our own depths, where we find the answer to our longings, the Trinity's tender love for us.

Through the Holy Spirit, the person of selfless gift-love at the heart of the Trinity, we become intimate also with the Father and Son. As we have seen, from all eternity, the Trinity is a family of love; eternally, the divine persons give themselves to one another in the ecstasy of selfless love. Not even the most passionate and unconditional of our human loves can compare with the intensity of the divine persons' love for one another. Yet Paul assures us that this very same love at the heart of God has been "poured into our hearts through the Holy Spirit that has been given to us" (Rom 5:5). Since the Spirit is the Father's and Son's tender bond of love the Spirit's first act of selflessness within us during prayer is to draw us closer to the Father and Son. We come to know Jesus, the Father's beloved Word, through the Holy Spirit who is united with the Son from all eternity: "No one can say 'Jesus is Lord'

---

[3] Yves Congar, O.P., *I Believe in the Holy Spirit*, trans. David Smith (New York: Seabury Press, 1983) 2:116.

except by the Holy Spirit" (1 Cor 12:3). In prayer, too, we sink into the abyss of love that is the Father's heart only through the Holy Spirit who is the very person of the Father's love for his Son: "God has sent the Spirit of his Son into our hearts, crying, 'Abba! Father!'" (Gal 4:6). We know Jesus in an intimate way only through his Holy Spirit, just as we come close to his beloved Father only through this same Spirit who is the secret of their love in person.

The Spirit's Light Shining on Jesus

Our experience of love as "light" within us helps us to understand how the Holy Spirit is the living light shining on Jesus and his Father, opening our heart to see them in faith and to draw close to them in prayer. When we feel loved, the whole world seems bathed in sunshine. Small matters that would otherwise disturb us fade into insignificance, and we greet even unpleasantness with a smile. Just as our human love is "sunlight" enabling us to see everything clearly in its radiance, the Holy Spirit is the "sun," love's light shining in our heart in prayer: "In your light we see light" (Ps 36:9). Our sacramental celebrations are the privileged times during which we can savor the Trinity's tenderness in a special way. But it is also at other times of prayer that the Holy Spirit deepens our union with the Trinity, and inspires our own self-giving to the divine persons who surrender themselves to us without reserve.

As the living light, the Holy Spirit shines first of all upon Jesus, showing us the Father's beloved Son, and opening us to see the tenderness of our Abba shining in Jesus. In order to "see" our unseen Father, we need to look at Jesus, for in his life and death we find unveiled our Father's gentle heart. Yet we "see" Jesus, who he really is as the Father's cherished Word, only if we are enlightened by the Holy Spirit, giver of every good gift.[4] Basil tells us that only this Spirit who is intimately united to Christ can fill us with the worship that the risen Lord deserves, for it is the Spirit who glorifies Jesus (John 16:14).[5] In prayer, then, the Holy Spirit unites us to Jesus and forms us into the Father's beloved image.[6]

The Holy Spirit in this way is our living bond with Jesus, uniting us so closely to him that only stark physical comparisons can suggest its reality.[7] Paul, for example, speaks of us as "members" of Christ's own body (1 Cor 12:27), while John pictures us as branches of the vine who

---

[4] Gregory of Nyssa, *On the Trinity;* NPNF 2.5, 329.

[5] Basil the Great, *On the Holy Spirit,* 18.46; NPNF 2.8, 29.

[6] Cyril of Alexandria, *Commentary on John;* PG 74, 541.

[7] Luis M. Bermejo, S.J., *The Spirit of Life: The Holy Spirit in the Life of the Christian* (Chicago: Loyola University Press, 1989) 55.

is Jesus (John 15:5). Gregory of Nyssa contemplates this inseparable union between the Son and Spirit by reflecting on the Spirit as the "oil" (Ps 45:7) with whom the Father intimately anoints Jesus. In order to touch Jesus through faith, we must first touch the "living anointing" who completely permeates Jesus. When we approach the Son in faith, on all sides we meet the Holy Spirit[8] who enables us to savor the risen Lord's presence, and to experience his gift of new life.

The Spirit Uniting Us to Our Abba

This same Spirit inspires us to pray not only "Lord Jesus" (1 Cor 12:3), but also "Abba Father" (Gal 4:6; Rom 8:15). Scripture tells us that we were "sealed with the promised Holy Spirit" in our baptism (Eph 1:13), and that the Father has put his own "seal" on us by giving us his Spirit as a guarantee (2 Cor 1:22). Cyril of Alexandria comments that the Holy Spirit so imprints himself in us like soft wax, that we become radiant with God's own splendor.[9] In being thus "sealed" with the Spirit, we are so completely claimed as the Father's beloved daughter or son that we hear in prayer our Abba's precious words to us, "You are Mine" (Isa 43:1).

Early Christians treasured the Aramaic word, "Abba," because Jesus himself has given us this unmerited gift of intimacy with the one he himself called "Abba." This expression of childlike tenderness—some have compared it with the word "Daddy"—belonged by right to Jesus alone. Inspired by the Spirit who is the secret of Jesus' love for his Father, however, we who are the Father's beloved children by adoption receive this tender form of address as Jesus' precious gift to us. United to Jesus, we use it in prayer because it is the very same intimate name which Jesus himself employed: "God has sent the Spirit of his Son into our hearts, crying, 'Abba! Father!'" (Gal 4:6).

The human intimacy of Jesus with his Father reflects the love story that transcends all time, the unfathomable closeness of the Father and his beloved Son from all eternity. In alluding to the depths of this intimacy that surpasses all our concepts, mystics have used affectionate images, picturing the Father as the beloved "couch," the familiar "easy chair" into which the Son sinks with complete abandon from all eternity. The Son's cherished "resting place" forever is the warmth of his Father's heart (John 1:18).[10] We ourselves grow secure as persons

---

[8] Gregory of Nyssa, *On the Holy Spirit;* NPNF 2.5, 321.

[9] Cyril of Alexandria, *Thesaurus* 34; PG 75, 609.

[10] Bernard of Clairvaux, *On the Song of Songs,* 42.10; in *The Works of Bernard of Clairvaux,* trans. Kilian Walsh, O.C.S.O. (Kalamazoo, Mich.: Cistercian Publications, 1976) 3:218.

through the prayer that places us, also, in the very center of the Father's and Son's tender love.[11] We sink into the heart of Jesus through prayer, and there feel the depths of closeness between Jesus and his Father. But as we do so, we savor the Father's infinite love also for us who are so united to Jesus. The Spirit of love in Jesus' heart now dwells deep within us. This same Spirit unites us so closely to Jesus that we can pray, in him and with him, the most intimate prayer of his own heart, "O Abba, my Father!" (Rom 8:15, Gal 4:6).

It is the Spirit of love who also fills us with the sense of the Father's affection for us, inspiring us with great love to sink into the warmth of his embrace. His heart is so familiar, so warm and inviting that we can speak of "resting" in the Father's heart, like children asleep with utter abandon and peace in their parents' arms. With child-like trust we rest in our beloved Father's arms; there we grow secure in our identity as the cherished son or daughter of our Abba. The Spirit who is the "kiss" of sharing enables us in this way to know our Father through love[12] and to pray the "Our Father" with deepened affection. The Father's heart, in turn, is filled with tenderness at hearing these words of his own Son, words which the Holy Spirit now inspires in our heart and places on our lips.[13] With all of his heart's affection, the Father then invites us, in St. Bernard of Clairvaux's mystical phrase, to the "sweet caresses of his Son."[14]

In prayer such as this, the gates of paradise are opened to us—the paradise that is the Father's and Son's own heart, the Holy Spirit. Even the most intimate human relationship can only suggest the infinite flood of tenderness with which the Father and Son cherish each other from all eternity. The wonder of their love, however, is that in prayer they give to us this same gift of their "heaven," their unfathomably sweet and good Holy Spirit, to be our heaven also, hidden deep in our heart and drawing us in love to them. Placed in the very center of the divine Family through prayer, we find ourselves at home, fully loved and blessed.[15] Jesus, our Savior and Lord, our brother and spouse, makes us well-loved members of the family who is the Trinity.[16] In prayer, our soul is filled with our Father's tender love healing our fear

---

[11] Bermejo, *Spirit of Life*, 132, 133.

[12] Bernard of Clairvaux, *On the Song of Songs*, 8.9; Walsh, 2:52.

[13] Cyprian, *On the Lord's Prayer*, 2–3; LH 236–37.

[14] Bernard of Clairvaux, *On the Song of Songs*, 8.9; Walsh, 2:52.

[15] Maurice Landrieux, *Le divin Méconnu* (Paris: Beauchesne, 1921); in Yolande Arsène-Henry, *Les plus beaux textes sur le Saint-Esprit*, rev. ed. (Paris: Lethielleux, 1968) 279.

[16] Bernard of Clairvaux, *On the Song of Songs*, 42.10; Walsh, 3:218.

and making us secure. We rest in the heart of Jesus, as the Holy Spirit's tenderness bathes our soul in peace. Basil the Great remarks that these blessings, which are the first fruits of the Spirit's kindness to us, let us taste even now the banquet of heaven's joy.[17]

Growing Close to the Spirit in Prayer

We draw close not only to the Father and Son but also to the Holy Spirit through prayer, for we have been promised the gift of knowing the Spirit intimately (John 14:17). In prayer to the Holy Spirit this promise is fulfilled. This is why Gregory Nazianzen urges us to pray not only "in" the Holy Spirit to the Father and Son, but also, with love and adoration, to the very person of the Spirit.[18] As we shall see, one of the most precious fruits of prayer to the Holy Spirit is tasting the Spirit's sweetness in our soul. Many of the most profound insights of Thomas Aquinas about the Holy Spirit are inspired by the Book of Wisdom which describes these delights of the "Spirit of wisdom" within us. The author prays for the spirit of wisdom, depicted in the most enchanting of feminine images, as the gift in whose company we gain intimate friendship with God: "I called on God, and the spirit of wisdom came to me. . . . All good things came to me along with her," for those who gain her "obtain friendship with God" (Wis 7:7, 11, 14). The author of the Book of Wisdom continues, "She is a breath of the power of God . . . she passes into holy souls and makes them friends of God . . . I determined to take her to live with me . . . in friendship with her, [I find] pure delight" (Wis 7:25, 27; 8:9, 18). Thomas Aquinas interpreted these verses as an allusion to the giver of wisdom, the Holy Spirit, in whose presence we find the most delicate contentment.[19]

The experience of the Holy Spirit's sweetness in prayer has inspired countless saints and mystics to speak of the Spirit's closeness in words of great tenderness. Many of their poems are used not only by individual believers in their personal prayer but also by the Church in its liturgical celebrations. Because we shall reflect more deeply in the following chapter on intimate friendship with the Holy Spirit, we simply call attention here to some of the most exquisite poems and prayers which have inspired Christian prayer to the Holy Spirit throughout the centuries. The beautiful images of the ninth-century hymn, *Veni Creator Spiritus*, are the first which come to mind. In this lovely poem

---

[17] Basil the Great, *On the Holy Spirit*, 15.36; NPNF 2.8, 22.

[18] *Fifth Theological Oration*, 18; NPNF 2.7, 323; Basil the Great, *On the Holy Spirit*, 23.54; NPNF 2.8, 35.

[19] *Commentary on John* 15, lect. 3; see also ST II–II, 45, 2 and 5.

we pray to the Holy Spirit who is our Paraclete and gift, the living water, flame of love, and spiritual anointing, the finger of God's right hand, and promise of the Father. We beg the Spirit to give speech to our voices, to inflame our senses with light, to pour love into our hearts, to strengthen us with power, and to grant us peace.

Another prayer of closeness to the Holy Spirit is the sequence *Qui procedis,* the enchanting poem of the medieval writer, Adam of St. Victor. In this prayer we praise the Holy Spirit as the living fire of love who fills the universe, guides the stars, and gives light and life to all. We call out to the Spirit of love who helps the oppressed, consoles the sad, gives refuge to the poor, and draws our hearts to God. Cleansing us of sin, the Holy Spirit reconciles those who are estranged, wipes out hatred, and brings peace and sweetness to our souls.[20]

There is perhaps no more inspiring liturgical prayer to the Holy Spirit than the exquisite thirteenth-century poem, *Veni Sancte Spiritus,* sung as the Sequence to the second reading at the Eucharistic Celebration of Pentecost. We ask the Holy Spirit, lover of the poor, to come to us as our most welcome guest, filling the depths of our heart, refreshing us, giving us light, and dwelling in us as the sweetest of all comforters. Without the Spirit we have no power for good; but with the Spirit filling us, our wounds are healed, our strength is revived, our guilt washed away, and our stubbornness melted by the Holy Spirit's warmth. Through the Holy Spirit guiding us and pouring out upon us the seven gifts, we are drawn to the joys of heaven itself.

Another prayer once attributed to Augustine expresses these same sentiments to the Spirit in words full of affection. We praise the Holy Spirit as the one who is strength for the weak, support for the fallen, teacher of the humble, lover of the abandoned, hope of the poor, guide of the lost, port of the shipwrecked, and salvation of the dying. We ask the Spirit of tenderness to come to us in our weakness, that our powerlessness may be made strong in the Spirit's strength.[21] In his own prayer to the Holy Spirit, the eastern mystic Symeon the New Theologian begs the Spirit to stay with us, to enfold and protect us as our light and life, our treasure and joy, and the awakening of those who have died. Symeon tells us that when evil spirits see the Holy Spirit at home in us, they take flight before the Spirit's mighty power. As our comforter, this sweet Spirit meets our every need, heals our loneliness, and purifies us with tears. When we dwell in the Spirit as our home, we find our true selves in the depths of the Spirit's warmth. The Spirit

[20] Arsène-Henry, *Les plus beaux textes,* 205.
[21] Ibid., 204.

who chooses us in love thus makes us also faithful in love. Possessing us totally, the Spirit who is the treasure of the poor lavishes on us the indestructible wealth of God's own life and holiness (Rom 15:16; 1 Pet 1:2).[22]

Echoing these same sentiments, Cardinal Manning urges us to pray for the grace of an intimate devotion to the Holy Spirit, and to give ourselves, with all of our freedom, mind, heart, and will, to the Spirit of love. Since belonging to ourselves is slavery, Manning implores us to surrender ourselves completely to the Spirit of Truth, doing and saying all that the Holy Spirit inspires in us, for to be bound to the Spirit is to be utterly free (2 Cor 3:17).[23] Cyril of Alexandria writes that we are united so completely with the Spirit who is holiness itself that we ourselves become holy.[24] This Spirit is not a created breath quickly dissolved like ours, but the uncreated breath who breathes into us the Trinity's own holiness. The Spirit's very presence in our heart, then, makes us holy.[25]

We may have thought that only churches are the "holy" places where the Trinity dwells and in which we can pray. But John assures us, "True worshippers will worship the Father in spirit and truth" (John 4:23). Eastern writers such as Basil the Great interpreted these beautiful words to mean that we pray "in" the Holy Spirit, for our heart is opened to believe in Jesus by the Spirit in whom we live and pray. Certainly, the Holy Spirit dwells in us, for we are the sacred "temple" of the Spirit: "You are God's temple, and . . . God's Spirit dwells in you . . . God's temple is holy, and you are that temple" (1 Cor 3:16, 17). Even more, however, we dwell in the Holy Spirit who is our home and "temple," the holy "place" where we live and pray, where we are plunged into the Trinity's love and made holy. In what "place," then, do we really pray? "In the Holy Spirit," Basil answers. Outside *this* temple, the Holy Spirit in whom we live, we cannot truly pray. We commune with the Holy Trinity, therefore, by making our home in the living temple who is the Holy Spirit.[26] And since this temple is not a material building but the very person of the Spirit, we need never leave our "holy place" of prayer.

[22] Symeon the New Theologian, "Prayer to the Holy Spirit preceding the *Hymns*," in Maloney, *Hymns of Divine Love*, 9, 10.

[23] Henry Edward Manning, *The Internal Mission of the Holy Ghost*, 5th ed. (New York: P. J. Kenedy, 1904) 33, 35.

[24] Cyril of Alexandria, *Thesaurus*, 34; PG 75, 958; *Commentary on John*, 10, 11; PG 74, 293, 553.

[25] Basil the Great, *On the Holy Spirit*, 18.46; NPNF 2.8, 29.

[26] Ibid., 26.62, 26.64; NPNF 2.8, 39–40.

The Spirit's Gift of Contemplative Prayer

As our desire for prayer grows, these beautiful words of Paul encourage us when we find it difficult to pray: "The Spirit helps us in our weakness; for we do not know how to pray as we ought." But the Spirit prays within us "with sighs too deep for words" (Rom 8:26). St. John of the Cross tells us that the deepest prayer is the Holy Spirit's activity in us, and that the Holy Spirit longs to give us the gift of contemplative prayer that transcends even our thoughts, words, and feelings.[27] Initially, we may think that such prayer means wonderful feelings of closeness to God. Yet the beginning of contemplative prayer may bring instead a painful emptiness, a great solitude that not even the best of human loves can assuage because it is an ache for God. We may feel that nothing is happening, and that we are wasting our time, because our prayer is dry and distracted. But our very helplessness is a precious gift to us, for it brings us face to face with our need for God. Often when we feel most helpless and unproductive, the Holy Spirit can take over in us, expanding our heart by attaching us not to good feelings but to God. We may try to flee the emptiness by using the time for prayer to think or to read. But meditating and reading, though valuable in quieting us for prayer, can also be used as an escape from the painful beginnings of deeper prayer. It may be helpful to begin our prayer with reading, especially prayerful reading of Scripture. As St. John of the Cross reminds us, however, the moment should come when we put aside our thoughts and reading in order to rest in the emptiness that is full of God's closeness, even if we do not yet feel it.[28]

Even problems and worries need not be a "distraction" in our prayer. On the contrary, the Holy Spirit can transform them into a means of drawing us closer to the Trinity. Prayer is a loving conversation in which we commune with the divine persons as we converse with our dearest friends. And just as we tell a loved one all that is in our heart, we can speak to Jesus, to our Abba, and to the Holy Spirit about our worries, our problems, and joys. As we express what is concerning us, we then can become quieted enough to listen to the divine persons speaking their love to our heart. In our dryness and distractions, we can learn from saints who prayed by gently repeating a word or phrase, perhaps from Scripture. Francis of Assisi would say again and again, "My Lord and my God," and Dominic would pray these words all night, "My God, have mercy on sinners." During our own prayer,

---

[27] John of the Cross, *Living Flame of Love*, 3.36, 41; in *The Collected Works of St. John of the Cross*, trans. Kieran Kavanaugh, O.C.D., and Otilio Rodriguez, O.C.D. (Washington, D.C.: ICS Publications, 1973) 624, 625.

[28] Ibid., 3.31–36; Kavanaugh and Rodriguez, 621–24.

words such as these may well up from our heart, as, on a deeper level, our soul rests without words in the divine persons' nearness: "Jesus, heal me, hold me close"; "Father, protect me"; "My God, I love you"; "Holy Spirit of Love, possess me." Eastern Christians, especially, have treasured for centuries "the Jesus Prayer": "Lord Jesus Christ, Son of God, have mercy on me, a sinner."

As we gently say words or phrases such as these in our heart, the Holy Spirit can transform our agitation into a quiet in which we do not want to think or say anything. We may fear that this inner stillness is not prayer, but John of the Cross tells us that it is profound prayer given by the Holy Spirit. Trying to think or meditate when we feel drawn to rest without words in the divine persons' closeness is to risk losing the Holy Spirit's delicate anointings.[29]

As we have seen, we may not feel at first the Spirit's sweet anointing hidden in the darkness of contemplative prayer. But our own experience of planting seeds can help us to see the fruitfulness of patient waiting when nothing seems to be happening in prayer. We plant seeds and day after day watch for them to sprout, only to find nothing. One day, however, we discover a little shoot budding from the ground. This surge of new life did not happen in a moment; the roots had been growing in the darkness of the earth. When we ourselves wait in the initial dryness of contemplative prayer, with time we begin to feel a quiet peace that increasingly draws us to rest without words in the center of our soul.

This inner quiet can be so restful that it sometimes leads to drowsiness. Yet, as we recall with a heart's smile, Scripture itself consoles us with the assurance that the Lord gives "sleep to his beloved" (Ps 127:2). The problem of drowsiness in prayer is helped also if we try to give the best part of our day to time with the Trinity in prayer rather than the time when we are psychologically and physically drained. This may demand a readjustment of our schedule so that we pray early in the morning. But if we begin our day by resting in the Trinity's love for us, the sweetness of the love we experience in prayer will permeate all that we do. By starting our day with prayer, we will find that our whole life becomes simpler, filled with the Trinity's closeness to us, and anointed with the Holy Spirit's peace in our heart.

Prayer that Becomes a Life of Joy

"Pray at all times in the Spirit" (Eph 6:18). Daily time in explicit prayer helps us to recognize the Trinity's presence with us at every moment. Mysticism inspired by the Holy Spirit becomes closeness to

---

[29] Ibid., 3.40–43, 46, 54; Kavanaugh and Rodriguez, 625–27; 631.

the Trinity in our everyday life. In a special way, we grow more conscious of the Holy Spirit's companionship with us at every moment, doing everything with the Holy Spirit as our beloved friend. And while we may feel only dryness and darkness during the time of explicit prayer, we may experience later a sweet quiet within us. We may be reading, for example, and find ourselves drawn to close our eyes and rest deep in our soul where the Trinity dwells.

Prayer sometimes may well up in our heart in the form of the Spirit's gift of tears cleansing and healing our soul.[30] At other times, we may run out of words, and our voice will want to keep praising. Paul then encourages us to "pray in tongues," allowing the Holy Spirit to pray within us. Echoing Paul, Augustine and Thomas Aquinas urge us to pray in "jubilation."[31] We are told that other saints, such as Romuald, would burst forth in "jubilant cries in the Spirit": "Dear Jesus, honey to my heart! Sweetness of the saints."[32] Augustine describes this "jubilation in the Spirit" when he urges us to "sing to the Lord a new song" (Ps 98:1). If we want to do just that, let us sing in "jubilation," Augustine tells us. He recalls the experience of those who sing as they harvest a bountiful crop. The joy of the song so fills them that words fail, yet their voices keep singing. Their hearts "raise a cry of jubilation." So, too, when we are unable to express in words our petition or praise, the Holy Spirit gives us the prayer in which our hearts "rejoice in a song without words," singing a "cry of jubilation."[33]

Those who have experienced the blessings of the Charismatic Renewal can identify with Augustine's sentiments. Praying in tongues is one beautiful way that the Holy Spirit prays within us with "sighs too deep for words" (Rom 8:26). In 1 Corinthians 14:1-25, Paul distinguishes between praying in tongues and speaking in tongues. This latter gift is a message from God inspired by the Spirit but spoken in non-verbal syllables which need interpretation. When this gift is followed by an interpretation, it serves the same purpose as the gift of prophecy, a message from God to build up the community. Cardinal Suenens explains that praying in tongues, unlike the gift of speaking in tongues, is "non-discursive prayer, a preconceptual expression of spontaneous prayer," available to every believer.[34] Praying in tongues

---

[30] Vladimir Lossky, *The Mystical Theology of the Eastern Church* (New York: St. Vladimir's Seminary Press, 1976) 205.

[31] Aquinas, *Commentary on the Psalms*, Ps 46:1.

[32] St. Peter Damien, *Life of St. Romuald*; LH 1601.

[33] Augustine, *Commentary on the Psalms*, Ps 32; LH 1788–89.

[34] Léon Joseph Cardinal Suenens, *A New Pentecost?*, trans. Francis Martin (New York: Crossroad Seabury, 1975) 101.

can be compared to expressions of our subconscious that rise to God in dreams, laughter, tears, painting, and dance. It is something like the syllables children use to speak when they have no words. They are not afraid to communicate with non-verbal sounds like those which we ourselves make when we run out of words—sounds such as "Ah, hooray, oh, uh huh, wow!"

Suenens comments that such surrender of ourselves to the Holy Spirit, allowing the Spirit to pray within us, is difficult for us at first. It is not easy for us to express our inmost self even to those closest to us. For this reason we often fail to experience the "warmth and enthusiasm" that should mark our prayer together, especially at the Eucharist. Yet it seems natural, Suenens continues, "that we should be able to praise, adore, glorify and love God with all the means at our disposal—using all the strings of our harp."[35]

The non-discursive prayer of tongues cuts through the reserve and defense systems which we use to protect ourselves. It heals our inner wounds and frees us to surrender ourselves more completely to God, for we humble ourselves and take the risk of appearing foolish or childish, even in our own eyes. Transcending all words, this kind of prayer fills us with peace, spiritual communion with others, and a humility that opens us to other gifts of the Spirit.[36] Praying in tongues ultimately teaches us that it is not our own efforts and activity but yielding to the Holy Spirit that makes us more fulfilled, creative, and self-giving than we could ever be through our own power alone.

The deepest effect of the Holy Spirit's unceasing prayer within us is a holy heart, a happy heart. It is true that we are promised this joy in heaven: "I have said these things to you, so that my joy may be in you, and that your joy may be complete" (John 15:11). In prayer inspired by the Spirit, however, we taste this joy even now: "You have tasted the sweetness of the Lord"; "O taste and see that the Lord is good" (1 Pet 2:3; Ps 34:8). We can feel this sweetness not only during explicit prayer, but also at other moments, perhaps as we walk in the peace of the evening, wrapt in wonder at a beautiful sunset. At times like this, we have no thoughts or words, no desire to think, yet the quiet in our heart makes our life feel sweet. The Spirit's gift of contemplative prayer thus greatly expands our capacity for delight in even the smallest blessings. We become more open to God's sweetness everywhere, tasting the Trinity's joy all around us, given to us in myriads of ways at every second.

[35] Ibid., 103, 104.
[36] Ibid., 102.

We begin to receive and to enjoy our life as a gift of God, taking time to look at flowers, to watch the sunset, to enjoy good music, to be creative. This joy of the Spirit within us sometimes wells up into spontaneous praise that yearns to be expressed in dance or song. Jesus' own profound intimacy with the Holy Spirit caused him to break into exultation in the Holy Spirit (Luke 10:21).[37] Augustine tells us that we ourselves need to let our joy inspired by the Spirit burst into praise here on earth, since our joy in heaven will be to extol God with complete abandon. As he reflects on the beautiful Easter cry, "alleluia," from the Hebrew phrase meaning "Praise the Lord," Augustine urges us to glorify God with all of our being, not only with our lips but also with our life and actions.[38] Prayer inspired by the Spirit in this way flowers in self-giving love not only to the Trinity but also to all those around us. As we grow close to the Trinity in prayer, we become the crowning work of the Holy Spirit, persons filled with joyful, generous hearts.

---

[37] Raniero Cantalamessa, O.F.M. Cap., *The Holy Spirit in the Life of Jesus: The Mystery of Christ's Baptism,* trans. Alan Neame (Collegeville: The Liturgical Press, 1994) 21, 54.

[38] Augustine, *Commentary on the Psalms,* Ps 148:1-2; LH 375–76.

10

INTIMATE FRIENDSHIP
WITH THE HOLY SPIRIT

Giving Ourselves to the Spirit of Love

We have been loved into life by the Trinity who is utter self-giving. For this reason, we cannot help wanting to give our own heart completely to another, without reservation or fear. We grow by such loving surrender of ourselves, as rich dimensions of our personality come to life through love's tenderness. This ability to give ourselves is the very heart of intimacy and our deepest fulfillment, for the more we bestow ourselves on one who is worthy of us, the more we gain who we are. Our growth through giving ourselves to one another, however, can only suggest the fulfillment we gain through giving ourselves to the Holy Spirit, the very person of love and the one through whom we also come close to Jesus and the Father.

As we have seen, the Holy Spirit first draws us to Jesus, the second divine person, in whom we find the tenderness of our Savior, brother, and Lord. In friendship with Jesus, we feel completely understood and accepted in all that we are. We know the joy of intimate companionship with the divine person who is flesh of our flesh, the one who has espoused us to himself in a covenant of his own blood shed for us. In addition to drawing us to Jesus, the Holy Spirit also gives us intimate friendship with the first divine Person whom Jesus taught us to call "Abba." In close relationship with the Father, we grow secure as we feel cared for with a love infinitely more provident than the dearest father or mother could give us. Through intimacy with the Father, we come to know our true identity: we are the precious daughter, the beloved son of our Abba in whose strong and tender arms we are always held safe.

Finally, we are meant to be close not only to Jesus and the Father, but also to the Holy Spirit, who is sweetness and joy itself. Indeed, our longing for closeness to another is rooted in our even deeper thirst to belong to this person of love at the heart of the Trinity. We are this thirst, however, only because of the Spirit's own unconditional self-giving to us; as Basil the Great assures us, the Holy Spirit is given to us completely and without reserve.[1] The Eastern saint Seraphim of Sarov adds that every means of holiness in our Christian life has this one key goal: to help us to possess and to be possessed by the Spirit of God (Gal 5:16).[2] The Holy Spirit's self-surrender to us thus invites us to surrender ourselves in return, offering love for love. The unconditional gift of ourselves to the Spirit of love is the very heart of our Christian life and the reason for which we were made.

Though the mutuality of friendship-love with the Holy Spirit is our deepest fulfillment, the Holy Spirit's love for us is at first completely one-sided. We think of parents who lavish unconditional love on their children long before their love can be returned. They care for their little ones' every need with a selflessness that is oblivious of their children's incapacity to love or to give anything in return. And they do so in the hope and trust that their selfless care will one day elicit their little ones' own response of love—not for their sake but for their children's own growth as self-giving persons.

The Holy Spirit's love for us is like this. From our baptism the Holy Spirit is intimately present in us, loving us unconditionally, giving us every blessing, and filling us also with the Father's and Son's presence. Often, however, we are unaware of the Holy Spirit's tender activity within us. Yet all the while the Spirit is preparing us for our own free self-surrender in return, for it is not unrequited love but the mutuality of intimate friendship-love that truly heals us. We know from experience that if we hold back who we are, in fear or selfishness, we wither into a self-absorbed existence. But when we freely entrust ourselves completely to another who is worthy of us, we attain the self-giving love that fulfills us as human persons. The Holy Spirit who is completely surrendered in love to us thus elicits our own self-surrender in return.

Paul urges us to "be filled with the Spirit" (Eph 5:18). We do so when we freely give ourselves to the Holy Spirit, letting the Spirit possess

---

[1] Basil, *On the Holy Spirit*, 9.22; NPNF 2.8, 15.

[2] Yves Congar, O.P., *I Believe in the Holy Spirit*, trans. David Smith (New York: Seabury Press, 1983), 2:69.

our thoughts and actions, our mind and heart, our body and soul. At first we may fear words like "surrendering" ourselves, and being "possessed" by the Holy Spirit, for we can give ourselves to others in a way that destroys our own autonomy. But surrendering ourselves to the divine persons can never rob us of our identity, since they are life itself and give us our own truest self in their life. Indeed, our own desire to give ourselves to another finds its source in their infinite self-giving to one another. They themselves lose nothing of who they are in their mutual self-surrender. On the contrary, the fullness of their personhood is precisely their ecstatic self-gift to one another. When we, too, give ourselves to another in love's freedom, we share in the self-giving love at the heart of the Trinity.

If this is true of our love for one another, it is infinitely more true of our self-giving to the Trinity, and especially to the Spirit who is the very person of intimate communion. This grace of surrendering ourselves in love to the person of love heals even the wounds of our loneliness. It fills us, too, with deepening peace and satisfaction, for the Spirit loves to delight, console, and fill us with God's own joy.[3] Furthermore, just as the sun generously shines on every one of us as if it were shining on us alone, the Holy Spirit draws close to each of us as if we were the only person in the world. The more we give ourselves to the Spirit of love the more we become the persons we were meant to be, saints made holy with the Trinity's own beauty.

The Joy of Surrendering Ourselves to the Holy Spirit

We ourselves delight in one who is the joy of our heart, and our delight is even greater when our own self-gift becomes mutual. No words, however, can describe the delight which the Holy Spirit takes in us when we give ourselves to the Spirit, the infinite "river of delights" (Ps 36:8) who is so completely surrendered to us. John of the Cross tells us that when we let this living "flame of love" possess us, we begin to know the joy of each divine person's self-surrender to us. They make us their "equals" through love, giving themselves completely to us with the greatest humility and esteem. Jesus comes close to us not only as our Redeemer but also as our spouse, showering us with his favor, and telling us with joy: "I am yours . . . and give myself to you."[4] Our beloved Father, too, surrenders himself to us only to

---

[3] Basil the Great, *On the Holy Spirit*, 9.22; NPNF 2.8, 15; Bernard of Clairvaux, *Sermons on Various Occasions, Sermon 5*; LH 608.

[4] John of the Cross, *The Living Flame of Love*, 3.6; in *The Collected Works of St. John of the Cross*, trans. Kieran Kavanaugh, O.C.D., and Otilio Rodriguez, O.C.D. (Washington, D.C.: ICS Publications, 1973) 613.

exalt us. Our Father's humility and sweetness are so profound that he cares for us as if he were our slave and we his God. Our Abba cherishes us like a mother nursing her child at her own breast: "You shall nurse and be carried on her arm, and dandled on her knees. As a mother comforts her child, so I will comfort you" (Isa 66:12-13).[5] Finally, as we come close to the Holy Spirit, the Spirit "overshadows" us (Luke 1:35) with infinite devotion to protect, cherish, and favor us.[6]

We find in the works of the thirteenth-century mystic Angela of Foligno a beautiful description of this grace of being cherished by the Holy Spirit. On a pilgrimage to Assisi, Angela had been praying to St. Francis that she might be faithful in her Franciscan vocation. As she prayed, she felt the Holy Spirit say to her heart that though she had asked for Francis, it was the Spirit who would care for her and console her. She then experienced the Holy Spirit's love and delight in her, and the Spirit's complete self-surrender to her. The Spirit who cherished her with an infinitely deep and tender love asked for her own love in return: "My delight, my temple, my beloved . . . love me, because you are very much loved by me; much more than you could love me . . . my sweet spouse." Angela was assured that the Holy Spirit longs to be completely given to us, working marvels of love for each of us. When she heard these tender sentiments which the Holy Spirit spoke to her heart, Angela felt an indescribable sweetness and joy well up within her. At the end of her journey, as she prayed in the Church of St. Francis, she saw a stained glass window depicting Francis resting in the arms of Jesus. She realized that this is how the Spirit of love held her close at every moment, and that the Holy Spirit was delighted by every dimension of her life, even her eating and sleeping.[7]

Angela protested that she was unworthy of such precious love. Yet she was assured that the Spirit is grieved not by our weakness but rather by the meagerness of our faith and love. The Holy Spirit wants to work even greater miracles for us than those experienced by the saints of old, for the Spirit of love wants only our love. This is surely the easiest, most joyful gift we can give to the Holy Spirit, for "everyone can love."[8]

---

[5] Idem., *The Spiritual Canticle*, 27.1, 2; *The Living Flame of Love*, 3.78; Kavanaugh and Rodriguez, 517, 641.

[6] Idem., *The Living Flame of Love*, 3.12; Kavanaugh and Rodriguez, 615.

[7] Angela of Foligno, *The Book of the Blessed Angela of Foligno*, 3; in *Angela of Foligno: Complete Works*, trans. and intro., Paul Lachance, O.F.M. (New York: Paulist Press, 1993) 139, 140, 141.

[8] Ibid., 4; Lachance, 153.

These last words from Angela's account assure us that every one of us is called to this joy of intimate friendship with the Holy Spirit. A dear friend of mine wrote to me about her own experience of being drawn close to the Holy Spirit:

> I had done everything I could to seek healing for a terrible hurt I had experienced, but nothing eased the pain. My heart was broken, and for months I could not enjoy anything; I was raw inside from the tears. Then one lovely evening as I was taking a walk, my heart became very quiet and I was moved to pray to the Holy Spirit with these words: "O Love, most Holy Spirit, give me *your* joy. You will have to give it to me because I will wear you down with my asking, just as the widow in the Gospel wore down the judge" (Luke 18:5).
>
> Spontaneously, I began to pray, "Holy Spirit, possess me." My heart smiled as I thought of the lines of the song, "My darling, possess me." "Yes," I said to the Holy Spirit, "My darling, possess me. My love, my treasure, my joy, I give myself to you. Free me, heal me, claim me as your own."
>
> At Mass a day or two later, I had the sense of being taken by the Holy Spirit to a special "room" in my heart where I felt completely protected, cherished, and loved by the Trinity. The three divine persons made me feel utterly secure in their love. I was like a little child in their presence as they bent over me, enrapt, lost in a gaze that was like "adoration." I think of how I myself feel as a mother when I bend over my sleeping children. As a nurse I also have seen young fathers gaze at their newborn children with a look of "adoration." I know from my husband's and my own experience that parents are so completely enraptured by their little one that they can talk about nothing but him or her. And the little one does absolutely nothing to gain this "adoration." When you think of it, an infant is absolutely helpless, utterly useless. Yet parents just "adore" their child; they cannot take their eyes off their newborn. This baby is theirs, and in their mind is the most precious, gorgeous gift God ever gave to the world.
>
> It is impossible to put into words the feeling I had as I thought of these things. The Holy Spirit made me realize that the divine persons not only love me but also "adore" me, cherish me, delight in me, and are enraptured by me in precisely this way. I knew in that moment that the reason that parents bend over their baby in rapt "adoration" is that the Trinity unceasingly bends over each one of us in this way. The divine persons have made us for this kind of total attention, to be "adored" as if we were the only one in the world, the most beautiful person ever made. Every one of us is that precious child, so beautiful to them that they cannot take their "adoring" gaze away from us. And we are loved in this way not in spite of but precisely because of our very weakness, which makes us all the more irresistible to the Trinity's infinite mercy.

"Ah, this is what I was made for," I cried out in my heart. "I can go here, to this secret place in my heart where the divine persons dwell, where they love and cherish me. I can enter at any time into the depths of my soul, where my aching heart can be filled by the Holy Spirit's "adoring" love for me. *This* is how I will be healed and made whole. Any time I want and need the Spirit's joy, I can enter the secret room of my heart and ask the Holy Spirit to let me feel how deeply loved and 'adored' I am." I see now that the Holy Spirit's joy for which I am asking is really the grace to be comforted by the Spirit's delight in me. And the most wonderful thing is that this joy is mine for the asking: "How much more will the heavenly Father give the Holy Spirit to those who ask. . . . Ask and you will receive, so that your joy may be complete" (Luke 11:13; John 16:24).

Docility to the Spirit: The Seven Gifts

As we have seen, the joy for which we are made is not a one-sided love but rather the reciprocity of friendship-love. In friendship, we give ourselves for our beloved's good, and share our hearts' secrets in a deepening "life together." This is precisely the kind of closeness we are meant to have with the Trinity (John 15:15). We have been created to surrender ourselves as completely to the divine persons as they have surrendered themselves to us, and to share ourselves and our hearts' secrets in an ever deepening "life together."

Of ourselves, however, we could never return to the divine persons the infinite love they pour out on us. Friendship is between equals, and we are only creatures. Yet through the Trinity's extraordinary tenderness, we are given, in the Holy Spirit, the astounding grace that will make the divine persons' love for us truly mutual. Through the Holy Spirit, we can love the Father and Son with the same love they have for each other and for us, the love who is the person of the Spirit.[9] In a special way, we are able to surrender ourselves to the Holy Spirit only because the Spirit is completely surrendered to us. The Spirit not only desires our love, then, but also gives us that love, enabling us to return the very tenderness with which we are cherished. We possess the Holy Spirit so that we might be possessed by the Holy Spirit.[10]

As we have seen, a key way that the Holy Spirit possesses us, making us true "equals" and friends of the Trinity, is through the seven gifts of wisdom, understanding, counsel, fortitude, knowledge, piety,

---

[9] John of the Cross, *The Spiritual Canticle*, 38.3, 4; Kavanaugh and Rodriguez, 553–54.

[10] Luis M. Bermejo, S.J., *The Spirit of Life: The Holy Spirit in the Life of the Christian* (Chicago: Loyola University Press, 1989) 207.

and fear of the Lord. These gifts soften our hearts, making them receptive to the Holy Spirit's work of love within us. The very person of the Spirit moves and guides us through these gifts which dispose us to follow the Spirit's leadings promptly, gladly, and with God's own ease and joy.[11]

We already have considered in chapter 8 the Spirit's gifts of wisdom, understanding, knowledge, and counsel in our lives. The gifts of fortitude, piety, and fear of the Lord also are wonderful means of deepening our self-giving to the Spirit. Through the gift of fortitude the Holy Spirit gives us an inner confidence that conquers our fear and enables us to face difficult situations with the Spirit's own strength. The gift of piety fills us with a tender affection for the Father as our own dear Abba, and deepens our desire to do good to all people as our Father's beloved children. Finally, the gift of fear of the Lord tempers our lust for pleasure and inspires us to avoid anything that could separate us from the Trinity.[12] These gifts of the Spirit transform even our sexuality, so that it becomes, in the Spirit of love, a gift of channeling our capacity for relationship into ever more pure and joyful self-giving to the divine persons and to one another.[13]

The Spirit Inspiring Our Thoughts and Actions

As the gifts of the Spirit blossom within us, we begin to draw our entire life from the Holy Spirit (Rom 8:14). The force for all that we do becomes not simply our own reason and desires, but rather the instinct of the Holy Spirit who acts within us through the seven gifts. Far from making us simply passive recipients, these gifts free us to reach our full potential. Since the Spirit is the very creator of our freedom, the more receptive we are to the Holy Spirit, the more we grow in our own identity and gifts. The seven gifts of the Spirit thus make us both receptive and active, inspiring in us quiet contemplation as well as loving service: we are "acted upon by the Spirit that we may act."[14] Through the gifts, we are drawn deep into ourselves where the Spirit intimately dwells, and also outward in love to one another where the Holy Spirit also abides in us as a community. As we surrender ourselves to the Spirit we become truly free, able to inspire and lead others by the example of our life.[15]

---

[11] Aquinas, ST, I–II, 68, aa. 1–8.
[12] Ibid., II–II, 139, 1; I–II, 68, 4; II–II, 19, 9.
[13] Bermejo, *Spirit of Life*, 221, 224, 246.
[14] Ibid., 225. See Aquinas, ST I–II, 68, 3, ad 2.
[15] Aquinas, ST, II–II, 52, 2, ad 3.

In the hymn for Terce we ask the Holy Spirit to "light up our mortal frame, 'til others catch the living flame." John of the Cross comments that just as the Trinity is all love, we begin to make all that we do an act of love. When we are surrendered to the Spirit of love, we desire only that the Holy Spirit become the "living flame," the delightful "wound" of love within us.[16] The rivers of the Spirit's love flow with greater force into the depths of our heart, drawing us to hasten in the ways of God (Cant 1:4). We increasingly do everything not by our own power but through the Holy Spirit who attracts us along the path of love. As we live in our heart where all is love, we begin to experience everything within and around us as love. The entire universe seems to be "a sea of love" in which we are engulfed, for the love within us appears to have no boundaries outside us. In this way we extract the Holy Spirit's sweetness from all that happens to us, and everything in our day leads us to love.[17]

We can see the fullness of this love in the saints, especially those whom the Holy Spirit has inspired to lead others—persons such as Dominic, Catherine of Siena, Ignatius of Loyola, Angela Merici, and Elizabeth Seton. Sometimes, as in Francis of Assisi, the wounds of the Holy Spirit's love break forth into their bodies and appear as the wounds of the stigmata.[18] These saints show us that the more we surrender ourselves to the Holy Spirit, the more our inner wounds of selfishness are healed by the Spirit's wounds of love, and the more healthy we become as persons. We begin to feel the exhilaration of receiving our life from the giver of life instead of living according to our own narrow plans. The Holy Spirit's love becomes sweet within us, as we feel the joy of no longer having to be in control. In the depths of our heart we love the divine persons, enjoying them in a way that allows us to taste heaven's bliss even now.[19]

We Share in the Breathing Forth of the Spirit

John of the Cross tells us that as we are united more and more intimately to the Trinity, the Holy Spirit completely transforms us. Through the Spirit's love, we become the divine persons' intimate companions and "equals," enjoying a "marriage" union in which we possess one another's goods. In a special way, we are joined to the

---

[16] *Spiritual Canticle,* 28.1; *Living Flame of Love,* 1.2–3, 8–9; Kavanaugh and Rodriguez, 520, 580, 582.

[17] John of the Cross, *Spiritual Canticle,* 25.4; 26.1; 27.8; *Living Flame of Love,* 2.10; Kavanaugh and Rodriguez, 507, 511, 519–20, 599.

[18] Idem., *Living Flame of Love,* 2.12, 13; Kavanaugh and Rodriguez, 599.

[19] Ibid., 2.7; 1.6; Kavanaugh and Rodriguez, 597, 581.

Lord who, as our spouse, dwells within us as in his own home, bed, and even heart. Through love's sharing, all that belongs to the Trinity now belongs to us, so that the words of Jesus to his Father are marvelously fulfilled in us: "All that is mine is yours, and all that is yours is mine" (see John 17:10).[20]

In an unimaginable gift of love, the Father and Son also share with us their most intimate activity, their eternal breathing forth of their Holy Spirit: "Father, I desire that those also, whom you have given me, may be with me where I am" (John 17:24). When John of the Cross reflects on these profound words, he interprets them to mean, "May they share in our breathing forth of the Holy Spirit." For "where" the Son is from all eternity is within the Father's heart, and it is here that they forever breathe forth to one another their Spirit of love. Because all that is theirs is now ours, Jesus and our Father breathe forth their Holy Spirit also within us, making our hearts their heaven. They fill us with their Spirit to lavish on us every good and glory. And in the most intimate return of love, the Holy Spirit breathed forth within us then enables us also to "breathe forth" back to them their same Spirit. This mystical grace is so deep a joy, John of the Cross tells us, that it transcends all that we could imagine. We ourselves delight in loving, enjoying, and drawing close to those dear to us. But our experience of intimate human love can only suggest the Father's and Son's ecstasy as they eternally breathe forth their Spirit of love to one another. Now, through the transforming union which the Holy Spirit lovingly works in us, we ourselves share in their "breathing forth" of the Spirit within us, so that the Father's and Son's own bliss becomes ours.[21]

Our love for the Trinity is thus enkindled in an unimaginable way within the very depths of the Trinity. Through love we possess the divine persons as our own and can "give" them to whomever we wish. We give them, therefore, to our beloved, the very God who is completely surrendered in love to us. In this way we return to the divine persons the only gift worthy of them, themselves. Through the Holy Spirit's transforming love, we give God as much as we receive from God; we give *God* to God, in a gift of love that exceedingly delights the Trinity's heart. Through love alone, the divine persons surrender themselves to us and do all that we desire, for we want only what they want.[22]

[20] Ibid., 3.79; 4.2–3; *Spiritual Canticle*, 39.5, 6; Kavanaugh and Rodriguez, 641, 643–44, 559.

[21] Idem., *Living Flame of Love*, 4.17; *Spiritual Canticle*, 39.3; Kavanaugh and Rodriguez, 649, 558.

[22] Idem., *Living Flame of Love*, 3.78; 4.17; *Spiritual Canticle*, 32.1; Kavanaugh and Rodriguez, 641, 649, 534.

Our Life Becomes a Sweet Fragrance in the Spirit

John of the Cross tells us further that those whom the Spirit so completely possesses exude an indefinable air of "greatness and dignity."
We are deeply touched by such persons, and cannot help being drawn
to them because of "their close and familiar conversation with God."
Since the Holy Spirit's sweetness in their hearts overflows outside of
them, in their presence we seem to be in a pleasant garden, filled with
God's own delights. When the Holy Spirit thus "breathes" within our
heart's garden, the Holy Spirit awakens virtues in us that enchant others with their sweet fragrance.[23] In his Commentary on the Canticle of
Canticles, John of the Cross writes, "Come South wind, you who
waken love, Breathe through my garden, Let its fragrance flow" (see
Cant 4:16). This lovely "South Wind" is the "Spirit of our Bridegroom,"
Jesus. As the delightful "breeze" within us, the Holy Spirit dispels our
dryness and deepens our love for Jesus as our spouse. In bringing rain
to our parched hearts, the Holy Spirit also opens the flowers in our
soul's garden, scattering their perfumed scent from deep within us to
everyone we meet.[24] Filled with the Holy Spirit's love, we radiate a
sweet fragrance that influences others.[25] As we are transformed by this
same love, the Holy Spirit also attracts us so irresistibly that we seem
unable to refuse the Holy Spirit anything. Because "sweet persuasion"
is the Spirit's own language, we learn that the only worthy response to
the Spirit of love is giving ourselves completely in return. We begin to
be so much the Holy Spirit's that the Spirit dwells and acts in us as in
a home which belongs entirely to the Spirit of love.[26]

We read of the woman who so lavishly anointed the feet of Jesus
with precious ointment that "the house was filled with the fragrance of
the perfume" (John 12:3). For Bernard of Clairvaux, this Gospel story
symbolizes the fragrance with which persons converted to the Lord
perfume the whole Church, drawing many others to the Trinity with
the Holy Spirit's sweet aroma.[27] Deep blessings in this way flow to the
world through those who draw their lives completely from the Spirit
of love. Marie of the Incarnation comments that the Holy Spirit fills us
with a sincerity and openness that enable us to live the beatitudes in

---

[23] Idem., *Spiritual Canticle,* 17.5, 7, 9; Kavanaugh and Rodriguez, 480, 481.

[24] Ibid., 17.1, 2–9; Kavanaugh and Rodriguez, 479, 480–81.

[25] Bernard of Clairvaux, *On the Song of Songs,* 12.5; in *The Works of Bernard of
Clairvaux,* trans. Kilian Walsh, O.C.S.O. (Kalamazoo, Mich.: Cistercian Publications,
1981) 2:81.

[26] Marie of the Incarnation, "Lettres à son fils"; in Yolande Arsène-Henry, ed., *Les
plus beaux textes sur le Saint-Esprit,* rev. ed. (Paris: Lethielleux, 1968) 242.

[27] Bernard of Clairvaux, *On the Song of Songs,* 10.6; Walsh, 2:64.

an extraordinary manner. Through the Spirit's anointing, we accomplish more in one day than we could do of ourselves in a month.[28] "Rich in the charity that no amount of self-giving can exhaust," we find ourselves full of peace even in difficult times. And because our hearts are anointed with the Spirit's peace, we cannot help pouring out its fragrance even on those who hate us.[29]

This sweetness of the Spirit's anointing produces myriads of wonderful effects in each person. Inspired by the Holy Spirit, the apostles, for example, proclaimed God's wonders, as they allowed the Holy Spirit to speak through them.[30] We ourselves may experience a deep sense of the Trinity's own love for others that makes us want to embrace every person in the world if we could. Sometimes we may rest in a deep spiritual calm, and at other times we may be filled with an inexpressible understanding, wisdom, or spiritual knowledge.[31] We may feel a profound grief at the sin in the world, or experience God's own strength within us to stand fast against temptations. Contemplating these sweet effects of the Holy Spirit's possessing us, Symeon the New Theologian cries out his praise to the Spirit who enkindles in us such boundless love. The same Spirit who teaches the prophets thus becomes the courage of the martyrs, the inspiration of the Church Fathers, and the holiness of the saints. Not only the saints of old but also we ourselves who have tasted the Spirit's love discover how inexpressibly sweet the Spirit is.[32]

Shining with the Spirit's Light

We know from our own experience that those who are in love "shine"; the tenderness within them radiates as light from their faces. This external manifestation of the love hidden in the heart especially marks those who live completely surrendered to the Spirit of love. We cannot see the Holy Spirit with our physical eyes, and yet the Spirit's radiance within us cannot help shining on our faces. This theme of light as the way in which the Spirit's sweetness becomes visible is especially dear to Eastern Christians. Symeon the New Theologian comments that when the "spring" who is the Holy Spirit bubbles up within

---

[28] Marie of the Incarnation, "Lettres à son fils"; Arsène-Henry, *Les plus beaux textes,* 242.

[29] Bernard of Clairvaux, *On the Song of Songs,* 10.9; Walsh, 2:68.

[30] Ibid.

[31] *Homily Eighteen,* by a Fourth-Century Writer; LH 164–65.

[32] *Homily Fifty-Three,* 2; in Vladimir Lossky, *The Mystical Theology of the Eastern Church* (New York: St. Vladimir's Seminary Press, 1976) 212, 213.

us, the light of grace flowing from the Spirit will be visible to those who look with faith.[33]

As we have seen, the Greek word for "gift" or "grace," *charis*, is also used of the Holy Spirit who is "Gift" in person. The word *charis* originally referred to the sparkling radiance of an object such as a precious jewel. The Hebrew and Christian Scriptures extend this idea of radiance to the gracious favor God bestows on a person.[34] Above all, God is envisioned as overflowing with beautiful light. We read, for example, that Moses' face shone with the reflection of God's radiant glory (Exod 34:29), and many psalm verses also speak of the "light of God's face" (Ps 4:6; 31:16; 67:1; 80:3, 19; 90:8). The Book of Numbers, too, contains this beautiful prayer: "The Lord bless you and keep you; the Lord make his face to shine upon you, and be gracious to you; the Lord lift up his countenance upon you, and give you peace" (Num 6:24-26). Finally, the evangelists themselves speak of the light of God's glory radiant in Jesus, and manifested especially at the Transfiguration (Matt 17:1-8; Mark 9:2-8; Luke 9:28-36).

This is the glory the Father endlessly shares with his Son, Jesus, and which Jesus now shares with us through the Holy Spirit: "The glory that you have given me I have given them"; "all of us, with unveiled faces, seeing the glory of the Lord as though reflected in a mirror, are being transformed into the same image from one degree of glory to another; for this comes from the Lord, the Spirit" (John 17:22; 2 Cor 3:18). John of the Cross gives us the example of light shining so intensely on a pure crystal that the crystal itself becomes indistinguishable from the light.[35] Basil the Great uses the same image to describe how we are so permeated by the Holy Spirit that we become "spiritual," radiating the Spirit's own glorious light.[36] In one of his prayers, Symeon the New Theologian writes that the Lord's living glory is the Holy Spirit who so fills us with light that we ourselves become light. Indeed, God the Word has become human for this very reason, that we might receive his Spirit and become "God" through grace: "O what dignity, what glory!"[37] John of the Cross uses still other images to convey this mystery of the Spirit's so completely filling us that we become like rays of love. The Spirit is like soft refreshing water satisfying our deepest

---

[33] Symeon, *Sermon Fifty-Seven*, 4; in Vladimir Lossky, *The Vision of God*, trans. Asheleigh Moorhouse (Bedfordshire: American Orthodox Book Service, 1963) 120.

[34] Bermejo, *Spirit of Life*, 150.

[35] John of the Cross, *Living Flame of Love*, 1.13; Kavanaugh and Rodriguez, 584.

[36] Basil the Great, *On the Holy Spirit*, 9.23; NPNF 2.8, 15.

[37] *Hymn 25*; in *Hymns of Divine Love*, trans. and intro., George Maloney, S.J. (Denville, N.J.: Dimension Books, 1975) 136.

thirst and flooding our being. And just as tongues of fire descended upon the Apostles (Acts 2:3), the Spirit's love, like immense living flames, warms and inflames our entire being.[38]

Transparent Icons of the Spirit

Many beautiful works of art and magnificent buildings, especially exquisite medieval cathedrals like Chartres, manifest this glorious light of the Spirit to us. Yet the Spirit is revealed still more wonderfully in the lives of those whom the Holy Spirit completely possesses. We know that the Father's perfect image or "icon" is the Son (Col 1:15), and that the Son's living "icon" is the Spirit; but there is no other divine person who is the Spirit's image. It is human persons filled with the Spirit who are the most brilliant icon revealing the Holy Spirit to the world.[39] This is surely one reason why Christian art of both East and West depicts light radiating from the saints. We do not look directly on the sun's brilliance but see it instead in the light it sheds all around us. In the same way, we do not see the Holy Spirit's glory directly, but we do see it reflected on the faces of those whom the Holy Spirit possesses. We can think, too, of a window perfectly cleaned; the sunlight so illumines it that the window itself seems to be identical with the ray of sunlight. John of the Cross tells us that we are like this transparent window through whom the Holy Spirit shines.[40]

The eastern writer Pseudo-Macarius assures us that when we are perfectly intermingled with the Spirit, we become all light and repose, all gladness and love, all goodness and mercy. We are like a rock in the depth of the sea, entirely encompassed by water; intermingled with the Holy Spirit, we become like Christ in every way.[41] Symeon the New Theologian also writes that through the Spirit's unreserved self-gift to us we are so filled with the Spirit's beauty that we radiate the Trinity's own glory. Our face shines like our Beloved's because every part of our body becomes a bearer of God's light.[42]

A beautiful story about the eastern mystic Seraphim of Sarov illustrates how the Holy Spirit illumines us with the Trinity's own radiance. Motovilov, a friend and disciple of Seraphim, had asked him how he could be sure of living in God's Spirit. Seraphim told him that

---

[38] John of the Cross, *Living Flame of Love*, 3.8; Kavanaugh and Rodriguez, 613.

[39] Yves Congar, O.P., *I Believe in the Holy Spirit*, trans. David Smith (New York: Seabury Press, 1983) 2:58.

[40] John of the Cross, *The Ascent of Mount Carmel*, 2.5.6; Kavanaugh and Rodriguez, 117.

[41] Pseudo-Macarius; in Arsène-Henry, *Les plus beaux textes*, 183–84.

[42] *Hymn Sixteen*; Maloney, *Hymns of Divine Love*, 58.

both of them already were permeated by the Holy Spirit. At that very moment Motovilov realized that he could not look at Seraphim's face because it had become as dazzling as the sun. Yet Seraphim assured his friend that he, too, was shining, for the Spirit's light, like a mother's tender love, enfolded them both. As Motovilov gazed upon Seraphim, Seraphim seemed to be encompassed by the sun's dazzling brightness. Motovilov himself felt an indescribable peace fill his soul. Seraphim explained that this was the peace the Lord himself has promised us, the peace beyond all words or understanding.[43]

Symeon the New Theologian had a similar experience of being illumined by the Holy Spirit's own light. As Symeon was praying, a divine light shone on him in great profusion, completely filling the place where he was standing. All that he could see was light, and it seemed to him that he himself had become light. Forgetting everything else, he was overwhelmed with tears and inexpressible joy. In his mind, however, he could see a heavenly light even brighter than the one that was visible to his eyes.[44] He was inspired to ask the Holy Spirit to so fill him that the Spirit's own light would grow ever more bright within him, engulfing him completely, and radiating from him to others.[45]

The Holy Spirit's beauty is too wonderful for our eyes to see. But if we look with love into our own and others' hearts, we will behold the unseen Spirit: "The kingdom of God is within you" (Luke 17:21; Vulgate). The Holy Spirit so intimately "penetrates" our being that at the very core of our own personhood we encounter the person of the Holy Spirit.[46] Gregory of Nyssa urges us to look in the transparent mirror of our own depths where we can see the radiant treasure that we seek,[47] for the Spirit's fire of love makes us glow like burning candles, just as Seraphim and Symeon did.[48] Filled with the Holy Spirit's anointing, we, too, are called to shine as the Spirit's radiant icons, manifesting the Trinity's glory to the world.

---

[43] Lossky, *Mystical Theology*, 227–29.

[44] Symeon the New Theologian, *Catecheses*, 22; in *Symeon the New Theologian: The Discourses*, trans. C. J. De Catanzaro (New York: Paulist Press, 1980) 245–46.

[45] *Hymn Twenty-Eight*; Maloney, *Hymns of Divine Love*, 151.

[46] *The Holy Spirit, Lord and Giver of Life*, prepared by the Theological-Historical Commission for the Great Jubilee of the Year 2000, trans. Agostino Bono (New York: Crossroad, 1997) 43.

[47] *Sixth Homily on the Beatitudes*; LH 461.

[48] St. Macarius of Egypt; in Lossky, *Mystical Theology*, 219.

11

PLEDGE OF HEAVEN'S GLORY

Having reflected on the Holy Spirit's presence within us here on earth, we contemplate in this final chapter the mystery of the Holy Spirit who is our fulfillment in heaven. We have seen how the Scriptures open with the Spirit of God gloriously giving life to all. The Scriptures also close, however, with the magnificent culmination of history in this same Spirit, the great dispenser of life. The Book of Genesis pictures God's *ruah* at the very beginning of time, hovering over the waters and bringing forth the miracle of life (Gen 1:2). By this same Spirit, everything is created and even more wonderfully renewed (Ps 104:30). The Spirit of life continues to be intimately present to the entire universe, and especially to us (Ps 139:7; Wis 1:7). In the power of the Spirit, Jesus' own human life both began (Luke 1:35) and attained its risen glory (Rom 8:11). As the New Testament closes, this same Spirit is intimately present to us as our inmost desire for the Lord's coming at the end of time (Rev 22:17).[1] The Spirit of God who filled the first person with life (Gen 2:7) thus brings the dead to life on the last day (Rom 8:11). The Scriptures in this way contemplate the mystery of the Holy Spirit as the completion of the Father's plan of love for us (Eph 1:14) and the very content of our joy in heaven. Intimately present to us as the giver of life at the beginning of history, the Holy Spirit is our glorious consummation at the end.

The Spirit Transforms Our Death in Jesus

We begin our reflections by considering the mystery of the Holy Spirit's presence to us at our death. We cannot help fearing death as

---

[1] F. X. Durrwell, *Holy Spirit of God: An Essay in Biblical Theology,* trans. Sr. Benedict Davies, O.S.U. (London: Geoffrey Chapman, 1983) 25, 5.

our great enemy, the destroyer of all that we hold dear. Luke describes the fear in Jesus' own human heart as he faced his death with an agony so intense that "his sweat became like great drops of blood falling down on the ground." Luke further recounts how Jesus' anxiety before the terror of his death forced to his lips these precious words: "Father, if you are willing, remove this cup from me; yet, not my will but yours be done" (Luke 22:44, 42). The Spirit of life, however, transformed not only Jesus' life but also his very death, so that it became the culmination of his life, the fulfillment of his human sonship, and the wondrous source of the Holy Spirit's outpouring to us.

We have already contemplated how the Spirit of love makes sweet every dimension of our life. The same Spirit who transformed Jesus' death, therefore, also transforms even the bitterness of our death into a gift infinitely sweet, a grace full of loving communion. Of itself, death renders us completely alone. We may be surrounded by those dear to us, but no one can enter our heart to accompany us in that final self-surrender to God. Even more, no other person can die our death for us. No one, that is, except God. Death, the most personal act of our life in which we are most alone, becomes, in the Holy Spirit, the gift of the most intense communion.[2]

Jesus' death was his alone, and yet he did not die alone, for the horror of his death was enfolded by the Spirit who is openness and love. In this Spirit, Jesus' death was transfigured into the most intimate communion with his Father and with us. At the crucifixion, the Holy Spirit broke open Jesus' human heart, so that from his heart, overflowing with love, the Spirit of love was poured out upon the world. The living fountain of the Spirit thus flowed from Jesus' pierced heart, where he is only love for his beloved Father and for us. In this same Spirit of love, Jesus not only shared our death but even died our death for us. It was our human death that he died, our suffering and fear before death's horror to which he submitted as the most precious gift of his union with us. Jesus died and was raised to life for us (2 Cor 5:15) so that the Spirit poured out by him could unite us not only to his life but most of all to his love-filled death. Jesus died our death, then; but in the Holy Spirit who transformed his death, we can now die his death, a death infinitely sweet, full of comfort and radiant life.

The Spirit of life conquers our death by enclosing it in the love-filled death of Jesus. The Spirit who vanquished death in Jesus thus unites us with Jesus in the mystery of a single death experienced by two together. Now, because of the risen Lord's Spirit-permeated presence within us, no one ever has to die alone. Paul himself calls our death a

[2] Ibid., 122.

"falling asleep" through the Lord (1 Thess 4:14). In these beautiful words Paul assures us that death means surrendering ourselves into the tender arms of Jesus, just as children completely abandon themselves to the sweet arms of their parents. There they are safe, and in that loving embrace they fall asleep, utterly secure. In these same sweet arms they awake, fully refreshed, eager to run and play with new vigor. So too, at our death we are taken not only into the arms of Jesus but also into his very death, into his own self-surrender into his Father's tender arms. In the Holy Spirit, Jesus makes our death his death, an act of infinite love and glorious birth to heaven's life, where no one will ever die again. In the Holy Spirit's love, we die "through" the Lord, who is, in person, our good death.[3]

Just as the Father comforted Jesus with the Spirit's tenderness at his death, the Father gives us the Holy Spirit at our death to be our comforter. The consolation of the Spirit floods our soul as we are held safe in our Father's arms where nothing can harm us, and where death itself is robbed of its power. The closer we draw to the Holy Spirit during our life, then, the more open and hungry we grow to experience fully the Holy Spirit's sweetness at our death. With St. John of the Cross, we begin to realize that the Spirit of love so transforms our death in Jesus that death itself becomes "very gentle and very sweet, sweeter and more gentle" than even our life lived in the Spirit. And though it may seem that we die of a physical cause, in the Holy Spirit, we do not die of old age or illness but rather of love.[4]

Even if our love is not yet perfect at our death, the Spirit of love can expand our heart at that last moment. Purgatory may be this purifying, healing experience of death itself, when we see in the Lord's eyes how much he loves us and how much we have refused his love. The Spirit's love flowing from Jesus then becomes the purification of our love, our purgatory. By softening the hardened places of our heart, the Holy Spirit opens our heart completely at death so that, finally, we can return the immensity of the Trinity's love for us. In this last great gift, the grace of our death, the Holy Spirit comes to us as our sweet comforter, transforming the isolation of our death into the most intimate and self-giving communion.[5]

Inspired by thoughts such as these, an early Christian author reflects on how the Spirit heals even our fear of death. Often, we cannot hold

---

[3] Ibid., 121.

[4] John of the Cross, *The Living Flame of Love* 1.35, 36, 30; in *The Collected Works of St. John of the Cross*, trans. Kieran Kavanaugh, O.C.D., and Otilio Rodriguez, O.C.D. (Washington, D.C.: ICS Publications, 1973) 594, 595, 592.

[5] Durwell, *Holy Spirit*, 122.

back the tears as we face our own death or the death of those close to us, for death's cruelty seems to rob us forever of the life we hold dear. But even in our grief the Holy Spirit comforts us with the promise that we shall hold our loved ones in our arms once more, and in heaven's joy nothing will ever separate us again.[6] In his beautiful poem on Pentecost, the poet Paul Claudel cries out in praise to this same Spirit by whose power Jesus himself was raised to life and through whom we ourselves, united to and enclosed in Jesus, will live again: "Ah, raise up the heart which sleeps! Come, devouring Spirit, come, O death of death!"[7]

The Holy Spirit and the Resurrection

"If the Spirit of him who raised Jesus from the dead dwells in you, he who raised Christ from the dead will give life to your mortal bodies also through his Spirit that dwells in you" (Rom 8:11). The resurrection of Jesus is the great feast of life, the pivotal point toward which all of history is moving, for, in the Spirit of life, Jesus' resurrection has become the cause of our own resurrection. It was in the Hebrew Scriptures that early Christians first saw illumined this intimate connection between the Holy Spirit, the Lord's resurrection, and our own resurrection. Isaiah tells us that the Spirit of God will be poured out on the messiah (Isa 11:2), the chosen servant of God (Isa 42:1), transforming even the desert wilderness into a paradise (Isa 32:16). Every one will be filled with the Spirit of life (Joel 3:1; Hag 2:5) who raises the dead from their graves, giving them new hearts and a whole new life (Ezek 36:26; 37:14). Early Christians began to understand that it was in the power of this very Spirit that Christ himself has become "life-giving spirit" (1 Cor 15:45).

In an exquisite homily for Holy Saturday, an early Christian writer ponders the marvel of the Lord's resurrection in the Holy Spirit's power. The author pictures the risen Lord descending to the place of the dead. The Lord Jesus who is the "life of the dead" seeks out our first parents and bids them to rise from the dead. He tenderly reminds them that he suffered a tortured death for our sake, because he wanted to be joined to us in the most intimate union possible: "You are in me and I am in you; together we form only one person and we cannot be separated. For your sake, I, your God, became your son." The cruelty of death itself now has been conquered by the risen Lord who raises

---

[6] St. Braulio of Saragossa, *Letter Nineteen*; in *The Office of Readings* (Boston: St. Paul Editions, 1983) 1814.

[7] Paul Claudel, *Hymne de la Pentecôte*; in Yolande Arsène-Henry, ed., *Les plus beaux textes sur le Saint-Esprit*, rev. ed. (Paris: Lethielleux, 1968) 308.

the dead through the Spirit of life: "The bridal chamber is adorned, the banquet is ready. . . . The kingdom of heaven has been prepared for you from all eternity."[8]

In this kingdom of heaven, the Holy Spirit completes the great work begun in us at our baptism. Enclosed in Jesus' death, our death is thus enclosed also in his glorious resurrection. As we have seen, though Jesus is God the Word from all eternity, his resurrection meant for him an entirely new human existence. Freed from the limitations of time and space, suffering and death, his risen body is completely permeated with the Spirit's glory. Through the Holy Spirit who transformed him, the risen Lord now lives within us even in his human existence, so that his risen power becomes the power of our own resurrection.

Here on earth, our own pre-risen bodies do not always manifest or give our inner goodness; our faces and actions can conceal rather than reveal our beautiful identity in God. When our death is transformed into the Lord's glorious life, however, our risen body will be "spiritual," permeated with the Spirit of life (1 Cor 15:42-44). It will no longer hide but rather unveil and give who we are; through its transparency, our soul's beauty will shine forth. Everything that our being has stored up as its inner treasure will appear outwardly in our body. "The heavenly fire" of God's life now at work within us invisibly thus will be manifested in its full glory. We will become radiant in beauty through the same Spirit who transformed the death of Jesus into unending life.[9]

In a sermon which he preached at the death of his own beloved young brother, Satyrus, St. Ambrose reflects on our Spirit-filled risen existence as enabling us to be closer than ever to our dear ones. Our death into the arms of Jesus and enfolded by the Spirit of love is a mystery not of the loss of our loved ones and of their absence from us but rather of their most intense and intimate presence to us. Speaking directly to Satyrus, Ambrose asks his brother to console him and all those present, for death has not torn them apart. On the contrary, it has enabled Satyrus to be with them in a far more intimate way and has infinitely deepened their means of enjoying his closeness. Before, because of their many pressing responsibilities, Ambrose could have Satyrus' presence only at limited times. But now, in his risen existence, Satyrus will be with them always through the intimate communion of saints formed by the Spirit of love.[10]

---

[8] *Ancient Homily on Holy Saturday;* in *The Office of Readings,* 483, 484.

[9] Vladimir Lossky, *The Mystical Theology of the Eastern Church* (New York: St. Vladimir's Seminary Press, 1976) 234, 235.

[10] St. Ambrose, *First Funeral Oration on His Brother, Satyrus.* In *Funeral Orations by Saint Gregory Nazianzen and Saint Ambrose,* trans. Leo McCauley, John J. Sullivan,

The young Jesuit Aloysius Gonzaga wrote to his mother about this same mystery of our deepened presence to each other through our Spirit-permeated risen bodies. Aloysius had been ministering to victims of the plague, but he soon caught the dread disease himself. In his final days he wrote to his mother, asking the Holy Spirit to console her heart, and telling her that he would help her powerfully through his prayer in heaven. Aloysius ends his letter by assuring her that our life seems to be taken away at death only so that God can give it back to us more wonderfully than we could ever desire. At our death, the Lord receives back the life he has lent to us as sheer gift, and returns it to us transformed and radiant.[11] Our risen bodies enable us to be incomparably close to those we love, and one day we shall hold one another again, for the Spirit joins us in a union that can never be broken.

The Communion of Saints Fulfilled in the Spirit

The Holy Spirit poured out by the risen Lord is both the source of our profound communion with one another now, and also its perfect fulfillment in heaven's joy. Here on earth our union with one another is so damaged by our weakness that, without the Spirit of love possessing us, we cannot live heaven's life.[12] But we can beg the Holy Spirit to break through our selfishness now, and to purify our love completely at death. Our hearts then will be opened perfectly, so that we will give ourselves to the Trinity and cherish one another with the Spirit's own love. In the power of this love, we will sink into the Trinity's embrace as our heaven, and in this same Spirit, we, too, will become heaven for one another. Dante ends his *Paradiso* with a vision in which he sees all that is now scattered in the universe finally united, bound by love.[13] No one is isolated or separated, and all divisions are healed. With the Spirit's own love enabling us to enjoy God and one another forever, our own hearts become the "place" of joy where every person is cherished.[14] Thérèse of Lisieux even writes that one of heaven's delights will be discovering that we owe to one another's help and prayer all of the blessings we have received here on earth.[15]

Martin R. McGuire, Roy J. Deferrari; Vol. 22 of *The Fathers of the Church*, ed. Roy J. Deferrari (New York: Fathers of the Church, 1953), 163, 191–94.

[11] Aloysius Gonzaga, *Letter to His Mother;* LH 1602.

[12] Irenaeus, *Against the Heresies,* 5.9.3.

[13] *The Divine Comedy: Paradiso,* 33; Congar, *I Believe,* 2:221.

[14] Durrwell, *Holy Spirit,* 127.

[15] See John Clarke, O.C.D., trans., *St. Thérèse of Lisieux: Her Last Conversations* (Washington, D.C.: ICS Publications, 1977) 100.

In heaven, the Holy Spirit unites us so perfectly that we become "one body and one Spirit" (Eph 4:4). Ephrem the Syrian reflects with special beauty on this mystery of our forming "one body" in heaven so that we live together without crowding. He considers how millions of light rays can exist in a single building, and thousands of scents can permeate a single room, just as an infinite number of thoughts can exist in one mind. And so it is with heaven. There will be ample space for all of us, for our risen bodies will be so permeated by the unbounded Spirit that even the most subtle thoughts will touch us.[16] With the one same life of the Trinity uniting us, both our uniqueness and our union will be enhanced, so that God will be "all in all" (1 Cor 15:28). Finally, our bond of unity will be the very person of the Spirit who is the Trinity's glory and our radiant glory forever.[17] This Spirit, who is so humble in our experience here on earth, will be gloriously revealed in heaven through us. For all of eternity, the saints themselves shine as the Spirit's luminous icon.[18]

The Spirit Perfects and Completes All

The Father and Son thus bring creation to its glorious culmination in the Spirit, the "third" divine person who is the Trinity's "completion" and our fulfillment as well.[19] This mystery reflects the beautiful "order" among the divine persons that expresses their unique personal identities. We are baptized and pray in the name of "the Father, and the Son, and the Holy Spirit." So, too, we worship the Trinity with the prayer, "Glory to the Father, and to the Son, and to the Holy Spirit." This order in which we name the divine persons implies no inequality but rather the unique relationship that they have and are to one another. The Father is the "first" divine person; Jesus, the Word, is the "second" divine person; and the Holy Spirit is the "third" divine person.

The Holy Spirit, then, is the Trinity's "completion" as the "third" divine person. On the other hand, the Spirit is the first divine person we encounter in our experience, even if we are not initially aware of this truth. When we receive gifts from the Trinity, Basil the Great tells us,

---

[16] St. Ephrem, *Hymns on Paradise*, 5, 9, 10; in Sebastian Brock, *The Harp of the Spirit* (London: Fellowship of St. Alban and St. Sergius, 1983) 24.

[17] Gregory of Nyssa, *Fifteenth Homily on the Canticle of Canticles*; Durrwell, *Holy Spirit*, 181.

[18] Lossky, *Mystical Theology*, 173.

[19] Basil the Great, *On the Holy Spirit*, 18.45; 16.38; NPNF 2.8, 28, 23; Gregory Nazianzen, *Fifth Theological Oration*, 4; NPNF 2.7, 318; Cyril of Alexandria, *Thesaurus*; PG 75, 608. Gregory Nazianzen tells us that the Father is *aitios*, the Son is *demiourgos*, and the Spirit is *telos*.

the first person we experience is the distributor, the Holy Spirit. Next, we encounter the sender, Jesus; finally, we lift our minds to the fountain of all blessings, the Father.[20] The wonderful order within the Trinity in this way is reversed in our experience of the Trinity. The Spirit, the third divine person in whom the mystery of the Trinity is eternally "completed," is also the one through whom the Trinity's life is opened out to us. This is why Basil calls the Holy Spirit the great "distributor" of the Trinity's life, the generous giver of God's good to all (1 Cor 12:11). Gregory of Nyssa, too, reflects on how every blessing comes from the Father through the Son and is completed by the Spirit who "works all in all." The Father's marvelous gifts to us are brought to fulfillment through Jesus and in the power of the Holy Spirit.[21]

Basil the Great describes this Spirit as the one who perfects not only us but also everything in the universe, for the Spirit does not need life but rather bestows it as the dispenser of life, drawing us to heaven as our true goal.[22] Basil also contemplates the Spirit as the divine person who preserves the glorious harmony of the angels. He pictures "ten thousand times ten thousand" ministering spirits (Dan 7:10), accomplishing their work by the power of the Spirit who is their fulfillment, the one in whom they were made perfect from the moment of their creation. From this Spirit who completes everything in the universe, the angels receive their perfection, joy, and confirmation in good. Basil adds that, unlike the angels, we are not perfect from the first moment of our creation. But the Holy Spirit does for us what we cannot do for ourselves: confirm, complete, and strengthen us in holiness. The Spirit's own boundless good makes us faithful in virtue, so that we find it increasingly difficult to abandon God's goodness by sin.[23]

In the Holy Spirit, then, we become fully mature as human persons. Bernard of Clairvaux paints a beautiful portrait of the Spirit's work in perfecting us as members of the Church. The Spirit gives gifts, like jewels, to the Church as the Bride of Christ, raising up prophets, instructing teachers, encouraging tongues, inspiring the Church's councils, and dispensing every gift of grace. The Church itself thus holds astonishing "heavens" of grace within her, and is herself an "immense heaven."[24] We see the Spirit's graciousness also in nature, especially in the sheer abundance that marks creation. Here on earth, however, we

---

[20] Basil the Great, *On the Holy Spirit*, 16.37; NPNF 2.8, 23.

[21] Gregory of Nyssa, *Not Three Gods*; NPNF 2.5, 335.

[22] Basil the Great, *On the Holy Spirit*, 9.22; NPNF 2.8, 15.

[23] Ibid., 16.38, 19.49; NPNF 2.8, 24, 31.

[24] Bernard of Clairvaux, *On the Song of Songs*, 27.12; in *The Works of Bernard of Clairvaux*, trans. Kilian Walsh, O.C.S.O. (Kalamazoo, Mich.: Cistercian Publications, 1981) 3:84, 85.

not only cherish and care for the earth's beauty, but also damage it by our sin. Yet just as the Holy Spirit now changes bread and wine into the body and blood of Christ in the Eucharist, the Holy Spirit is continually at work among us to heal our sin and to transform the cosmos into a heavenly banquet for us at the end of time.[25] This miracle of grace is happening even now, as the Holy Spirit works through us to bring greater love, peace, and justice to the world. The Spirit who is active everywhere in the world[26] thus performs wonders among us, binding us together in relationships of faithful love.

In the Spirit, Heaven's Joy Begins Now

Finally, the Holy Spirit is at work within us as the "Spirit of the Promise" (Eph 1:14), the "gift" (Acts 2:38) and "promised" one (Luke 24:49, Acts 1:4, 2:33, Gal 3:14) in whom all of God's promises will be completely fulfilled at the end of time. When we ourselves make promises to those we love, our promise is a pledge of something good in the future. It is an expression of our love, a giving in some way of ourselves. But because we are weak, some of the promises we make we do not or cannot keep. The promises of God to us, however, come from a heart infinitely powerful, faithful, and true. The Trinity's promises to us are always fulfilled, and beyond our wildest dreams. And Jesus has promised to give us nothing less than his own heart, the Spirit who is the very person of the Father's and Son's love.

At Pentecost Peter preached that this Spirit is the "eschatological gift" (Acts 2:38) whose fullness we will experience in the joy of heaven. But even now we possess the Spirit deep in our hearts as the *arrha*, the "pledge," first-fruits, and guarantee of our inheritance until we possess it completely in heaven (Rom 8:23; 2 Cor 1:22, 5:5; Eph 1:14, 4:30). As we wait for our adoption as children of God, we "groan inwardly" (Rom 8:23), "that what is mortal may be swallowed up by life." God has prepared us for this very thing and "given us the Spirit as a guarantee" (2 Cor 5:4-5). A "pledge" or "guarantee" of a promised future good is its beginning possessed by us even now. We might think of a marvelous treasure which its owner promises to give us. As a pledge that we can trust this promise, the owner gives us the key which alone will open the treasure. In some way, then, the whole treasure is already ours, and we are assured that one day we will have it fully. Jesus' resurrection has so completely inaugurated the eschaton (Acts 2:33), that

[25] Walter Kasper, *The God of Jesus Christ*, trans. Matthew J. O'Connell (New York: Crossroad, 1986) 226.

[26] Irenaeus, *Against the Heresies*, 3.11.8.

the Spirit poured out by him is the "pledge" within us, the beginning of heaven even now in our hearts (2 Cor 1:22).

The Holy Spirit dwelling within us, therefore, is not only the "promise of the paschal feast of heaven," but even more the "fore-taste" in our hearts of heaven here on earth.[27] As the Father's and Son's living "ecstasy," the Holy Spirit is eternally givable, the person of overflowing love and grace.[28] In this Spirit all the gifts promised to us in the future already are ours. We enjoy them through faith, even as we await their fulfillment in heaven. Paul describes some of these marvelous gifts, delicious to our soul, as the "fruit" of the Spirit: "love, joy, peace, patience, kindness, generosity, faithfulness, gentle-ness, and self-control" (Gal 5:22). Blessings such as these are a fore-taste of heaven's own sweet joy. Yet we can and are meant to enjoy, at every moment of our lives, not only the sweet gifts of the Spirit, but also the heavenly sweetness of the Spirit, the very person of joy. Symeon the New Theologian assures us that, as children of the light (1 Thess 5:5), we live even now "with God and in God,"[29] for the risen life is not only future hope but also present reality. The Spirit who gives us communion with the Trinity and one another in heaven thus becomes the pledge and heart of heaven within us even now (Eph 1:14). As we enjoy and surrender ourselves to the Holy Spirit here on earth, we also begin to live the beatitudes as a share in the life of heaven:[30] "Blessed are the poor in spirit, for theirs is the kingdom of heaven . . . Blessed are the merciful, for they will receive mercy . . . Blessed are the peacemakers, for they will be called children of God!" (Matt 5:3, 7, 9). Basil the Great cries out in praise that if such blessings are the foretaste, what must their fulfillment be![31]

Gregory Nazianzen writes that this Spirit who is the "pledge of our inheritance" (Eph 1:14) draws us to our fulfillment by inspiring us to long for heaven's joy. God the Word gave us his life by placing in our hearts the Spirit both as his living glory and the desire within us for heaven's joy.[32] Symeon the New Theologian adds that our intimate sharing in the Holy Spirit is the very kingdom of God in our midst (Luke 17:21).[33] This is surely why, in place of the words "Thy kingdom

---

[27] Preface Thirty-Four, Sundays in Ordinary Time, VI.

[28] Kasper, *God*, 226.

[29] Vladimir Lossky, *Orthodox Theology: An Introduction*, trans. Ian and Ihita Kesarcodi-Matson (New York: St. Vladimir's Seminary Press, 1978) 118.

[30] Aquinas, ST, I–II, 69, aa 1–4.

[31] Basil the Great, *On the Holy Spirit*, 15.36; NPNF 2.8, 22.

[32] Gregory Nazianzen, *On the Soul*; PG 37, 452; in Lossky, *Orthodox Theology,* 121.

[33] *Catecheses*, 6; in Yves Congar, O.P., *I Believe in the Holy Spirit*, trans. David Smith (New York: Seabury Press, 1983) 2:70.

come" (Luke 11:2), several early manuscripts of Luke read, "May your Spirit come upon us and purify us." Maximus Confessor remarks that when we pray, "Thy kingdom come," in reality we are asking for the Holy Spirit who is the kingdom of God in person.[34] John of the Cross further tells us that if we live in the Holy Spirit's tenderness now, we will die in those same sweet bonds of love. The Spirit who "sighs" within us (Rom 8:26) thus inspires us to desire God (Ps 16:2) and to long for heaven's joy as a bride longs to see her bridegroom: "Arise, my love, my fair one, and come away" (Cant 2:10).

Such impatient yearning for God can so fill us that we even begin to pray, "Tear the thin veil of this life and do not let old age cut it naturally," for we long to cherish God with the perfect love that is heaven's own joy.[35] Cyprian gives us a beautiful description of the Spirit enticing us to heaven's bliss when he compares us to travelers longing to "hasten homeward." Our loved ones tenderly await us, anxious for us to arrive safely home. What ecstasy it will be to rush into their arms and linger there, never to be separated again.[36] We see the Spirit inspiring this same thirst for heaven's joy in Christians such as the early bishop, Ignatius of Antioch. As he was being taken by soldiers to his martyrdom in Rome, he wrote to the Christian community there begging them not to save him: "A living spring flows in me and it says, 'Come to the Father.'"[37] This "living spring" is the Holy Spirit within us, drawing us home to heaven's ecstatic joy.

Through the gracious gift of this same Spirit, we ourselves hope to hear at our death the glorious invitation, "Enter into the joy" of your Lord (Matt 25:21). Saints such as Augustine, Thomas Aquinas, and Bernadine of Siena tell us that heaven's joy is so immense that we cannot contain it; rather, we must enter into it. The Trinity's joy, then, will not only be within us; it will surround and penetrate us, absorbing us as into a limitless ocean.[38] At our death, the Father, Son, and Spirit will welcome us with exquisite love, drawing us into the warmth of their embrace. Filled with the Spirit's love, we will sink into the heart of our Father, as the Spirit of Jesus within us cries out with indescribable tenderness, "Abba, my Father" (Rom 8:15; Gal 4:6). We will gather in a great throng with all of heaven, jubilantly praising our Abba who

---

[34] Maximus Confessor, PG 90, 884b; see also Gregory of Nyssa, *On the Lord's Prayer*, 3; PG 44, 1157c; Congar, *I Believe*, 2:57.

[35] John of the Cross, *Living Flame of Love*, 1.28, 36; Kavanaugh and Rodriguez, 590, 595.

[36] Cyprian, *Sermon on Our Mortality*, 26; LH 771.

[37] Ignatius of Antioch, *Letter to the Romans*, 6; LH 425.

[38] Aquinas, *Commentary on Matthew*, 25, lect. 2; ST II–II, 28, 3; Bernadine of Siena, *Second Sermon: on St. Joseph*; LH 1535.

raised us with Jesus and gave us eternal life in the Spirit.[39] Possessed by the Spirit of Jesus, we will rush into the arms of Jesus, our beloved Lord and spouse. Finally, we who have been sealed with the Spirit unto the day of redemption (Eph 4:30) will receive as our radiant crown the Spirit's own glory.[40] Just as the Holy Spirit is the Father's and Son's very "heart," their living heaven, this same Spirit of love will become our heaven forever.

Augustine interprets the story of Martha and Mary as a promise of the Holy Spirit as the very heart of our joy in heaven. We read that when Jesus visited his beloved friends Martha and Mary, Martha served Jesus while Mary sat at his feet, listening to his word (Luke 10:38-42). Augustine comments that Martha fed Jesus with earthly food, but Jesus wanted to feed her with the Holy Spirit. In heaven, this is exactly what will happen. Here on earth, we feed Jesus in the poor and hungry, but in heaven there will be no hungry people to feed, no sick people to visit, no quarrelsome people to reconcile, no dead loved ones to bury. No longer will we feed one another, for God will feed us (Luke 12:37). On earth Mary gathered the crumbs from the lavish table of the Lord's word, but in heaven the Lord himself will make us sit at table and feed our hearts on the banquet who is the Holy Spirit.[41]

This Spirit who overshadowed Mary, sanctified John the Baptist, and filled the apostles and countless others for their missions,[42] is also the one through whom everything in the universe is consummated. As the living pledge and very heart of heaven, the Holy Spirit is drawing us to the wonderful surprises of the future, and finally to heaven's bliss:[43] "The Spirit and the bride say, 'Come!'" (Rev 22:17). Just as the Gospel itself spreads only in the Holy Spirit's power (1 Thess 1:5), everything we do in the Holy Spirit sings of ever new life and vigor. Pope Paul VI urges us to surrender ourselves to this Spirit of love, to "open the window" of our heart to the Spirit's breath and light: "We must all of us place ourselves windward of the mysterious breath of the Holy Spirit" so that the "sails of the Spirit may bring us to our eschatological port."[44]

---

[39] Irenaeus, *Against the Heresies*, 5.8.1.

[40] Basil the Great, *On the Holy Spirit*, 16.40; NPNF 2.8, 25.

[41] Augustine, *Sermon 103*, 2; LH 1649.

[42] Victor Dillard, S.J., *Au Dieu inconnu* (Paris: Beauchesne, 1928); in Yolande Arsène-Henry, ed., *Les plus beaux textes sur le Saint-Esprit*, rev. ed. (Paris: Lethielleux, 1968) 322.

[43] Congar, *I Believe*, 2:57.

[44] *The Teaching of Pope Paul VI* (Washington, D.C.: U.S. Catholic Conference, 1975) 200, 76, 68.

An eastern Christian mystic once wrote to his friends, "May the Holy Spirit be your last reward."[45] As we ourselves await the Holy Spirit's ecstatic joy which will be our bliss in heaven, let us also, as Augustine urges us to do, advance in virtue, and sing as we go.[46] May our very lives become a song of joy to the Trinity, drawing others with the melody of the Spirit who is the unbounded gift of joy.

[45] Nicholas of Flüe; Congar, *I Believe*, 2:69.
[46] Augustine, *Sermon 256*, 3; LH 773.

Select Bibliography

Primary Texts

Ambrose of Milan. *First Funeral Oration on His Brother, Satyrus.* Trans. Leo McCauley, John J. Sullivan, Martin R. McGuire, Roy J. Deferrari. In *Funeral Orations by Saint Gregory Nazianzen and Saint Ambrose.* Vol. 22 of *The Fathers of the Church,* ed., Roy J. Deferrari. New York: Fathers of the Church, 1953.

_____. *On the Holy Spirit.* Trans. H. De Romestin. In *A Select Library of Nicene and Post-Nicene Fathers of the Christian Church,* Series II, Vol. 10. Grand Rapids, Mich.: Wm. B. Eerdmans, 1976.

Angela of Foligno. *Complete Works.* Trans. and intro., Paul Lachance. New York: Paulist Press, 1993.

Athanasius of Alexandria. *Letters Concerning the Holy Spirit.* Trans., intro. and notes, C.R.B. Shapland. New York: Philosophical Library, 1951.

Augustine of Hippo. *On the Trinity.* Trans. Stephen McKenna. New York: Fathers of the Church, 1954.

Basil the Great. *On the Holy Spirit.* Trans. Blomfield Jackson. In *A Select Library of Nicene and Post-Nicene Fathers of the Christian Church,* Series II, Vol. 8. Grand Rapids, Mich.: Wm. B. Eerdmans, 1983.

Bernard of Clairvaux. *On the Song of Songs.* 4 vols. Trans. Kilian Walsh, O.C.S.O. and Irene M. Edmunds. In *The Works of Bernard of Clairvaux.* Vols. 4, 7, 31, and 40 of *The Cistercian Fathers Series.* Spencer, Mass. and Kalamazoo, Mich.: Cistercian Publications, 1971–80.

Book of Prayer: A Short Breviary. 4th rev. ed. Trans. Monks of Saint John's Abbey. Collegeville: Saint John's Abbey Press, 1975.

Burns, J. Patout, and Gerald M. Fagin, eds., *The Holy Spirit.* Message of the Fathers of the Church 3. Wilmington: Michael Glazier, Inc., 1984.

Catechism of the Catholic Church. Dubuque, Ia.: Brown-Roa, 1994.

Catherine of Siena. *The Dialogue.* Trans. Suzanne Noffke, O.P. New York: Paulist Press, 1980.

Cyril of Jerusalem. *Catechetical Lectures.* Trans. Edwin Hamilton Gifford. In *A Select Library of Nicene and Post-Nicene Fathers of the Christian Church,* Series II, Vol. 7. Grand Rapids, Mich.: Wm. B. Eerdmans, 1983.

Eusebius of Caesarea. *The History of the Church from Christ to Constantine.* Trans. and intro. G. A. Williamson. Baltimore, Md.: Penguin Books, 1965.

The Holy Spirit, Lord and Giver of Life. Prepared by the Theological-Historical Commission for the Great Jubilee of the Year 2000. Trans. Agostino Bono. New York: Crossroad, 1997.

Gregory Nazianzen. *Orations.* Trans. Charles Browne and James Swallow. In *A Select Library of Nicene and Post-Nicene Fathers of the Christian Church,* Series II, Vol. 7. Grand Rapids, Mich.: Wm. B. Eerdmans, 1983.

Gregory of Nyssa. *On the Holy Spirit.* Trans. W. Moore and H. A. Wilson. In *A Select Library of Nicene and Post-Nicene Fathers of the Christian Church,* Series II, Vol. 5. Grand Rapids, Mich.: Wm. B. Eerdmans, 1976.

John Chrysostom. *Homilies on the Gospel of St. Matthew.* Trans. George Prevost. In *A Select Library of Nicene and Post-Nicene Fathers of the Christian Church,* Series I, Vol. 10. Grand Rapids, Mich.: Wm. B. Eerdmans, 1986.

John of the Cross. *The Collected Works of St. John of the Cross.* Trans. Kieran Kavanaugh, O.C.D., and Otilio Rodriguez, O.C.D. Intro. Kieran Kavanaugh. Washington, D.C.: ICS Publications, 1973.

John Paul II. *Dominum et Vivificantem: Lord and Giver of Life.* Encyclical on The Holy Spirit in the Life of the Church and the World, May 30, 1986. Washington, D.C.: United States Catholic Conference, 1986.

Patrologia cursus completus. Series Graeca. Jacques Paul Migne, ed. Paris: J. P. Migne, 1857–87.

Symeon the New Theologian. *Hymns of Divine Love.* Trans. and intro. George Maloney, S.J. Denville, N.J.: Dimension Books, 1975.

_____. *The Discourses.* Trans. C. J. De Catanzaro. Intro. George Maloney, S.J. New York: Paulist Press, 1980.

Thomas Aquinas. *On Charity.* Trans. Lottie H. Kendzierski. Milwaukee: Marquette University Press, 1960.

_____. *Commentary on the Epistle to the Ephesians.* Trans. M. L. Lamb, O.C.S.O. Vol. 2 of Aquinas Scripture Series. Albany: Magi Books, 1981.

_____. *Commentary on the Gospel of St. John.* Part I. Trans. James A. Weisheipl, O.P., and Fabian R. Larcher, O.P. Vol. 4 of Aquinas Scripture Series. Albany: Magi Books, 1980.

_____. *Commentary on Saint Paul's First Letter to the Thessalonians and the Letter to the Philippians.* Trans. F. R. Larcher and Michael Duffy. Vol. 3 of Aquinas Scripture Series. Albany: Magi Books, 1969.

_____. *On the Truth of the Catholic Faith.* Trans. Pegis, Anderson, Bourke, O'Neil. 5 vols. New York: Doubleday, 1955–57. Reprint, Notre Dame University Press, 1975.

_____. *S. Thomae Aquinatis Opera omnia ut sunt in Indice Thomistico.* Curante R. Busa. Stuttgart, 1980.

_____. *The Sermon-Conferences of St. Thomas Aquinas on the Apostles' Creed.* Trans. from the Leonine Edition, ed. and intro., Nicholas Ayo, C.S.C. Notre Dame: University of Notre Dame Press, 1988.

_____. *Summa Theologiae.* Latin text and English translation. 61 vols. London: Blackfriars in conjunction with Eyre & Spottiswoode; New York: McGraw-Hill, 1963–81.

Vatican Council II: The Conciliar and Post Conciliar Documents. Rev. ed. Austin Flannery, O.P., ed. Northport, New York: Costello Publishing Company, 1996.

Related Studies

Adam, Karl. *Christ Our Brother.* Trans. Justin McCann. London: Sheed and Ward, 1937.

Arsène-Henry, Yolande, *Les plus beaux textes sur le Saint-Esprit.* Rev. ed. Paris: Lethielleux, 1968.

Austin, O.P., Gerard. *Anointing with the Spirit: The Rite of Confirmation.* Vol. 2 of *Studies in the Reformed Rites of the Catholic Church.* New York: Pueblo, 1985. Reprint: Collegeville: The Liturgical Press, 1992.

Bermejo, S.J., Luis M. *The Spirit of Life: The Holy Spirit in the Life of the Christian.* Chicago: Loyola University Press, 1989.

Brock, Sebastian. *The Harp of the Spirit.* London: Fellowship of St. Alban and St. Sergius, 1983.

Burgess, Stanley. *The Holy Spirit: Eastern Traditions.* Peabody, Mass.: Hendrickson, 1989.

Cantalamessa, O.F.M. Cap., Raniero. *The Holy Spirit in the Life of Jesus: The Mystery of Christ's Baptism.* Trans. Alan Neame. Collegeville: The Liturgical Press, 1994.

Chennici, Joseph P., ed. *Devotion to the Holy Spirit in American Catholicism.* New York: Paulist Press, 1985.

Comblin, José, *The Holy Spirit and Liberation.* Trans. Paul Burns. Maryknoll: Orbis, 1989.

Congar, O.P., Yves. *I Believe in the Holy Spirit.* 3 vols. Trans. David Smith. New York: Seabury Press, 1983.

De Celles, Charles. *The Unbound Spirit.* New York: Alba House, 1985.

Dobson, Theodore Elliott. *Inner Healing: God's Great Assurance.* New York: Paulist Press, 1978.

Durrwell, F. X. *Holy Spirit of God: An Essay in Biblical Theology.* Trans. Sr. Benedict Davies, O.S.U. London: Geoffrey Chapman, 1983.

Elliott, Peter J. *What God Has Joined: The Sacramentality of Marriage.* New York: Alba House, 1990.

Fatula, O.P., Mary Ann. *Catherine of Siena's Way.* Wilmington: Michael Glazier, 1987. Reprint and revised ed.: Collegeville: The Liturgical Press, 1990.

_____. *Thomas Aquinas, Preacher and Friend.* Collegeville: The Liturgical Press, 1993.

_____. *The Triune God of Christian Faith.* Collegeville: The Liturgical Press, 1990.

Fortman, S.J., Edmund J. *Activities of the Holy Spirit.* Chicago: Franciscan Herald Press, 1984.

Galtier, S.J., Paul. *Le Saint Esprit en nous d'après les Pères Grecs.* Rome: Gregorian University, 1946.

Gaybba, Brian. *The Spirit of Love: Theology of the Holy Spirit.* London: Geoffrey Chapman, 1987.

Gelpi, S.J., Donald L. *The Divine Mother: A Trinitarian Theology of the Holy Spirit.* Lanham, Md.: University Press of America, 1984.

_____. *The Spirit in the World.* Wilmington: Michael Glazier, 1988.

Gerard Manley Hopkins. *The Major Poems.* Ed. Walford Davies. New York: E. P. Dutton & Co., 1979.

Kavanagh, Aidan. *The Shape of Baptism: The Rite of Christian Initiation.* New York: Pueblo, 1978. Reprint: Collegeville: The Liturgical Press, 1992.

Kasper, Walter. *The God of Jesus Christ.* Trans. Matthew J. O'Connell. New York: Crossroad, 1986.

_____. *Jesus the Christ.* New York: Paulist Press, 1977.

Lewis, Warren, ed. *Witnesses to the Holy Spirit.* Valley Forge: Judson Press, 1978.

Lossky, Vladimir. *In the Image and Likeness of God.* New York: St. Vladimir's Seminary Press, 1976.

_____. *The Mystical Theology of the Eastern Church.* New York: St. Vladimir's Seminary Press, 1976.

_____. *The Vision of God.* Trans. Asheleigh Moorhouse. Bedfordshire: American Orthodox Book Service, 1963.

_____. *Orthodox Theology: An Introduction.* Trans. Ian and Ihita Kesarcodi-Matson. New York: St. Vladimir's Seminary Press, 1978.

Manning, Henry Edward. *The Internal Mission of the Holy Ghost.* 5th ed. New York: P. J. Kenedy, 1904.

_____. *The Holy Ghost, the Sanctifier.* London: Burns and Oates, 1880.

Marmion, Columba. *Fire of Love: An Anthology of Abbot Marmion's Published Writings on the Holy Spirit.* Ed. Chas Dollen. St. Louis: Herder, 1964.

Marshall, Catherine. *The Helper.* New York: Avon, 1978.

Martinez, Luis. *The Sanctifier.* Trans. Sr. M. Aquinas. Paterson, N.J.: St. Anthony Guild Press, 1957.

Martos, Joseph. *Doors to the Sacred: A Historical Introduction to Sacraments in the Catholic Church.* Garden City, New York: Doubleday Image Books, 1982.

Massabki, O.S.B., Charles. *Who Is the Holy Spirit?* New York: Alba House, 1979.

McDonnell, O.S.B., Kilian, ed. *The Holy Spirit and Power: The Catholic Charismatic Renewal.* Garden City: Doubleday, 1975.

_____. "A Trinitarian Theology of the Holy Spirit?" *Theological Studies* 46(1985) 191–227.

McDonnell, O.S.B., Kilian, and Montague, S.M., George T. *Christian Initiation and Baptism in the Holy Spirit: Evidence from the First Eight Centuries.* Collegeville: The Liturgical Press, 1991.

Montague, S. M., George. *The Holy Spirit: Growth of a Biblical Tradition.* New York: Paulist Press, 1976. Reprint: Peabody, Mass.: Hendrickson, 1994.

Moltmann, Jürgen. *The Spirit of Life: A Universal Affirmation.* Trans. Margaret Kohl. London: SCM Press, 1992.

_____. *The Church in the Power of the Spirit.* Trans. Margaret Kohl. New York: Harper and Row, 1977.

_____. *The Crucified God.* Trans. R. A. Wilson and John Bowden. New York: Harper and Row, 1973.

Mühlen, Heribert. *Der Heilige Geist als Person: in der Trinität bei der Inkarnation und im Gnadenbund: Ich, du, wir.* 2nd ed. Paderborn, 1966.

_____. *L'Esprit dans l'Eglise.* 2 vols. Trans. A. Liefolghe, M. Massart, R. Virrion. Paris: Cerf, 1969.

Newman, John Henry. *Meditations and Devotions.* London: Longmans, Green and Co., 1953.

O'Carroll, C.S.Sp., Michael. *Veni Creator Spiritus: A Theological Encyclopedia of the Holy Spirit.* Collegeville: The Liturgical Press, 1990.

O'Connor, Edward E. *Pope Paul and the Spirit: Charisms and Church Renewal in the Teaching of Paul VI.* Notre Dame: Ave Maria Press, 1978.

Rahner, S.J., Karl. *The Spirit in the Church.* New York: Crossroad Seabury, 1979.

_____. *The Trinity.* Trans. Joseph Donceel. New York: Herder and Herder, 1969.

_____. "The Episcopate and the Primacy," in Karl Rahner and Joseph Ratzinger, *The Episcopate and the Primacy. Quaestiones Disputatae* 4. New York: Herder and Herder, 1962, 11–36.

Ranaghan, Kevin and Dorothy, eds. *As the Spirit Leads Us.* Paramus, N.J.: Paulist Press, 1971.

Schmemann, Alexander. *The Vespers of Pentecost.* Orthodox Church in America, Department of Religious Education, n. d.

Shlemon, Barbara Leahy. *Healing the Hidden Self.* Notre Dame: Ave Maria Press, 1982.

Suenens, Léon Joseph Cardinal. *A New Pentecost?* Trans. Francis Martin. New York: Crossroad Seabury, 1975.

St. Thérèse of Lisieux: Her Last Conversations. Trans. John Clarke, O.C.D. Washington, D.C.: ICS Publications, 1977.

Tillard, O.P., J. M. R. *The Bishop of Rome.* Trans. John de Satge. Wilmington, Delaware: Michael Glazier, 1983.

_____. *Eglise d'Eglises: L'écclésiologie de communion.* Paris: Cerf, 1987.

INDEX OF SUBJECTS

INDEX OF NAMES